Technological Advancement in Internet of Medical Things and Blockchain for Personalized Healthcare

Technological Advancement in Internet of Medical Things and Blockchain for Personalized Healthcare presents an overview of the innovative concepts, technologies, and various biomedical applications of the Internet of Medical Things (IoMT).

Features:

- Provides insights into smart contracts, healthcare monitoring equipment, and the next generation of Internet of Things sensors to improve adherence to chronic disease management programs and patient health.
- Discusses the IoMT for personalized healthcare, security, and privacy issues of the IoMT in the healthcare sector.
- Elaborates on the opportunities and challenges of blockchain technology in the healthcare system.
- Focuses on the convergence of the IoMT and blockchain for emerging personalized healthcare systems.
- Presents techniques and methods to secure IoMT devices to protect them from cyberattacks.

This book is primarily written for graduate students and academic researchers working in the fields of computer science and engineering, biomedical engineering, and electrical engineering.

Technological Advancement in Internet of Medical Things and Blockchain for Personalized Healthcare

Applications and Use Cases

Edited by
A. Prasanth, Lakshmi D, Rajesh Kumar Dhanaraj,
Balamurugan Balusamy, and Sherimon P.C

CRC Press
Taylor & Francis Group
Boca Raton London New York

CRC Press is an imprint of the
Taylor & Francis Group, an **informa** business

First edition published 2024
by CRC Press
2385 Executive Center Drive, Suite 320, Boca Raton, FL 33431

and by CRC Press
4 Park Square, Milton Park, Abingdon, Oxon, OX14 4RN

CRC Press is an imprint of Taylor & Francis Group, LLC

© 2024 selection and editorial matter, A. Prasanth, Lakshmi D, D Rajesh Kumar, Balamurugan Balusamy, and Sherimon P.C; individual chapters, the contributors

ISBN: 9781032521541 (hbk)
ISBN: 9781032521602 (pbk)
ISBN: 9781003405450 (ebk)

DOI: 10.1201/9781003405450

Typeset in Times
by Newgen Publishing UK

Contents

About the Editors

Dr. A. Prasanth is currently working as an Assistant Professor at Vel Tech Rangarajan Dr. Sagunthala R&D Institute of Science and Technology, Chennai, Tamil Nadu, India. He received the B.E. degree in Electronics and Communication Engineering , the M.E. degree in Computer Science and Engineering (with specialization in Networks) and the PhD degree in Information and Communication Engineering, all from Anna University, Chennai, India. Recently, he has received the Young Scientist Award from the International Scientist Award 2020 for his excellent research performance. He has also received Researcher of the Year Award 2020 from "2nd International Business and Academic Excellence Awards (IBAE)" at Delhi, held on 26 December 2020. Moreover, he has received the Young Researcher Award from the "Institute of Scholars Awards" 2020. He has published more than 45 research articles in reputed international journals, among which 15 articles are indexed in SCI and 30 articles are indexed in Scopus. He has published and granted two patents. Further, he has published more than 12 books under reputed publishers. He has served as Resource person in 25 Faculty development programmes. Moreover, he has served as Editorial Board Member in various reputed SCI journals. He has 9 years of teaching experience and his research interests include Internet of Things, Edge Computing, Cloud Computing, and 5G network.

Lakshmi D is presently working as Senior Associate Professor (Grade 2) in the School of Computer Science and Engineering at VIT Bhopal University, Madhya Pradesh, India. Till February 2021, she was designated as an Educational Research Officer at Vishnu Educational Development and Innovation Centre and Associate Professor at B V Raju Institute of Technology run by Shri Vishnu Educational Society, Hyderabad, from 2016 to February 2021. She has been working in the educational sector since 1998. Her key research focus is on exploring the dynamics of learning, the dynamics of learner, and classroom dynamics, suitable to accelerate the learning efficacy of higher education students. With her expertise she has delivered a session more than 150 on various titles. Her research areas include machine learning, deep learning and Internet of Things, educational technology, educational data mining, virtual education, and educational psychology. She holds a PhD degree in Information and Communication Engineering from Anna University, Chennai, India. She has published 28 articles in various journals and conference proceedings and contributed chapters to the books. She has won two best paper awards: one in IEEE and another in Springer conference. She has to her credit one book publication titled on "Theory of Computation" and seven Indian patents provisionally published and waiting for examinations.

Rajesh Kumar Dhanaraj is Professor at Symbiosis Institute of Computer Studies and Research (SICSR), Symbiosis International (Deemed University), Pune, India. He obtained his PhD degree in Information and Communication Engineering from Anna University, Chennai, India. He has presented research papers at conferences, published articles and papers in various journals, and contributed chapters to books. His research interests include Wireless Sensor Networks and Cloud Computing. He is an Expert Advisory Panel Member of Texas Instruments Inc., USA.

Balamurugan Balusamy has served up to the position of Associate Professor in his stint of 14 years of experience with VIT University, Vellore. He had completed his bachelors, Master's, and PhD degrees from top premier institutions in India. His passion is teaching and adapts different design thinking principles while delivering his lectures. He has published more than 30 books on various technologies and visited over 15 countries for his technical course. He has several top-notch conferences in his resume and has published over 150 of quality journal, conference, and book chapters combined. He serves in the advisory committee for several startups and forums and does consultancy work for industry on Industrial IOT. He has given over 175 talks in various events and symposium. He is currently working as Associate Dean, at Shiv Nadar University, and teaches students and does research on Blockchain and IoT.

Sherimon P.C is presently working as a Faculty of Computer Studies, Arab Open University, Oman. He has 22 years of international experience in administration, teaching, and research in universities. He has completed numerous research projects and consultancy projects too. His Google Scholar citation is 316, h-index is 7, and i10 index is 6.

Contributors

Prasanth A.
Vel Tech Rangarajan Dr.
Sagunthala R&D Institute of
Science and Technology, Chennai, India

Chidhambararajan B.
SRM Valliammai Engineering College
Chennai, India

Sangeetha B.
AVS Engineering College
Salem, India

Wasana Boonsong
Rajamangala University of Technology
   Srivijaya
Thailand

Rajesh Kumar Dhanaraj
Symbiosis International (Deemed
   University),
Pune, India

Lakshmi D
VIT Bhopal
India

MohanaPriya D.
KIT-Kalaignarkarunanidhi Institute of
   Technology
Coimbatore, India

Rajalakshmi D.
Sri Sairam Institute of Technology
Chennai, India

Nguyen Tien Dung
Thai Nguyen University of Medicine
   and Pharmacy
Thai Nguyen, Vietnam

Ahmed A. Elngar
Beni-Suef University
Egypt

Arthi K.
SRM Valliammai Engineering College
Chennai, India

Kannan K.
Annapoorana Engineering College,
   Salem, Tamil Nadu, India

Meena K.
GITAM University
Bengaluru, India

Thamarai Selvi K.
SRM Medical College Hospital and
   Research Centre
Kattankulathur, India

Umapathy K.
Sri Chandrasekarendra Saraswathi
   Viswa Maha Vidyalaya (SCSVMV)
   Deemed University, Kanchipuram,
   Tamil Nadu, India

Veena K.
Sathyabama Institute of Science and
   Technology
Chennai, India

Yamuna K.S.
Sona College of Technology
Salem, India

Fathima M.
Sri Krishna College of Engineering and
   Technology
Coimbatore, India

Vetrivel M.
R P Sarathy Institute of Technology,
    Salem, Tamil Nadu, India

Senthamil Selvi M.
Sri Ramakrishna Engineering College
Coimbatore, India

Archana M.A.
Sri Chandrasekarendra Saraswathi
    Viswa Maha Vidyalaya (SCSVMV)
    Deemed University, Kanchipuram,
    Tamil Nadu, India

Deepa N.
Saveetha University
Chennai, India

Mariya Ouaissa
Moulay Ismail University
Meknes, Morocco

Manjula P.
Saveetha Institute of Technical and
    Medical Sciences,
Chennai, India

Mathivanan P.
KIT-Kalaignarkarunanidhi Institute of
    Technology
Coimbatore, India

Deepa P.V.
Arunachala College of Engineering
    for Women
Kanyakumari, India

Kavitha P.V.
Sri Ramakrishna Engineering College
Coimbatore, India

Janhvi Rajyaguru
VIT Bhopal University India

Hari Krishnan Ramachandran
SASTRA Deemed to be University
Thanjavur, Tamil Nadu, India

Aravind Krishnaswamy Rangarajan
Ghent University
Belgium

Omkumar S.
Sri Chandrasekarendra Saraswathi
    Viswa Maha Vidyalaya (SCSVMV)
    Deemed University, Kanchipuram,
    Tamil Nadu, India

Shreya Kakkar
VIT Bhopal University
India

Devi T.
Saveetha University
Chennai, India

Dineshkumar T.
Sri Chandrasekarendra Saraswathi
    Viswa Maha Vidyalaya (SCSVMV)
    Deemed University, Kanchipuram,
    Tamil Nadu, India

Kokilavani T.
Sri Krishna College of Engineering and
    Technology
Coimbatore, India

Pham Chien Thang
TNU-University of Sciences
Thai Nguyen, Vietnam

Ta Thi Nguyet Trang
International School, Thai Nguyen
    University
Thai Nguyen, Vietnam

Saranya V.
Saveetha University
Chennai, India

Ranju Yadav
VIT Bhopal University
Bhopal, India

1 Advanced Enabling Technologies of IoMT in Personalized Healthcare

K. Arthi and *B. Chidhambararajan*
Department of Electronics and Communication Engineering,
SRM Valliammai Engineering College, Chennai, India
*Corresponding Author: K. Arthi (arthikalidasan@gmail.com)

1.1 INTRODUCTION

The rapid increase in the aging population, the prevalence of chronic health issues, and the rise in the spread of pandemic diseases pose a strict need for healthcare services for people affected by economic conditions and reachability. The lack of immediate attention to people affected by prolonged illness and accidents increases the number of deaths every year. Informational communication between people and doctors remains a major hindrance in such cases. To avoid such provocations, many researchers started to keep on exploring new technologies to provide innovative solutions.

The Internet of Medical Things (IoMT) has played a significant role in transforming traditional healthcare services into digitized healthcare platforms to enhance the quality of lives and improve patient outcomes [1]. IoMT is a medical network infrastructure that has the potential to bring interaction between people, processes, things, and networked objects connected through the Internet. IoMT ensures a promising solution by providing remote monitoring of people's health status and reporting to hospitals, medical experts, caretakers, etc.

Before the evolution of the Internet of Things (IoT), patients' visits to hospitals were restricted and there was no way to provide continuous monitoring and diagnosis [2]. The IoT has transformed healthcare services, unleashing their potential by connecting medical devices to the Internet to collect information from invaluable data. IoMT empowers physicians to promote continuous patient engagement and remote monitoring of patients' health, reducing the length of hospital stays at reduced costs.

Due to the increase in demand for a 5G network, the design and production of healthcare devices like smartwatches, fitness trackers, smart gadgets, and smartphones are getting dramatically more attention. A survey based on Fortune Business Insights predicts that the global IoMT market would expand from \$30.79 billion to \$187.60 billion between 2021 and 2028, with an average annual growth rate of 29.5%, down from 71.3% in 2020. The convergence of communication technologies and its fusion of advanced enabling technologies like artificial intelligence (AI) and blockchain technology deliver 4P services, namely, predictive, preventive, personalized, and participative, to shift traditional healthcare to a new era of digitalized healthcare [3]. Collaboration of emerging technologies facilitates remote monitoring, chronic disease management, electronic health records management, medication adherence, and so on.

1.2   IOMT COMMUNICATION PROTOCOLS

Connectivity is necessary for data from the sensors to be exchanged through networks to share information locally or centrally. The communication protocols employed in the healthcare system are also based on its performance and functional requirements. A communication protocol can be chosen based on use cases and distances, which may be for short-range or long-range communications. For sending data gathered from sensors to a smartphone nearby, short-range protocols like ZigBee and Bluetooth are recommended. The information from the patient's wearable sensors can be sent to the doctor or healthcare provider via SMS or the Internet via long-range connectivity such as Long-Term Evolution (LTE). Wireless body area networks are utilized for inter-body communication. Table 1.1 shows the important communication protocols widely used in IoMT applications [4].

1.3   FOG-BASED ARCHITECTURE OF IOMT

IoMT is the concentrated embodiment of IoT technology in the medical field. In general, components of the IoMT system architecture comprise medical devices, medical applications, data management servers, and patient monitoring systems connected through the Internet within the network. The author presented a fog–cloud architecture for COVID-19 detection that comprises three layers, namely, user, fog, and cloud layers [5]. An in-depth knowledge of IoMT architecture is essential in knowing the significance of the technological components involved and how the association between components of the medical ecosystem was established. As medical applications are latency-sensitive, a tri-layer IoMT architecture was proposed to provide real-time monitoring to save lives by reducing the latency and enhancing the quality of healthcare services. Figure 1.1 depicts a fog-based IoMT architecture.

1.3.1   Perception Layer

In IoMT architecture, the uppermost layer is referred to as the perception or physical layer, or sensing layer. The main functions of the perception layer were to provide data collection and provide data access by transporting the data to the next higher layer [6]. The key elements of the perception layer include sensors, actuators, medical

TABLE 1.1

Communication Protocols for IoMT Applications

Protocols	Features	Definition	Uses
IEEE 802.15.4	• Topology: star or peer-peer • Supports 16-bit and 64-bit addressing • Very limited battery consumption	standard	• To obtain information from body area networks and hospital environments
Infrared	• Works up to the line of sight or within a few meters • Used for point-of-care devices	Protocol	• Used in thermometers and cameras
RFID	• Eliminates the need for an external power source. • Real-time location tracking	Technology	• Autonomous RFID tags to develop body area healthcare systems. • Passive RFID tag used for ambient monitoring of the patient's environment
Near Field Communication	• Supports in the range of a few centimeters. • Ensures fast and secure communication between two devices	Technology	• Used in ingestible or implantable sensors
Bluetooth/BLE	• Data transmission over short distances • Security enhanced within the limited range • Low initialization time	Technology	• Fitness monitors • Portable medical devices
Wi-Fi	• Provides long-range communication. • Require high power consumption • Robust connection in indoor environments	Protocol Standard	• Wireless Body Area Network • Wearable handheld devices
ZigBee	• Low-cost and low-power protocol • Transfer data up to 200 m range. • Designed for personal area networks	Protocol	• Noninvasive healthcare
6LoWPAN	• Media access control protocol • Low bandwidth • Covers a range of about 10–100 m	Technology	• Internet-connected routers

(continued)

TABLE 1.1 (Continued)
Communication Protocols for IoMT Applications

Protocols	Features	Definition	Uses
LoRaWAN	• Supports long-range communication of 10 km • Battery-operated device and supports low-power • Used for both public and private networks	Protocol	• Health monitoring system
COAP	• Application protocol • Lightweight mechanism of COAP suits well for resource-constrained nodes and lossy networks	Architecture	• Health domain • Remote monitoring system
MQTT	• Supports lightweight communication protocol • Works well for poor connections. • Constrained processing and memory resources	Architecture	• Facilitates connection between a user device and the cloud
HTTP	• Used for communication between the cloud and the doctor	Architecture	• Wearable thermometer • Remote monitoring systems

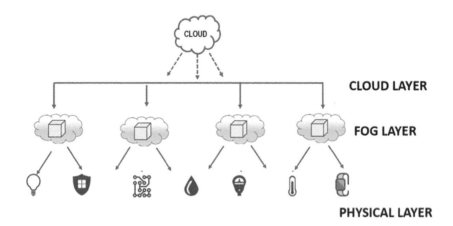

FIGURE 1.1   Fog-based IoMT architecture.

devices, and processing elements to acquire the desired data from the physical world. The main component that drives the physical layer is sensors which mainly comprise environmental, physiological sensors and motion sensors to sense the data about the patient along with contextual awareness. The heterogeneous data captured by different sensors will be processed through hardware development platforms or single-board computers like Arduino or Raspberry Pi. The healthcare experts can have direct access to the generated data by employing local routers and servers in and around the premises. The collected data are passed to the fog layer for further data processing.

1.3.2   Fog Layer

The fog layer acts as a connecting layer located between the things layer and the cloud layer. The main functions of the fog layer are to provide data aggregation, distributed data processing, real-time response, and secured storage of medical data. Fog nodes comprise local servers, access points, routers, set-top boxes, and local and border gateways [6]. Fog nodes fill the gap between devices and the cloud as they lie close to the users, so an immediate response was achieved. Communication between fog-to-fog nodes and fog-to-cloud nodes is wired or wireless based on network connectivity. Distributed architecture, mobility, low latency, and bandwidth efficiency are additional benefits of fog computing. The fog layer reduced the computational workload of devices in the physical layer as it was resource constrained. Fog nodes collect the data from sensors and devices to perform data pre-processing and decision-making. It enables alerts and notifications in case of emergencies or abnormalities noted in patients' data.

1.3.3   Cloud Layer

The cloud layer is considered the service layer that contains repositories, computational resources, and centralized cloud servers to store and process the data received from the fog layer. The cloud presents a virtual dynamic storage platform to interconnect devices and perform computations on the generated massive heterogeneous data [7]. Other than data storage, the cloud provides data analytics and data visualization services that present the data in a structured format.

Cloud technology acts as a promising solution for warehousing the enormous data generated by healthcare services. cloud platforms are used to provide efficient on-demand availability of cloud services, computation, and storage resources. The cloud-based medical information interfaces help healthcare experts derive insights and take action from the generated data.

1.4   CLASSIFICATION OF IOMT DEVICES

IoMT is a connected infrastructure made up of an amalgamation of sensors, medical devices, computing technologies, and medical applications interconnected through the Internet. IoMT devices could be wearable devices, blood glucose monitors, kiosks, or implants for medical treatment. Based on the application used, IoMT is classified as on-body segments, in-body segments, community segment devices, and asset management.

1.4.1 ON-BODY SEGMENT MEDICAL DEVICES

On-body devices are used to assess physical activity or track the health metrics of an individual day-to-day. These devices are mostly clinical-based or consumer-grade wearable devices used in the form of wristbands, smart apparel, textiles, and smartwatches for collecting vital stats through medical apps and smartphones [8]. The devices equipped with sensors are used to track fluctuations in vital parameters and make clinical evaluations using the collected on-body data.

1.4.1.1 Consumer-Based Medical Devices

Consumer-based medical devices equip users to track longitudinal information of a person's heart rate and rhythm, blood pressure, daily activity, etc. Increasing use of consumer-based medical devices skyrocketed once people started to monitor their health after the emergence of the pandemic situations. The most frequently used on-body wearables include FitBit Flex, Garmin vívosmart 4, iWatch, Move ECG – a wearable ECG monitor, HeartGuide – a blood pressure monitor, and bio-sensors.

1.4.1.2 Clinical-Grade Wearables

Clinical-grade medical devices are devices approved by medical regulatory authorities and referred by clinicians for enhancing quicker diagnosis and treatment. Examples of clinical-grade wearables include smart belts for detecting falls, and gait and for alleviating chronic pain in sensory nerves.

1.4.1.3 Implantable

An artificial implantable device is a biomedical device implanted into a human body through an in vitro or surgical procedure used to treat a specific disorder. The most common examples of implantable medical devices are artificial joints, cardiac pacemakers, cochlear implants, and left ventricular assist devices (LVADs).

1.4.2 IN-HOME MEDICAL DEVICES

In-home devices comprise remote patient monitoring (RPM) devices, medical alert systems, and telehealth platforms to carry out constant remote monitoring of patients without unnecessary visits to hospitals. The use of in-home devices helps the patients take care of their health from home and restore their lives with a faster recovery time. Medical alert systems comprise wearable devices synchronized with a medical call center to provide emergency services to those in need. They are used mainly for the elderly or physically challenged people with a lack of mobility. RPM devices facilitate the healthcare management of people with chronic disorders by allowing them to monitor, analyze, and report critical indicators to healthcare experts [9]. The tele-medicine application aims to deliver epidemiological surveillance through medical conference consultation. Telemedicine is used to deliver virtual clinical services to patients, such as diagnosis and monitoring, via the convergence of information technology.

1.4.3 COMMUNITY SEGMENT MEDICAL DEVICES

The community segment encompasses the medical devices used for mobility services, AI-based emergency response intelligence systems, computerized kiosks, point-of-care devices, and pharmaceutical logistics dispersed in cities or over a range of geographic areas to enable mobile, emergency, and remote services. Mobility services are used to track the vital parameters of patients in transit. Medical personnel utilize emergency response intelligence systems to track vital parameters in ambulance services or safety-restricted zones in the event of emergencies outside the hospital's perimeter. Point-of-care devices are used to eliminate laboratory visits by conducting screening procedures and tests from distant locations [10]. Kiosks are customizable computerized self-service structures embedded with touch-screen displays used to get services without staff interaction. It is used to reduce patient waiting time, schedule appointments, and dispense medicines. IoMT devices in logistics help sense temperature, shock, vibration, and humidity for the effective delivery of medical supplies and pharmaceuticals needed by hospitals.

1.4.4 IN-HOSPITAL SEGMENT MEDICAL DEVICES

The in-hospital segment of medical devices comprises medical devices that were inside hospital premises to handle asset management, patient flow management, environmental and energy monitoring, and personnel management. These devices provide a vast array of functions in several operational zones as shown in Figure 1.2.

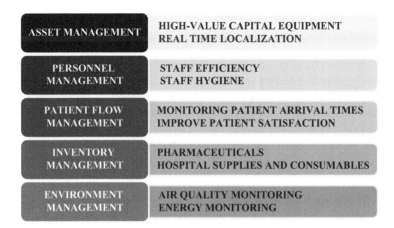

FIGURE 1.2   Functions of in-hospital segment medical devices.

1.5   ENABLING TECHNOLOGIES

1.5.1   Fog Computing

The rapid development of healthcare led to a rise in the number of IoMT devices, which resulted in a massive quantity of data generated from sensors and medical devices. Cloud computing offers data computation resources, processing facilities, and data storage for the massive amounts of data generated by IoT devices. Though it acts as a data warehouse, it still suffers from severe shortcomings like a lack of immediate response, high data transmission costs, and security issues. Health data processing demands low latency, real-time tracking, and data heterogeneity issues. Cloud computing fails to handle latency-sensitive and real-time applications in minimum response time as its data transmission back and forth across multiple hops makes it unfit for applications like vehicular networks, healthcare, etc.

Fog computing was introduced as an alternative approach to cloud computing that delivers data services effectively in both spatial and temporal dimensions [11]. Fog computing is a technological paradigm located close to the end users to provide instantaneous data analysis and results within milliseconds or seconds. It is a decentralized architecture of computing between devices and the cloud that facilitates data transmission with improved quality of service in terms of mobility, low latency, bandwidth conservation, data privacy, and security [12].The author proposed a lossless Electroencephalography (EEG) data compression technique enabled by edge-fog architecture that aims to predict epileptic seizures [13]. The data reduction from edge to fog and fog to cloud was obtained by a unique hybrid approach of KCHE, i.e., a combination of k-means clustering and Huffman encoding. The author used Naive Bayes algorithm to predict epileptic seizures of patients at the fog gateway. The proposed method attains an accuracy range of 99.53% to 99.99%. Machine learning (ML) algorithms were employed to detect disease and determine diagnosis options from clinical data analysis. The author presented IoMT-based patient-centric monitoring for the prediction of heart disease [14]. ML classification algorithms were used in the fog layer for quick analysis and prediction of heart disease, with improved performance compared with other models.

In a remote health monitoring system, efficient and secure data transmission and aggregation were presented to protect the data against security threats and privacy issues from distant locations in a secure manner [15]. The proposed system comprises (i) data encryption and decryption techniques; (ii) sensor, mobile, and fog nodes; and (iii) a single cloud server. Data compression and lightweight symmetric key-based encryption are used for secured data communication. The secure message aggregation (SMA) algorithm at the mobile node is used to enhance aggregation efficiency. The secure message decryption (SMD) algorithm at the fog node is used to enhance data security at the fog nodes.

1.5.2   Blockchain Technology

Blockchain technology has a profound impact on the medical field in information security management, digitalized tracking, health record management, and accelerating clinical health flow [16]. Blockchain technology is a public digital immutable ledger technology distributed across peer-to-peer networks that prevent the healthcare system from being hacked by improving security and transparency within the blockchain ecosystem [17]. A block is a container that comprises data, the hash of the previous block, and the hash of the block to be linked together to form a blockchain. The hash contains the timestamp of the new block created and transactional information. Each time the patient visits the doctor, results or records are recorded as a new block on the ledger that is appended to the preceding block to form a chain that cannot be modified later.

Blockchain facilitates patient health records and drug supplies with improved accessibility and accountability at the appropriate time without any data manipulation. Blockchain cryptographic hash algorithms convert the records into a unique pattern of codes, or hash function, that can be accessed only by the person who owns the data [18]. Blockchain helps medical experts track the results and alert the caretakers in case of emergencies by keeping health records. Blockchain technology documents all kinds of transactions to provide a good deal of accountability, versatility, flexibility, and immutability without any falsification in clinical trials.

Integration of blockchain technology in medical devices poses some problems in terms of processing, storage, mobility, and bandwidth consumption as they are highly resource-constrained in terms of power, memory, and computational resources. An ML-based blockchain task scheduling method, is to protect data against fraud and threats at various levels, including fog nodes and remote servers [19]. The performance was evaluated both in terms of hard and soft constraints for different medical applications. PSLA^{2}P, an authentication key agreement protocol, was proposed for the IoMT architecture-deployed in-hospital and emergency conditions to establish communication between cloud servers and edge devices securely [20]. It also allows legitimate users to access the data from cloud servers with low computational overheads and better functionality. The author presented a fog-enabled automated patient monitoring scheme that enables remote monitoring in fog to detect critical anomalies [21]. In addition, optimization of the fog nodes with blockchains facilitates the secured exchange of information among diverse entities at reduced latency and computational costs.

1.5.3 ARTIFICIAL INTELLIGENCE

AI is steadily revolutionizing multiple domains, like smart voice assistants, self-driving cars, robots, and healthcare. The amalgamation of AI and IoT steers the IoT systems into smart devices by incorporating intelligence algorithms into systems and converting the data into actionable insights to improve the quality of human lives. IoMT sheds light on many breakthroughs to transform traditional healthcare into a smart healthcare service by delivering proactive care to patients with the new era of modern medical applications like precision medicine, drug discovery, and management, robotic surgeries, etc. AI algorithms were used in the IoMT system to secure the data and alert healthcare experts and caretakers when there were any contradictions or abnormalities in the marginal vital parameters. AI is used in point-of-care devices to avoid the spreading of infectious diseases and track disease progression.

Machine learning and deep learning are subsets of AI used to derive insights and make predictions from sensor-generated data with improved speed and accuracy in data analysis [22]. They are used in drug discovery, patient data analysis, medical imaging, and disease anomaly detection. Integration of AI with blockchain technology achieves a good level of trade-off between energy and load by balancing load between fog and cloud nodes using task scheduling. Personalized deep-learning approaches were used for the early diagnosis of diseases and to make clinical decisions.

An IoT-based deep learning architecture was used to estimate the fetal Q wave, R wave and S wave (QRS) complex in the abdominal Electrocardiography (ECG) [23]. A deep learning model based on transfer learning allowed to run on the cloud consists of three phases: (i) data processing and segmentation, (ii) time frequency and representation, and (iii) training of the deep learning model and classification. A deep learning model was used to predict if decompression surgery was recommended or if it was curable by nonsurgical procedures [24]. The model performance was evaluated by classical and generalizability evaluation, whereas logistic regression was used as a benchmark model for results comparison.

1.5.4 WEARABLE TECHNOLOGY

Wearable devices are small wearables that comprise a wearable part and an electronic counterpart that can be incorporated into the clothing and accessories of the users to keep track of vital health parameters. Nowadays, humans use wearables like pedometers, smart watches, hearing aids, fitness trackers, and eyewear in their daily lives. As noninvasive wearable devices are hands-free, it simplifies repairing and replacing them without any pain. Wearable technologies exist in forms such as sewing thread, accessories, garments, and portables.

The wearables are also portable in nature. Examples include mobile phones, cameras, and microphones. Compact, portable devices track and monitor fitness measurements such as walking and running distances, counting steps, calculating calories burned, measuring heart rate and pulse rate, and so on. Another form of wearable technology is in smart garment form that can be worn as a jacket and provides feasible solutions to the unobtrusive measurement of new parameters. Wearables, in the form of accessories, can supplement daily style with items such as smart jewellery, smart headsets, or smart shoes. Monitoring and assistive technology are used for chronic disease management, tracking Parkinson's disease progression, and monitoring bio-signal waveforms.

1.6   ADVANCEMENTS OF IOMT

The proliferation of IoMT gained massive momentum in the field of healthcare to offer benefits to people in the medical ecosystem in many ways. It has a lot of calibers to redefine traditional healthcare services into modern digital healthcare using seamless connectivity. IoMT made a huge step forward in recent years by offering smart services to clinicians, patients, medical equipment, hospitals, and community segments. For example, apart from the basic functions of a smartphone, it got improvised concerning health by providing information about location, mobility metrics, track

FIGURE 1.3   Advancements in the IoMT.

workouts, heartbeat irregularity, calorie tracker, and heart rate notifications [25, 26]. Some of the unique advancements of IoMT that outshined the previous innovations are explained next and outlined in Figure 1.3.

1.6.1   HEALTH MONITORS [B HEAD]

Most people are susceptible to diabetes due to sedentary lifestyles and poor eating habits, which need recurrent monitoring to track glucose levels. FreeStyle Libre 2 is a small, unobtrusive continuous glucose monitoring system used to monitor glucose levels for adults and children. Walgreens TrueMetrix Bluetooth Blood Glucose Meter, Eversense, and Dexcom G6 are some of the best glucose monitors for diabetes management. These devices activate alarms and alert the caretakers when the levels cross the threshold limit.

Many blood pressure monitors are available on the market in the form of fitness trackers, smart watches, wristbands, bracelets, etc. People like to use devices that are conspicuous and unobtrusive in nature. In that scenario, Valencell Ear Pressure Devices in the form of earbuds and Vivae Blood Pressure Ring took a huge market to monitor blood pressure and vital signs. The University of California, San Diego (UCSD) developed a stretchable epidermal patch for tracing and monitoring heart rate, lactate, blood pressure, and metabolites of glucose. KEYAR is a wireless intrapartum monitoring device used to monitor uterine contraction, fetal heart rate, and maternal heart rate at the time of labor to avoid complications.

1.6.2   SEIZURE MANAGEMENT

Seizure management is necessary as it may cause the sudden death of a person at any time, even while sleeping. Proper monitoring avoids it by using seizure alert devices in the form of headband wearables, smart watches, wearable bracelets, mattresses, and cameras. For seizure management, MedPage movement alarm, seizure alert camera-SAMi, EpiWatch App, Sleep-Safe pillow, and Emfit MM sleep monitor are used.

A brain sentinel device is used to detect uncontrollable and convulsive seizures using an EMG recording with nigh-on perfect accuracy. An IoMT-based epileptic seizure predictor, ForeSeiz, is designed as a wearable headband for patients with generalized epileptic seizures [27]. The proposed system consists of threeElectromyography (EMG) electrodes, NodeMCU ESP8266, and Firebase as the cloud. It uses Enhanced Convolutional Neural Network for classification along with the Artifact Removal Technique to avoid artifact contamination in EEG recordings. The authors evaluated the proposed design on 12 real-time subjects for validation and showed the results with 97% accuracy.

1.6.3 WEARABLE

iRhythm Technologies designed a wearable Patch that detects atrial fibrillation and prevents stroke. Reebok CheckLight is a wearable skullcap used as a sports activity indicator to monitor the impact of head injuries. A Holter monitor is a noninvasive wearable device recommended by doctors to keep track of heart rate and rhythm for patients with arrhythmia.

1.6.4 PERSONAL ASSISTANTS

Voice-controlled personal assistants like Amazon Echo and Google Home provide elderly people with assisted living and retrieval of information from electronic health records. AI-enabled smart speakers can be employed in home and infirmary rooms to follow proper medical adherence and make patients friendly by getting engaged.

1.6.5 IMPLANTABLE

Smart pills taken orally travel through the body, capturing images that help to ease colon cancer at its early stages. The pills send information to peripheral devices through the Internet or Bluetooth. Imec developed a smart pill used to examine the gastrointestinal system along with muscle contractions. Capsule endoscopies have become the best alternative for endoscopies without sticking a tube down into the body. Pillcam COLON eliminates the necessity of a complex colonoscopy. Proteus Patch keeps track of medication adherence to enhance the diagnosis rate. ABILIFY MYCITE is a combination medicine of an antipsychotic tablet for the treatment of schizophrenia or depressive disorders in adults with an ingestible sensor to record and transmit time-logged data.

1.6.6 ROBOTS

Due to the recent advancements in medical technology, medical Robots are used in many medical applications like robot-assisted surgeries, prosthetics, robotic nurses, clearing infections in clinical areas, and rehabilitation. ReWalk Personal 6.0 is developed for personal use by those who have paralyzed or poorly handed arms or hands. Surgical robot daVinci, a multi-armed wonderbot, assists surgeons in the operating rooms by accessing magnetic resonance imaging (MRI) data of similar cases. Xenex Germ-Zapping Robot, an automated robot, is trained to kill infectious bacteria in hospitals using ultraviolet (UV) rays. The PARO Therapeutic Robot is used to reduce stress for elderly patients suffering from dementia and mood disorders.

1.6.7   PROSTHETICS

The tremendous growth of wearable technology and mobile platforms has put forward its step in the field of prosthetics into reality by making suitable limb and skin replacements in patients. TracPatch, a wearable device, OrthyoApp, and BMPpathway, an RPM system, are used in treating orthopedic patients after surgery and sharing the data to improve recovery progress. Knee prosthetics with data transmission enable clinician and patient contact to increase the mobility of patients in real time.

1.6.8   HYGIENE MANAGEMENT

Implementation of proper hygiene practices among medical personnel in hospitals and organizations is essential to preventing the spread of infectious diseases. IoT-based hygiene management systems are used to provide automatic alerts to medical personnel to sanitize their hands on time in areas that demand higher standards of hand hygiene.

1.7   CONCLUSION

In the Industrial 4.0 era, IoMT is on its way to transforming traditional medical services into automated digital health services in every walk of life around us. Different emerging technologies go hand in hand with IoMT to promote medical amenities like telehealth services, sending reports, personalized care, and notification alerts. Different medical requirements have opened the door to diverse types of medical devices according to the needs of the well-being of people.

In summary, this chapter developed the architecture of the IoMT that is suitable for healthcare applications with low latency. A summary of IoMT communication protocols and their application areas were discussed. IoMT was thoroughly reviewed in the chapter with examples of healthcare applications. It also looked at some of the essential enabling technologies that will help IoMT to reach new heights in the future. The chapter ends by highlighting some recent and significant developments in IoMT in the healthcare industry.

REFERENCES

1.   Wagan, S. A., Koo, J., Siddiqui, I. F., Attique, M., Internet of medical things and trending converged technologies: A comprehensive review on real-time applications. *Journal of King Saud University–Computer and Information Sciences*, 34, 9228–9251, 2022.

2. Kumar, D. R., Krishna, T. A., Wahi, A., Health monitoring framework for in time recognition of pulmonary embolism using Internet of Things. *Journal of Computational and Theoretical Nanoscience*, 15(5), 1598–1602, 2018.

3. Firouzi, F., Jiang, S., Chakrabarty, K., Farahani, B., Fusion of IoT, AI, edge–fog–cloud, and blockchain: Challenges, solutions, and a case study in healthcare and medicine. *IEEE Internet of Things Journal*, 10, 3686–3705, 2022.

4. Aruchamy, P., Gnanaselvi, S., Sowndarya, D., An artificial intelligence approach for energy-aware intrusion detection and secure routing in internet of things-enabled wireless sensor networks. *Concurrency and Computation: Practice and Experience*, 1–33, 2023.

5. Akram, K. M., Sihem, S., Okba, K., Harous, S., IoMT-fog-cloud based architecture for Covid-19 detection. *Biomedical Signal Processing and Control*, 76, 103715, 2022.

6. Cheikhrouhou, O., Mershad, K., Jamil, F., Mahmud, R., A lightweight blockchain and fog-enabled secure remote patient monitoring system. *Internet of Things*, 22, 100691, 2023.

7. Jayachitra, S., Prasanth, A., Hariprasath, S., AI enabled internet of medical things in smart healthcare. *AI Models for Blockchain-Based Intelligent Networks in IoT Systems: Concepts, Methodologies, Tools, and Applications*, 6, 141–161, 2023.

8. Dao, N., Internet of wearable things: Advancements and benefits from 6G technologies. *Future Generation Computer Systems*, 138, 172–184, 2022.

9. Boikanyo, K., Zungeru, A. M., Sigweni, B., Yahya, A., Remote patient monitoring systems: Applications, architecture, and challenges. *Scientific African*, 20, e01638, 2023.

10. Aljabr, A., Kumar, K., Design and implementation of Internet of Medical Things (IoMT) using artificial intelligent for mobile-healthcare. *Measurement: Sensors*, 24, 100499, 2022.

11. Elhadad, A., Alanazi, F., Taloba, A. I., Abozeid, A., Fog computing service in the healthcare monitoring system for managing the real-time notification. *Journal of Healthcare Engineering*, 5337733: 1–19 2022.

12. Wang, X., Wu, Y., Fog-assisted internet of medical things for smart healthcare. *IEEE Transactions on Consumer Electronics*, 1: 391–399 2023.

13. Idrees, A. K., Idrees, S. K., Couturier, R., Ali-Yahiya, T., An edge-fog computing-enabled lossless EEG data compression with epileptic seizure detection in IoMT networks. *IEEE Internet of Things Journal*, 9, 13327–13337, 2022.

14. Chakraborty, C., Kishor, A., Real-time cloud-based patient-centric monitoring using computational health systems. *IEEE Transactions on Computational Social Systems*, 9, 1613–1623, 2022.

15. Azeem, M., Ning, H., Ashraf, H., Zaman, N., Humayun, M., Fog-oriented secure and lightweight data aggregation in IoMT. *IEEE Access*, 9, 111072–111082, 2021.

16. Bhaskar, K.B., Prasanth, A., Saranya, P, An energy-efficient blockchain approach for secure communication in IoT-enabled electric vehicles. *International Journal of Communication Systems*, 35, 1–30, 2022.

17. Taherdoost, H., Blockchain-based Internet of Medical Things. *Applied Sciences*, 13, 1287, 2023.

18. Andew, J., Isravel, D. P., Sagayam, K. M., Bhushan, B., Sei, Y., Blockchain for healthcare systems: Architecture, security challenges, trends and future directions. *Journal of Network and Computer Applications*, 215, 103633, 2023.

19. Lakhan, A., Mohammed, M. A., Nedoma, J., Martinek, R., Federated-learning based privacy preservation and fraud-enabled blockchain IoMT system for healthcare. *IEEE Journal of Biomedical and Health Informatics*, 27, 664–672, 2023.

20. Abdussami, M., Amin, R., Vollala, S., Provably secured lightweight authenticated key agreement protocol for modern health industry. *Ad Hoc Networks*, 141, 103094, 2023.

21. Cheikhrouhou, O., Mershad, K., Jamil, F., Mahmud., A., Lightweight blockchain and fog-enabled secure remote patient monitoring system. *Internet of Things*, 22, 100691, 2023.

22. Kavitha, M., Roobini, S., Prasanth, A., Sujaritha, M., Systematic view and impact of artificial intelligence in smart healthcare systems, principles, challenges and applications. *Machine Learning and Artificial Intelligence in Healthcare Systems*, 21, 25–56, 2023.

23. Krupa, A. J. D., Dhanalakshmi, S., Lai, K. W., Tan, Y., An IoMT enabled deep learning framework for automatic detection of fetal QRS: A solution to remote prenatal care. *Journal of King Saud University–Computer and Information Sciences*, 34, 7200–7211, 2022.

24. Jujjavarapu, C., Suri, P., Pejaver, V., Friedly, J. L., Predicting decompression surgery by applying multimodal deep learning to patients structured and unstructured health data. *BMC Medical Informatics and Decision Making*, 23, 1–24. 2023.

25. Bhatt, M. W., Sharma, S., An IoMT-based approach for real-time monitoring using wearable neuro-sensors. *Journal of Healthcare Engineering*, *2023*, 1–10, 2023.

26. Subhan, F., Mirza, A., Su'ud, M. B. M., Alam, M. M., AI-enabled wearable medical internet of things in healthcare system: A survey. *Applied Sciences*, 13, 1394, 2023.

27. Prathaban, B. P., Balasubramanian, R., Kalpana, R., ForeSeiz: An IoMT based headband for Real-time epileptic seizure forecasting. *Expert Systems with Applications*, 188, 116083, 2022.

2 Deep Learning Interpretation of Biomedical Data in IoMT

M. Senthamil Selvi,[1] P.V. Kavitha,[2] P.V. Deepa,[3] and Ahmed A. Elngar[4]*
[1]Department of Information Technology, Sri Ramakrishna Engineering College, Coimbatore, India
[2]Department of Artificial Intelligence and Data Science, Sri Ramakrishna Engineering College, Coimbatore, India (Email: kavitha.krishna@srec.ac.in)
[3]Department of Electronics and Communication Engineering, Arunachala College of Engineering for Women, Kanyakumari, India (Email: pv.deepa.me@gmail.com)
[4]Faculty of Computers and Artificial Intelligence, Beni-Suef University, Egypt (Email: elngar_7@yahoo.co.uk)
* Corresponding Author: M. Senthamil Selvi (Email: senthamilselvi@srec.ac.in)

2.1 INTRODUCTION

To live a joyful and prosperous life, every individual in the universe deserves good health. According to the World Health Organization, health is "a state of physical and mental well-being free of disease and disability." Healthcare is the practice of upholding and assessing one's health through disease and illness prevention, treatment, and improvement of well-being and life quality. Medical errors are common in traditional healthcare, posing a severe public health risk and threatening patient safety.

In today's healthcare system, faulty diagnosis, prescription errors, improper treatment, inadequate and insecure clinical facilities, or physicians' lack of adequate training can all lead to failure in emergency situations. These medical concerns are prevalent in the majority of countries. To address the challenges that the medical domain faces, IoMT plays a major role in saving patients' lives through accurate disease detection. IoMT replaces the traditional medical system and acts as a crucial element in creating the upcoming healthcare industry.

DOI: 10.1201/9781003405450-2

2.1.1 IoMT

IoMT is a networked environment composed of software packages and medical equipment that interact with patients and healthcare professionals over the Internet [1]. IoMT devices allow doctors to care for patients remotely, saving patients from having to visit them in person. It connects patients with their doctors and allows medical data to be transferred over a secure network, reducing the number of unnecessary hospital visits. After the COVID-19 outbreak, IoMT has been a hot topic in the rising healthcare and telemedicine market. The Internet of Things (IoT) is sometimes known as "Smart Healthcare." The IoT has improved the way we engage with doctors [2].

2.1.2 IoMT Architecture

IoMT devices connect patients, physicians, hospital equipment, and wearable technologies to send health records over a secure network. IoMT is a smart healthcare system made up of five components [3]. They are:

- Sensors Unit: This unit gathers biomedical signals from the patient.
- Processing Unit: This unit is used to process biomedical signals.
- Network Unit: This unit is used to send biomedical data via the Internet.
- Data Storage Unit: This is a device that temporarily or permanently stores data.
- Visualization Unit: Based on medical data, this unit uses artificial intelligence (AI) algorithms to make decisions about diagnosis and therapy.

The components of the IoMT architecture are illustrated in Figure 2.1.

2.1.3 IoMT Technology

IoMT is also known as "Connecting Medical Devices to Networks." It is built upon three technologies. They are [4] discussed next.

Sensor Technology: The biosensor senses the patient's health factors. It is of two types: biological medical sensors and nonbiological medical sensors.

- ✓ Blood, respiratory, tissue, and other body parts are detected by a biological medical sensor.
- ✓ Body temperature, mobility, electrical activity of the cardiac and muscles, as well as other patient factors are all measured using a nonbiological medical sensor.

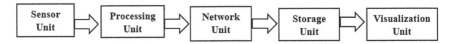

FIGURE 2.1 IoMT Architecture.

Internet of Things Connectivity: IoMT data is transmitted directly and saved in a repository (i.e., database). Clinicians can access the data over the Internet, allowing them to provide better care to their patients.

Artificial Intelligence: Data is intelligently managed by IoMT devices [5]. It makes intelligent decisions by removing irrelevant data from the medical system and forecasting medical diagnoses using complicated analysis algorithms. This allows medical practitioners to focus on patients instead.

2.1.4 ADVANTAGES OF IoMT

The benefits of IoMT are listed as follows:

- **Accessibility:**
  - It is the ability to access patient health data by doctors more quickly and accurately.
- **Low Per-Patient Cost:**
  - It reduces costs by taking treatments at home and avoids unnecessary hospital visits.
- **Fast Per-Patient:**
  - IoMT devices are faster and easy to implement.
- **Improved Efficiency:**
  - Waiting time and visiting time to look into patients have been reduced, which in turn improves efficiency because IoMT captures data from anywhere.

2.1.5 CHALLENGES OF IMPLEMENTING IoMT

The following challenges are faced during the implementation of IoMT:

High-Cost Infrastructure:
The cost of setting up IoMT infrastructure is very large.

Vulnerabilities in IoMT Security:
Securing millions of patient medical records is a challenge in maintaining the quality of care.

Strain on Existing Networks:
Existing hospital networks have to be ready with additional support for connecting devices and an information technology backbone that makes hospital networks fast and secure. This is an ongoing issue because most hospitals are generally slow to equip themselves with expensive IoMT devices.

2.1.6 APPLICATIONS OF IoMT IN HEALTHCARE

IoMT serves as a smart remote monitoring system that detects early signs of disease and provides patients with suitable treatment. Some of the healthcare applications of IoMT [6] are prognostication of genetic disorders, anticipating the evolution of the cardiovascular disease, irregular heartbeats, bone disorder, tumor prediction, and early diagnosis of contagious ailments like dengue fever, coronavirus, malaria, etc. It is used for identifying bone loss, precise peptides, and initial periodontal diseases, detecting teeth areas affected by clenching and grinding, handling asthma issues, measuring blood oxygen saturation, heart rate, and pulse measurements, sensing dental problems, tracking blood glucose and levels of pressure, trying to identify dental disease in the primitive phase, assisting in the pre-diagnosis of diabetes, real-time tracking of viral and bacterial infections, and detecting tooth cavities. It is also used to detect high body temperature associated with coronavirus infection, which is useful for environment-assisted living facilities, detecting adverse drug reactions, and monitoring viral and bacterial infections in human body fluids such as sweat, urine, and saliva in real time.

2.2 ROLE OF MACHINE LEARNING IN IOMT

IoMT's AI technology plays a major role in detecting accurate early-stage diagnoses of diseases, which could save patients' lives by allowing them to be cured. Machine learning is frequently applied in the IoMT domain to assist the medical profession in making accurate diagnoses, treating diseases, and providing high-quality service to patients. IoMT devices collect medical data from patients and transfer it to the cloud, where a machine learning algorithm does the actual diagnosis. Machine learning uses three important steps: pre-processing, feature extraction, and classification for the diagnosis process. The report is provided to medical practitioners after the diagnosis process is completed.

In the healthcare industry, IoMT is currently quickly expanding due to the vast volume of data. Owing to the processing and analysis volumes of patient health data, machine learning methods in IoMT are taking a back seat in the healthcare industry. Feature extraction is done manually throughout the diagnosis phase in machine learning approaches. The workflow of machine learning is illustrated in Figure 2.2.

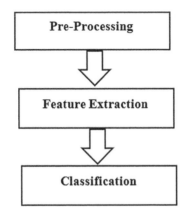

FIGURE 2.2 Machine learning.

2.3 DEEP LEARNING IN IOMT

2.3.1 DEEP LEARNING OVERVIEW

Deep learning comes under the discipline of AI capable of dealing with extremely complicated medical data and producing highly accurate diagnoses. [7]. It can manage a vast amount of data and perform well. Without the assistance of a programmer, it pulls the features from the data automatically. It necessitates more hardware support in order to solve complex problems with high precision. It concentrates on high-level attributes rather than low-level data attributes. It solves the issue from beginning to end, rather than breaking it down into bits. It necessitates a longer execution time because it incorporates a huge amount of constraints during the training phase. The following layers are used to build deep learning algorithms:

1. *Input layer*: This is the initial layer, and it is where each node receives its data.
2. *Output layer*: This is the final layer, and it contains the problem's output.
3. *Hidden layer*: Between the first and last levels, there lies a hidden layer. It is made up of neurons that use an activation function to produce a response after getting a collection of weighted inputs. When an image of a car is passed through the initial layer (input) and middle layer (hidden), the final layer (output) provides the result of a hatchback car or a sedan car.

Figure 2.3 illustrates the different layers of deep learning.

2.3.2 DEEP LEARNING IN IOMT

Deep learning plays a vital role in IoMT since it handles a massive volume of healthcare records in the medical field. Deep learning' inculcation into the IoMT domain keeps an eye on enhancing the accuracy of disease diagnosis, medical image processing, medical data analysis, and other related medical applications [8]. Figure 2.4 depicts the structure of the deep learning IoMT framework.

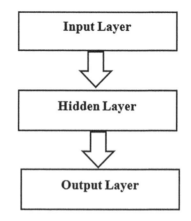

FIGURE 2.3   Deep learning.

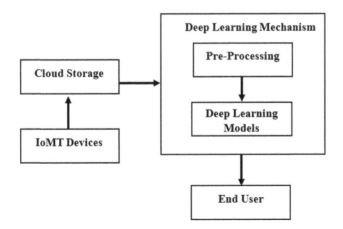

FIGURE 2.4   Deep learning IoMT framework.

The deep learning IoMT framework comprises four layers [9]:

- Layer 1: Data collection from IoMT
- Layer 2: Cloud storage
- Layer 3: Deep learning mechanism
- Layer 4: End users

A. DATA COLLECTION FROM IoMT

This layer collects data from the human body's wearable gadgets. Wearable devices may consist of sensors and electronic circuits that monitor critical patient functions such as blood pressure level, blood sugar level, oxygen level, breathing and pulse rate, body temperature, urine report, and so on.

B. CLOUD STORAGE

This layer sends health data from IoMT devices via a secure network to the cloud, where it is kept for further analysis. Raw, unlabeled, and unfiltered data samples will be collected.

C. DEEP LEARNING MECHANISM

The stages included in the deep learning mechanism are as follows: Pre-processing is the initial step in deep learning. The cloud data is preprocessed to eliminate noise from the input, improve the required features, or resize the input. Upon preprocessing, the data can be put into clever deep learning models, which extract features and conduct classification without the need for human intervention. The proposed system detects early disease symptoms and delivers essential treatment to patients, thereby saving their lives. It paves the way for more intricate health issues to be resolved in emergency situations, as well as very accurate disease diagnoses for patients. The next section discusses various deep learning models.

D. END USER

Hospitals and medical practitioners could be the final users. In this layer, doctors have access to patients' medical records. The physician can notice the patient's health difficulties by using a graphical user interface.

2.4 DEEP LEARNING ALGORITHMS IN IOMT

The various types of deep learning models employed in remote patient monitoring for the prediction of extremely accurate diagnoses are as follows:

2.4.1 DEEP NEURAL NETWORK (DNN)

It involves input layer, intermediate layer, and output layer. The data is transmitted between the processing layers via intermediate levels. The term "deep" represents a higher number of hidden levels of processing. To deliver an efficient output, the DNN collects the input data and processes it by using a linear or nonlinear connection. When the DNN receives the input, it calculates its probability function for each layer's probable output. The input is labeled based on the likelihood value.

DNNs can be used to address issues that have a lot of nonlinear relationships. When the input data is represented as primitives in numerous layers, DNN uses additional layers to composite aspects of the difficult problem. Deep architectures reveal a plethora of new varieties not found in traditional neural designs. DNNs are feedforward networks with only one direction of data flow (input layer to output layer). To make a connection between virtual neurons, DNN first involves a series of virtual neural connections and assigns weights to them at random. The random weights are multiplied by those of the specified inputs to get an output between 0 and 1. If the input data is not recognized by the network, an algorithm can automatically alter its weight until it finds the correct mathematical mapping.

2.4.2 RESTRICTED BOLTZMANN NETWORKS (RBNS) OR AUTO ENCODERS

RBN [10] is a stochastic network used in deep learning. It is made up of two units and there is no output unit. They are a visible layer and concealed/hidden layer. Each node of the visible layer is connected with its counterpart inside the concealed/hidden layer. The observation is aligned to the visible layer, while the feature extractor is aligned to the hidden layer.

The RBN framework is depicted in Figure 2.5.

For learning the distributions of unlabeled training data, the RBN functions as a generative model. It is a discriminative model that is used to classify labeled data. They are called auto encoders, and they encode and decode data. The inputs are encoded and converted into a list of numbers using a forward pass. A backward pass

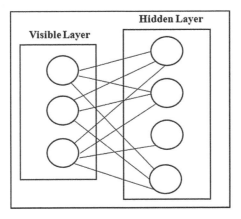

FIGURE 2.5 RBN.

decodes the inputs by taking these sets of integers to convert back into reconstructing input data.

2.4.3 DEEP BELIEF NETWORKS (DBNs)

DBNs are feed-forward neural networks made up of RBM models stacked one on top of the other [11]. It solves the vanishing gradient problem. It consists of two RBM models. The second visible layer of RBM is taken from the first hidden layer of RBM model, then the output of the first RBM model can be used to train the second RBM model. This approach is repeated until all of the network's layers have been trained. This network is more easily expandable. It consists of input and output units. The visible layer is known as the input unit. The hidden layer is known as the output unit.

DBNs allow for the extraction and classification of features. Layer-by-layer pre-training is used for feature extraction, back-propagation is employed for classification, and other tasks are tuned using a small labeled data set. The block diagram of DBN is depicted in Figure 2.6.

2.4.4 GENERATIVE ADVERSARIAL NETWORKS (GANs)

It is a kind of deep neural network made up of two networks [22]: generators and discriminators. Adversarial training is another name for GAN. There are two feedback loops in each network. Generator creates data whereas discriminator determines if the data generated is authorized. The steps of GAN process are explained as follows:

- The generator network accepts random numbers as input and outputs an image.
- The discriminator network receives the output of the generator, as well as sample images from the original dataset.

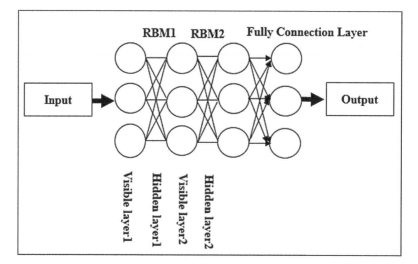

FIGURE 2.6 DBN.

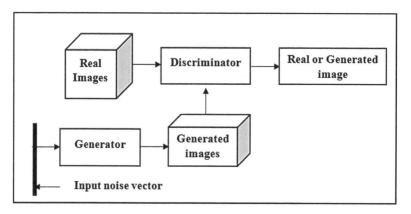

FIGURE 2.7 GAN.

- The discriminator outputs probabilities of 0 or 1, where 1 indicates true prediction (i.e., authentic) and 0 indicates false prediction (i.e., fake). For example, 1 indicates a brain tumor prediction while 0 indicates a non-tumor prediction.

The block diagram of GAN is depicted in Figure 2.7.

2.4.5 RECURRENT NEURAL NETWORKS (RNNs)

As in the intensive care unit (ICU), clinical medical data is often composed of a multivariate time sequence of observations. The sensory data and lab test results are recorded as part of the IoMT framework's health monitoring of patients. The health

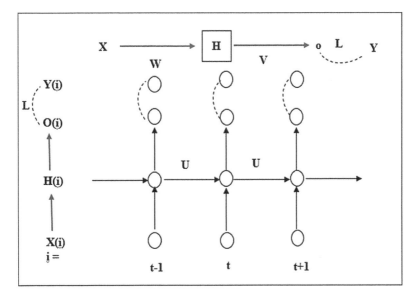

FIGURE 2.8 RNN.

records have sporadic sampling, missing data, and differ in length. The common models for learning from sequence data are Long Short-Term Memory (LSTM) and RNN [23].

RNNs deal with sequential data, which can flow in any direction. In an RNN, all inputs and outputs are dependent on each other. It contains a memory that stores the information from previous computations. The output depends on previous computations to predict the next word sequence. The illustration of the RNN [12] workflow is depicted in Figure 2.8.

The model parameters collected as output from various RNN model time steps are shared. RNNs consist of a circuit that contains hidden to input and hidden to output units.

RNNs resemble to the following equation:

$$H(t) = a(v + UH(t - 1) + WX(t)) \qquad (2.1)$$

$$O(t) = h + VH(t) \qquad (2.2)$$

where
- t stands for time.
- v indicates the offsets of the visible layer and h indicates the offsets of the hidden layer.
- W denotes the weight joining the hidden and hidden units.
- V denotes the weight joining the hidden and output units.
- a represents the activation function.
- U represents the weights of hidden units at time $t-1$ and t.
- X indicates the network's input, whereas Y indicates the network's output.

RNN is normally used in Natural Language Processing applications. Image captioning applications employ the convolutional neural network (CNN)–RNN framework. The encoder uses CNN and the decoder uses RNN. The encoder encodes the image automatically. From the encoded image, the decoder creates word captions.

2.4.6 LONG SHORT-TERM MEMORY

The output from the previous step is used as a source in the next phase in RNN [21]. It makes reliable forecasts based on recent data. RNN's problems include:

- No provision for long-term dependencies
- As the gap length grows, performance becomes inefficient

The aforementioned difficulties are dealt with by LSTM, which keeps the data for a long time. It's used for time-series data processing, prediction, and classification. The outcome of LSTM is determined by three factors:

1 *Cell state*: It comprises the network's current long-term memory.
2 *Hidden state*: It stores the output from the preceding time interval.
3 *Input state*: The current time step's input data.

These three gates make up the LSTM module. They are.

Forget gate: This gate is in charge of eliminating unimportant data.
Input gate: This gate is in charge of adding data.
Output gate: This gate is in charge of transmitting data to the next hidden state.

The LSTM network is depicted in Figure 2.9. In LSTM, $X(t)$ combined with previous output from cell $h(t\text{-}1)$ is passed to the input gate. "tanh layer" squashes the input combination. This input combination is then sent to sigmoid-activated nodes. The squashed input is multiplied by sigmoid activated output and it is passed to the forget gate.

In LSTM cells, state variables like $S(t)$ and $S(t\text{–}1)$ are applied to input data to reduce the risk of vanishing gradients and to assist the network in remembering or forgetting the information. The output gate generates the output $h(t)$ by multiplying the tanh squashing function with a sigmoid-activated node.

2.4.7 CONVOLUTIONAL DEEP NEURAL NETWORKS – CNNs

CNN is a kind of neural network used to classify images [13]. It simplifies images into a form that retains all of their attributes, making accurate prediction simple. CNNs take multidimensional arrays as input data, such as two-dimensional images having three color channels. It consists of convolutional and pooling layers.

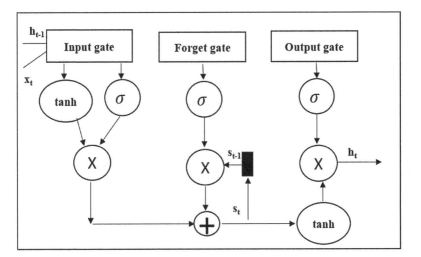

FIGURE 2.9 LSTM architecture.

i. **Convolutional Layer:**
The input image is dealt with a filter (3 matrix) in this layer to produce a convolved feature. The convolved features (Feature Maps) are transferred to the next layer. The first layer gathers fundamental information like diagonal or horizontal edges. The first layer's output acts as input for the next layer. As it progresses deeper into the network, it finds increasingly complicated features.

ii. **Pooling Layer**
This layer shrinks the Convolved Feature's spatial size. The data processing time is sped up by reducing the dimensions. Down sampling is the term for this method. On CNN, there are three different forms of pooling. They are
- Maximum/Max Pooling
- Minimum/Min Pooling
- Average/Avg Pooling

- The highest value for every patch on that feature map is returned by Max Pooling.
- The minimal value for every patch on that feature map is returned by Min Pooling.
- Return the overall average for every patch on that feature map when using Average Pooling.

However, Max Pooling outperforms both Min and Average Pooling in terms of performance. The pooling layer generates a flattened two-dimensional matrix, which is sent into the Fully Connected layer for classifying the image.

The CNN architecture is depicted in Figure 2.10. The color blocks of the input patch "A" are multiplied by the convolution kernel "K" to produce feature maps in

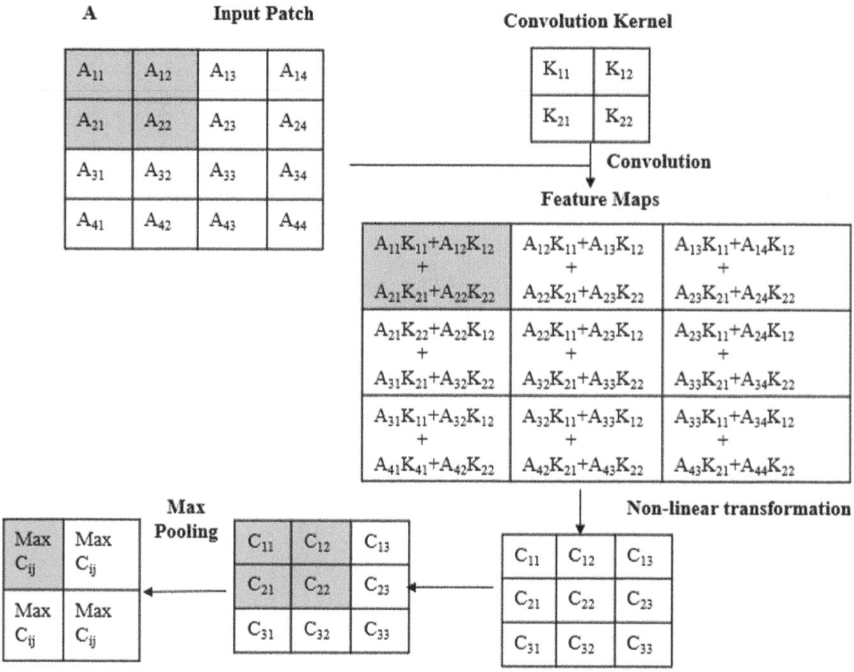

FIGURE 2.10 CNN architecture.

the convolution layer. The final output is generated using Max Pooling. Feature Maps represent the matrix A_{ij} and K_{ij} Convolutional matrix represents C_{ij}. i and j indicate the rows and columns of the matrix, respectively.

2.4.8 TRANSFER LEARNING MODELS

Transfer learning model trains a neural network for a specific problem and then uses it to solve different problems by adding extra layers [14]. It reduces the time it takes to train a neural network model and lowers the generalization error. The following are common types of transfer learning models:

2.4.8.1 ResNet-34

ResNet is an acronym for Residual CNN [24]. It overcomes the problem of vanishing gradients. If the system is excessively lengthy, the gradients will be zero when the loss function is computed. As a result, there is no learning and the weight is not updated. The benefit of ResNet is that gradients can flow backward via later layers to the starting filters. IoMT is utilized to detect the early phase diagnosis of leukemia patients using the ResNet-34 model. It is a CNN with 34 layers.

ResNet is an acronym for ResidualCNN. It overcomes the problem of vanishing gradients. It is a CNN with 34 layers.

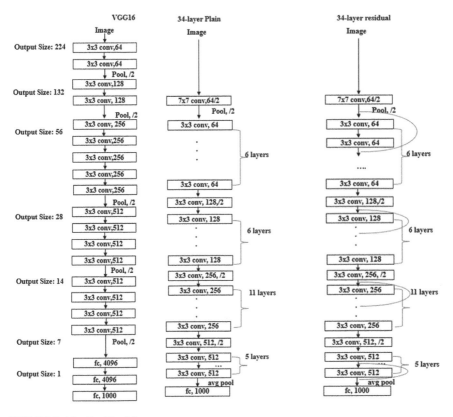

FIGURE 2.11 ResNet-34.

ResNet-34's architecture is depicted in Figure 2.11. VGG19 is the first layer. The 34-layer plain network is the second layer, while the 34-layer residual network is the third layer. Other ResNet models, such as ResNet-50 and ResNet-101, are employed in biomedical image categorization tasks.

2.4.8.2 DenseNet-121

DenseNet is known as Densely Connected Convolutional Networks [15]. Deep convolutional networks' depth is increased. Because every layer has its own weights to learn, ResNet has a vast number of parameters. DenseNet layers, on the other hand, only have a few parameters (e.g., 12 filters) and contribute a few additional feature-maps. DenseNet joins the layer's output and incoming feature maps. ResNet sums the layer's output feature maps with the incoming feature maps instead of concatenating them. DenseNet is divided into four categories: DenseNet121, DenseNet169, DenseNet201, and DenseNet264. This chapter discusses DenseNet121 and DenseNet201.

The DenseNet-121 model can be used to diagnose COVID-19 disease and to identify the early-stage detection of leukemia patients remotely using IoMT. The following components make up DenseNet-121:

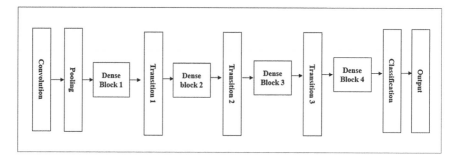

FIGURE 2.12   DenseNet-121.

- 1 – 7×7 convolution layer
- 58 – 3×3 convolution layer
- 61 – 1×1 convolution layer
- 4 – AvgPool layer
- 1 – Fully connected layer

Every dense block of DenseNet-121 architecture contains two convolution operations with various numbers of layers: a 1×1 sized bottleneck layer and a 3×3 kernel to conduct convolution operations. Figure 2.12 illustrates the diagram of DenseNet-121.

The layers of DenseNet-121 are described as follows:

1. *Convolution Layer*: It consists of 64 7×7 filters and a 2 stride.
2. *Pooling Layer*: It uses Max Pooling of 3×3 and a 2 stride.
3. *Dense Block 1*: It consists of two Convolutions that are repeated sixfold.
4. *Transition Layer1*: It consists of one Convolutional layer and one Average Pooling layer.
5. *Dense Block 2*: It consists of two Convolutions that are repeated 12-fold.
6. *Transition Layer 2*: It consists of one Convolutional layer and one Average Pooling layer.
7. *Dense Block 3*: It consists of two Convolutions that are repeated 24-fold.
8. *Transition Layer 3*: It consists of one Convolutional layer and one Average Pooling layer
9. *Dense Block 4*: It consists of two Convolutions that are repeated 16-fold.
10. *Classification*: It uses Feature maps and Global Average Pooling layer for classification.
11. *Output Layer*: It generates the output.

2.4.8.3   DenseNet-201

The DenseNet-201 model [16] is used to diagnose COVID-19 disease, as well as breast abnormalities and pneumonia. It consists of 201 layers and gives each layer direct control over the actual input image and loss function gradients. It is a better

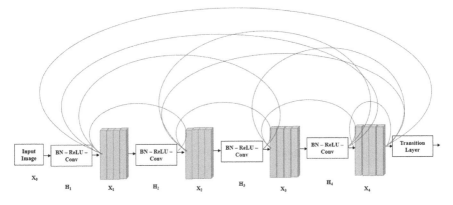

FIGURE 2.13   DenseNet-201.

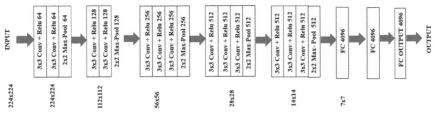

FIGURE 2.14   VGG16.

option for image classification because it saves time and money. The DenseNet-201 architecture is shown in Figure 2.13.

Because it employs fewer parameters and has a lower computational cost, DenseNet gives better results than ResNet.

2.4.8.4   VGG16

VGG16 is a biomedical image classification model. It is a kind of CNN [17]. VGG16's architecture is shown in Figure 2.14.

VGG16 comprises three fully connected layers and five convolutional blocks. Each block is made up of two or more convolutional layers as well as a Max Pool layer. The RGB input image is 224 × 224 pixels in size. VGG16 is made up of two layers: convolutional blocks and fully connected layers.

i.   Convolutional Blocks
- *Convolutional Block 1*: It consists of two convolutional filters, each with 64 filters, and is based on Max Pooling.
- *Convolutional Block 2*: This block contains two convolutional filters. Max Pooling uses 128 filters.
- *Convolutional Block 3*: This block contains three convolutional filters. Max Pooling uses 256 filters.

- *Convolutional Block 4*: This block contains three convolutional filters. Max Pooling uses 512 filters.
- *Convolutional Block 5*: This block contains three convolutional filters. Max Pooling uses 512 filters.

ii. **Fully Connected Layers**

This layer is made up of three layers. A total of 4,096 hidden units and ReLU activation make up the first and second layers. The final output layer contains 1,000 hidden units and Softmax activation.

2.4.8.5 InceptionResNetV2

CNN Inception ResNetV2 [18] incorporates the Inception and ResNet architectures. The input image is 299 by 299 pixels, with a list of computed class probabilities as the output. The inclusion of the ResNet network reduces the training time. Multiple filters' convolutional sizes are merged with a residual network. The layout of InceptionResNetV2 is shown in Figure 2.15.

InceptionResNetV2 contains modified Inception-Resnet blocks such as A, B, and C blocks for extracting the features to classify the image.

2.4.8.6 U-Net

The conventional CNN, which is used to handle biomedical image classification, has developed into U-Net [19]. U-Net assists in locating and recognizing borders while classifying each pixel. Both the input and output are of equal size. It has a U-shaped design [16]. It is divided into two sections. When it comes to biological applications, U-Net performs admirably.

- **Contracting Path:** The left section of the path is handled by the basic convolutional process.
- **Expansive Path:** The right section of the path is used for segmentation purposes.

Figure 2.16 shows the architecture of the U-Net.

2.4.8.6.1 Contracting Path

Each step has two convolutional layers, and the number of channels ranges from 1 to 64 as the depth of the picture is increased via the convolution process. The

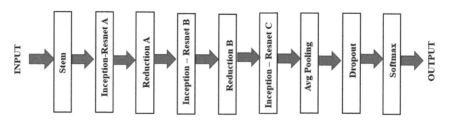

FIGURE 2.15   InceptionResNetV2.

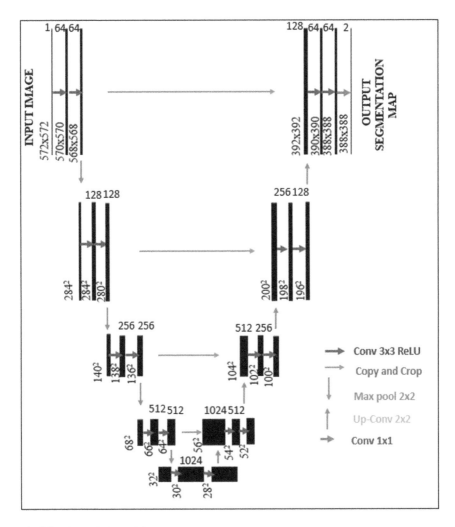

FIGURE 2.16   U-Net architecture.

max pooling procedure minimizes the image size from 572×572 to 568×568 pixels. The procedure is performed three more times. Without max pooling, two convolution layers are created once more. At this time, the image has been scaled to 28×28×1024.

2.4.8.6.2   Expansive Path

To get a precise prediction, the image upsizes to its original size in the expanding path. The transposed convolution method expands the image's size. The image is resized from 28×28×1024 to 56×56×512 and then concatenated with the contracting path image to create a 56×56×1024. This is followed by the addition of two more convolutions, and the procedure is repeated three times more.

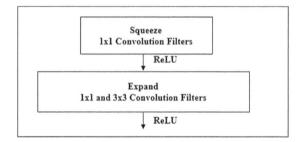

FIGURE 2.17   Fire Module–SqueezeNet.

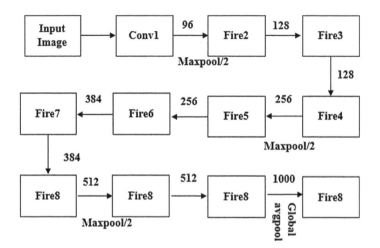

FIGURE 2.18   SqueezeNet architecture.

2.4.8.7 SqueezeNet

The essential element of this structure contains Squeeze unit and Expand unit, both units together known as Fire Module [20]. The squeeze unit is made up of 1×1 convolution filters. The expanded unit is made up of a mixture of two convolutional filters, 1×1 and 3×3 convolution filters. It is a pre-trained model for detecting pneumonia and classifying it as bacterial or viral. The fire module and SqueezeNet structure are depicted in Figures 2.17 and 2.18, respectively.

2.5 CONCLUSION

This chapter discussed the overview of IoMT in the medical industry. It highlighted the IoMT architecture and the various components involved within the architecture. It also provides an in-depth understanding of IoMT technologies and the challenges in the healthcare industry. Furthermore, it discussed the pros and cons of machine learning models incorporation into IoMT in the medical field. It emphasizes the benefits of inculcating deep learning models into IoMT. It explained how deep learning works in IoMT and discusses various deep learning algorithms used in IoMT.

Deep learning models discussed in this chapter include DNN, RBN, DBN, GAN, CNN, RNN, LSTM, and transfer learning. It emphasizes the significance of transferable learning paradigms. The transfer learning models described in this chapter are the ResNet34, DenseNet121, DenseNet201, VGG16, InceptionResNetV2, U-Net, and SqueezeNet architectures. Finally, it goes over a few assessment metrics for evaluating the performance of deep learning approaches. Transfer learning models of deep learning into IoMT enhance the medical industry in data analysis, processing, and accurate disease diagnosis.

REFERENCES

1. Dwivedi, R., Mehrotra, D., and Chandra, S., Potential of Internet of Medical Things (IoMT) applications in building a smart healthcare system: A systematic review, *Journal of Oral Biology and Craniofacial Research*, 12, 302–318, 2022.
2. Ramasamy, M.D., Periasamy K., Krishnasamy, L., Dhanaraj R.K., Multi-Disease Classification Model using Strassen's Half of Threshold (SHoT) Training Algorithm in Healthcare Sector, *IEEE Access*, 9, 112624–112636, 2021.
3. Al-Dhaen, F., Hou, J., Rana, N.P., Weerakkody, V., Advancing the understanding of the role of responsible AI in the continued use of IoMT in Healthcare, *Information Systems Frontiers–A Journal of Research and Innovation*, 1–20, 2021.
4. Arvindhan, M., Rajeshkumar, D., Anupam Lakhan Pal, A., Review of Challenges and Opportunities in Machine Learning for Healthcare, *Exploratory Data Analytics for Healthcare*, 67–84, 2021.
5. Kavitha, M., Roobini, S., Prasanth, A., Sujaritha, M., Systematic View and Impact of Artificial Intelligence in Smart Healthcare Systems, Principles, Challenges and Applications, *Machine Learning and Artificial Intelligence in Healthcare Systems*, 21, 25–56, 2023.
6. Jayachitra, S., Prasanth, A., Hariprasath, S., AI Enabled Internet of Medical Things in Smart Healthcare, *AI Models for Blockchain-Based Intelligent Networks in IoT Systems: Concepts, Methodologies, Tools, and Applications*, 141–161, 2023.
7. Zemouri R., Zerhouni N., Racoceanu, D., Deep learning in the biomedical applications: Recent and Future status, *MDPI Applied Sciences*, 9, 1–40, 2019.
8. Greff, K., Srivastava, R.K., Koutník, J., Steunebrink, B.R., Schmidhuber J., LSTM: A Search Space Odyssey, *IEEE Transactions on Neural Networks and Learning Systems*, 28, 2222–2232, 2017.
9. Jayachitra, S., Prasanth, A., Multi-Feature Analysis for Automated Brain Stroke Classification Using Weighted Gaussian Naïve Bayes Classifier, *Journal of Circuits, Systems and Computers*, 30, 2150178:1–23, 2021.
10. Yu, X., Zeng, N., Liu, S., Yu-Dong, Z., Utilization of DenseNet201 for diagnosis of breast abnormality, Machine Vision and Applications, *Springer*, 30, 1135–1144, 2019.
11. Huang, G., Liu, Z., Pleiss, G., Maaten, L.V., Kilian Weinberger, Q., Convolutional Networks with Dense Connectivity, *IEEE Transactions on Pattern Analysis and Machine Intelligence*, 1–12, 2019.
12. Liu, F., Tan H., Song, D., Deep learning and its applications in biomedicine, *Genomics Proteomics Bioinformatics*, 16, 17–32, 2018.

13. Tawsifur, R., Muhammad Chowdhury, E. H., Amith, K., Khandaker Islam, R., Khandaker Islam, F., Transfer Learning with Deep Convolutional Neural Network (CNN) for pneumonia detection Using Chest X-Ray, *Applied Sciences*, 10, 1–15, 2020.

14. Aayush, J., Neha, G., Dilbag, S., Vijay, K., Manjit, K., Classification of the COVID-19 infected patients using DenseNet201 based deep transfer learning, *Journal of Biomolecular Structure and Dynamics*, 39, 5682–5689, 2021.

15. Yang, Z., Xu, P., Yang, Y., Bao, B.K., A Densely connected network based on U-Net for Medical Image Segmentation, *ACM Transactions on Multimedia Computing, Communications, and Applications*, 17, 1–14, 2021.

16. Gao, H., Zhuang, L., Laurens Van Der, M., Densely connected convolutional networks, *IEEE Conference on Computer Vision and Pattern Recognition (CVPR)*, 1–6, 2017.

17. Sathish, R., and Ezhumalai, P., Intermodal sentiment analysis for images with text captions using the VGGNET technique, *ACM Transactions on Asian and Low-Resource Language Information Processing*, 20, 1–14, 2021.

18. Nguyen, L. D., Lin, D., Lin, Z., Cao, J., Deep CNNs for microscopic image classification by exploiting transfer learning and feature concatenation, *IEEE International Symposium on Circuits and Systems (ISCAS)*, 1–7, 2018.

19. Siddique, N., Paheding, S., Elkin, C., Devabhaktuni, V., U-Net and its variants for Medical Image Segmentation–A review of theory and applications, *IEEE Access*, 9, 82031–82057, 2021.

20. Krizhevsky, A., Sutskever, I., Hinton, G.E., Imagenet classification with deep convolutional neural networks, *Advances in Neural Information Processing Systems(NIPS)*, 25, 1106–1114, 2012.

21. Nandhini, P.S., Malliga, S., Monisha Sri, N., Jeevitha, K., LSTM: A Deep learning-based approach for the classification of intrusions in IoT based networks, *International Journal of Advanced Science and Technology*, 29(9s), 26–33, 2020.

22. Alankrita, A., Mamta, M., Gopi, B., Generative adversarial network: An overview of theory and applications, *International Journal of Information Management Data Insights, Springer*, 1, 1–19, 2021.

23. Sherstinsky, A., Fundamentals of Recurrent Neural Network (RNN) and Long Short-Term Memory (LSTM) Network, *Physica D: Nonlinear Phenomena Journal: Special Issue on Machine Learning and Dynamical Systems, Elsevier*, 404, 1–16, 2020.

24. Sajja Tulasi, K., and Hemantha Kumar, K., Deep learning and transfer learning approaches for image classification, *International Journal of Recent Technology and Engineering*, 7, 427–432, 2019.

3 Machine Learning for Decision Support Systems in IoMT

T. Kokilavani,[1]* K. Kannan,[2] K.S. Yamuna,[3] B. Sangeetha,[4] and M. Vetrivel,[5]
[1]Department of Electrical and Electronics Engineering, Srikrishna College of Engineering and Technology, Coimbatore, Tamil Nadu, India
[2]Department of Electrical and Electronics Engineering, Annapoorana Engineering College, Salem, Tamil Nadu, India
[3]Department of Electrical and Electronics Engineering, Sona College of Technology, Salem, Tamil Nadu, India
[4]Department of Electrical and Electronics Engineering, AVS Engineering College, Salem, Tamil Nadu, India
[5]Department of Electrical and Electronics Engineering, R P Sarathy Institute of Technology, Salem, Tamil Nadu, India
*Corresponding Author: T. Kokilavani (Email: kokilavani@skcet.ac.in)

3.1 INTRODUCTION

Hospitals utilize health prediction systems to monitor their patients and enable the patients to get proposed treatment. Mostly, the healthcare services are mainly utilized for the ambulance system during emergency events like natural disasters, etc. Some of the hospitals lack real-time data on the patient flow [1]. Under this situation, the Internet of Things (IoT) establishes communication between virtual computers and physical objects and provides real-time data collection [2]. Healthcare is the process of improving and maintaining people's health through the diagnosis and prevention of diseases.

The abnormalities in the body can be detected using diagnostic devices like Computed tomography (CT) and Magnetic Resonance Imaging (MRI), etc. [3]. However, the modern healthcare systems have been affected by population increase. Similarly, the demand for medical resources, such as nurses, physicians, and so on, has also increased. It necessitates the development of standard healthcare systems with high quality [4]. This can be achieved with the help of IoT. Doctors may readily monitor patients' information using healthcare monitoring schemes, which help them to carry out an accurate diagnosis [5]. To transmit the patent data to the doctor, wireless data transmission using handheld devices has been developed. While implementing this, despite the advantages of the IoT, data security has to be maintained [6]. As a

DOI: 10.1201/9781003405450-3

37

result, a number of studies have concentrated on the utilization of IoT and machine learning (ML) together to monitor medical issues and preserve data integrity.

In the health sector, IoT accompanied a new era, to communicate patients with experts more proactively [7]. Hence, doctors can easily monitor patients' information through healthcare monitoring schemes. Various handheld gadgets have been formulated to provide frequent wireless data transmission. IoT in conjunction with ML evaluates emergency care requests and establishes a strategy for dealing with the problem. In some hospitals, patients who need immediate medical attention have been delayed because of improper control. This problem is more common in developing countries, where hospitals are under-equipped. In this situation, IoT with ML topology assists hospitals to monitor the signs and symptoms of patients [8]. IoT sensors monitor the health status of the patient and forecast illness trends and abnormalities. This, in turn, will help patients to receive suggestions from different hospitals where they can get treatment [9].

A medical monitoring platform with Zigbee Technology and BSN has been developed for monitoring patients from the remote using sensors. To assess the state of patients, modules like Zigbee protocol (IEEE 802.15.4) and sensors are incorporated. The data is subsequently transferred through radio waves and visualized via computers [10]. IoT uses sensor networks which are a combination of software and hardware to enable patient monitoring and surveillance.

Devices such as the Raspberry Pi card, and blood pressure (BP), temperature, and heart rate sensors fall under this category. Among these, Raspberry Pi cards are companionable with cloud systems. Patient forecasting techniques are based on ML and allow for fast sharing of patient data between hospitals. Historical data of patients are utilized to estimate their future and help the hospital to predict their health condition. While implementing ML, training classifiers can detect health events using IoT devices. Clustering algorithms can identify and indicate the abnormalities of the patient to the healthcare providers [11]. It will be very useful for old age people.

3.2 WORKING OF IOMT

The integration of IoMT into our daily lives has revolutionized healthcare, enabling smarter and more connected medical systems. IoMT systems consist of several interconnected layers that work together seamlessly, incorporating various devices, sensors, and communication technologies (both wired and wireless). Figure 3.1 represents the structure and functionality of the layers involved in the IoMT layer.

3.2.1 PERCEPTION LAYER

The perception layer in the IoMT continues to play a crucial role in gathering data from a wide array of sources. These sources include smart objects, monitoring devices, mobile apps, and various types of sensors like infrared (IR), medical based, smart devices, radio frequency identification (RFID) tags, cameras, Global Positioning System, etc. The primary function of the perception layer is to collect real-world

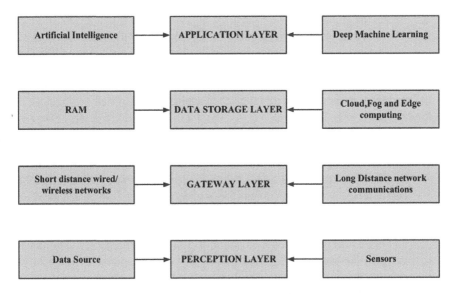

FIGURE 3.1 Different layers involved in IoMT framework.

information from these diverse sources and then digitally communicate it through a reliable transmission infrastructure. This infrastructure can consist of either wired or wireless networks, offering high-performance indices for data transport.

3.2.2 GATEWAY LAYER

The sensor must be linked to the gateway, as previously stated. Over networks, gateways are set up to interact and store data locally or centrally. The gateways such as RFID, WSN, cloud computing, etc., utilize different frequencies for communication [12–15]. The devices like ZigBee, Bluetooth/Ultra-wideband (UWB)/

Local Area Network (LAN), Ethernet, or WiFi connection can be used as the network. Wide Area Networks (WAN) such as Global System for Mobile Communications (GSM), which do not need connections but employ Wireless Sensor Network (WSN) that can support back-end servers/applications and vast numbers of sensor nodes, can be beneficial in some circumstances. Due to the stable connectivity of multiple devices at the same time, 4G and 5G cellular networks are gaining popularity.

Huge communication potential has the ability to propel healthcare IoMT applications forward and become a key driver. The many types of gates are listed below. RFID is a technique for identifying a person. The short-range communication gateway, with a range of 10 cm to 200 m, is equipped with a microprocessor and an antenna. This gateway serves a dual purpose – it can identify a specific object and function as a reader that communicates with RFID tags using radio waves. The information and data exchanged between the gateway and the tags are typically in the form of an Electronic Product Code (EPC). RFID is unsecure even though the power consumption is low. Therefore, it is not compatible with smartphones.

a. Bluetooth

The short-range communication system, designed for distances less than 100 m, employs ultra high frequency (UHF) waves operating at 2.4 GHz. This system ensures secure data transfer between devices. While being a cost-effective solution, it is specifically optimized for short-range communication and may not be suitable for long-range applications.

b. *Zigbee*

Zigbee is a low power communication protocol (wireless) which operates on the IEEE 802.15.4 standard. It is designed for short-range and low-data-rate applications in the field of home and industrial automation, smart energy, healthcare, and other IoT applications. Zigbee provides a reliable, secure, and cost-effective solution for connecting a wide variety of devices in a mesh network topology.

c. *Near-Field Communication (NFC)*

NFC is a short-range communication topology which enables data transfer between devices over a very close proximity, typically within a few centimeters. It operates on RFID principles and is an extension of the ISO/IEC 14443 standard for contactless smart cards.

d. *Wi-Fi*

In IoMT, Wi-Fi plays a crucial role in enabling seamless and reliable communication between medical devices, sensors, and systems. It facilitates the exchange of vital health data and information in real time, enhancing healthcare processes and patient monitoring.

e. *Satellite*

Satellite technology can play a significant role in IoMT by extending connectivity and communication capabilities to remote and underserved areas. Additionally, integrating satellite communications with other technologies like terrestrial networks, wireless protocols, and cloud services can create a comprehensive and efficient IoMT ecosystem that improves healthcare accessibility and quality globally.

3.2.3 MANAGEMENT SERVICE LAYER

This layer is a critical component in the architecture of complex systems, including IoT and other distributed networks. It is responsible for overseeing and controlling various aspects of the system, ensuring efficient operation, monitoring performance, and facilitating communication between different layers and components. The management service layer typically consists of software and services that provide centralized management and coordination.

The management/application layer serves as a critical component, providing user management, data management, and data analysis functionalities. It employs memory analytics to cache extensive data in Random Access Memory (RAM), enhancing data queries and decision-making speed. Real-time data analysis, known as streaming analytics, enables rapid decision-making. Scalability and flexibility are ensured through web servers and associated gateways like Flask and Apache 2. MongoDB, a NoSQL database, enables storage of diverse data types. Secure communication is facilitated using the Secure Socket Layer (SSL) Application Programming Interface (API) . Data can be stored locally or centrally on a cloud server.

Cloud-based computing offers centralized and scalable solutions [16], making it conducive to collecting and transmitting data from patient portals. It leverages IoT devices and smartphone apps to aid therapeutic strategies and decision-making. However, the distance between these devices and centralized data centers poses challenges like excessive data buildup and security concerns. To tackle these issues, researchers are exploring the decentralized approach of the "edge cloud" for data networking. This technique allows IoT sensors to analyze data autonomously. Consequently, it enriches the scalability of IoT devices and reduces the data burden on centralized sites.

Indeed, "blockchain storage" is another decentralized solution that offers a unique approach to data management. By implementing blockchain storage in the healthcare domain, patients can have more control over their medical data. They can grant permission to healthcare providers or researchers to access specific information while ensuring the privacy and security of their sensitive data. The combination of "Edge cloud" and blockchain in the medical field is an exciting and promising direction. The integration of these technologies can offer enhanced data processing capabilities at the network's edge, improving real-time data analysis and decision-making. Additionally, blockchain's immutable nature ensures data integrity, which is essential for maintaining accurate medical records.

3.2.4 APPLICATION/SERVICE LAYER

The application layer indeed plays a crucial role in understanding data and delivering application-based services in various systems, including healthcare applications like electronic medical records (EMR). This layer utilizes AI and ML to analyze and interpret EMR data, enabling advanced functionalities and services [17]. Based on these observations, diagnosis and/or treatment of the disease can be decided. Apart from image analysis, other scientific applications including drug design, mental health management, benign and malignant tumors, etc., can be carried out. The modernized lifestyles and oversaturated work schedules of human beings result in disorders. The advancement in the healthcare monitoring system aims to provide the best patient care. The unexpected incursion of coronavirus disease 2019 (COVID-19) has caused accountable changes in individuals' actions and priorities, as well as regulatory policies, functioning, and emphasis of governments in all countries throughout the world, and has been a catalyst for technological, social, and economic progress. Digital technology has revolutionized healthcare, contributing to significant innovations and digital transformation in various areas such as remote monitoring, telemedicine, and health evaluations through smart wearables.

Following COVID-19, the US Food and Drug Administration granted fast recognition to Emergency Use Authorization certificates for a number of COVID-19-related devices. Examples include biosensors formulated by Philips (detect COVID-19), Scripp's "DETECT" (a testing and tracing architecture developed by Taiwan that can gather data using smart wearable devices), Aidoc Medical's AI-CT algorithms, and many other ultrasound devices. Because of the fast adoption of IoMT in the healthcare industry, revenue from the IoMT sector was about $66 billion in 2020, representing a 20% increase from 2019. It has multiple applications in the healthcare sector, including health monitoring functions such as heart rate, mobility monitoring, etc.

Nutritional conditions and rehabilitation of old/infected patients are more important, resulting in a longer life expectancy and lower sickness and mortality rates. A smart hospital has been developed in which various technologies, such as MRI/CT scanners, may be integrated to improve the diagnosis, thereby assisting doctors for better monitoring and making treatment decisions. By implementing smart equipment in hospitals, costs could be decreased. The early detection of irregularities could also reduce the accuracy of medical devices, resulting in greater maintenance costs. The rise of IoMT-based "smart" technologies has also benefited dentistry.

Newer improvements attempt to speed up the dentist's work while also providing comfort and assurance to the patient about the process's reliability. To revolutionize dentistry, AI algorithms, ML techniques, and cloud computing can also be utilized. Tele dentistry advanced a step of distant care during the epidemic. For example, Mouth Watch's TeleDent service is a tele-dentistry platform through which patients can send the information to a dentist through pictures who is located remotely for a live consultation. ML has been created in the field of oncology to exactly measure the vicinity of cancer cells to provide improved insights into dissemination and resistance, aiding prognosis prediction.

3.3 ML ALGORITHMS AND THEIR CLASSIFICATION

The ML strengthens the ability of a system to assess and understand its inputs without any human intervention [18]. During the training phase, the ML model is exposed to a large data set of labeled or unlabeled inputs. Once the model is trained, it is evaluated and tested using a separate data set, often called the test data set. The test data set contains input features but does not include the corresponding target labels. During testing, the model attempts to predict the outcomes for these unlabeled inputs based on what it has learned from the training phase. The predicted outcomes are then compared to the true (known) target labels to assess the model's performance.

The accuracy of the ML model is determined by how well it predicts the outcomes for the unlabeled data in the test data set. The closer the model's predictions are to the true target labels, the higher its accuracy. In recent years, ML systems have emerged as indispensable tools in healthcare applications, playing a vital role in improving clinic-based systems. Among the various ML techniques used in healthcare, Artificial Neural Networks (ANN) and Support Vector Machines (SVM) stand out as prime examples. These models have been leveraged in cancer applications to enable precise diagnosis, analyzing data from diverse sensors and data sources to accurately identify patients' health conditions.

ML algorithms, such as SVM and ANN, have proven effective in capturing patient habits, including daily routines and sleeping patterns. By analyzing this data, these algorithms can suggest personalized lifestyle modifications and prescribe specialized therapies to optimize patient health. This capability empowers clinicians to formulate tailored care plans that enhance patient outcomes and well-being [19].

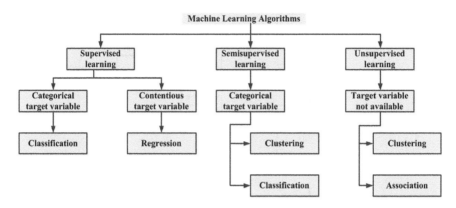

FIGURE 3.2   Machine learning algorithm.

In the realm of ML models, three primary types are commonly used:

- Supervised
- Semi-supervised
- Unsupervised

As shown in Figure 3.2, each ML type contains multiple algorithms. This section discusses the most widely used ML algorithms for prediction and categorization. In supervised learning, these techniques include K-nearest neighbor (KNN), decision trees, Naive-Bayes, SVM, ANN, regression tree, and random forest.

3.3.1   DATA IN ML

Figure 3.3 demonstrates that data must be gathered from a variety of sources to construct an ML-based model. The gathered data sets are stored centrally in the cloud in a traditional way. The fundamental units of a data set are data points, also commonly referred to as samples or observations. A system is represented by these data points. To create the training data sets, this system is examined. A data point can be used to represent a patient's information. Today, there has been significant growth in the accessibility of data points. Data points can be labeled or unlabeled. A characteristic feature (called a label) is assigned as labeled data, which is considered as output or response.

In the classical statistical literature, the features are referred to as a dependent variable. Thus, a label can either be ordinal or categorical. In this, categorical has no preset values whereas the ordinal has predetermined values. A label can also be a numerical value. Although most of the ML models can utilize both labeled and unlabeled data under appropriate contexts, supervised learning uses labelled data. On the other hand, unsupervised learning utilizes unlabeled data, whereas semi-supervised learning utilizes both labeled and unlabeled data.

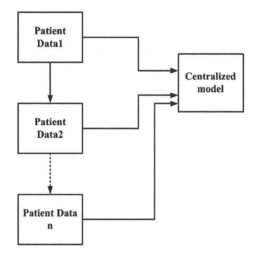

FIGURE 3.3 Centralized learning topology.

3.4 MACHINE LEARNING APPLICATIONS

The first step in developing an ML solution is the identification of the relevant problem. Healthcare is a data-driven industry. Even if a model is built to provide insight, it must have the ability to influence patient treatment.

3.4.1 MEDICAL IMAGING

Medical imaging encompasses a range of procedures and advanced technologies used to create visual representations of various body components, serving both diagnostic and therapeutic purposes. MRI and X-ray are two imaging modalities that are used nowadays. Currently, these are manually examined by a health professional to evaluate any anomalies. This procedure is time-consuming and also error-prone. The implementation of ML algorithms enhances disease prediction, detection, diagnostic accuracy, and timeliness [20]. Researchers have shown how ANN and other ML techniques may be associated with medical imaging and enable disease prediction, diagnosis, and detection. Convolutional neural networks (CNNs) have proven to be powerful tools for image and video interpretation. CT scans and X-rays are the most common input data types for medical imaging applications. The supervised learning approach is widely used in medical imaging diagnosis using ML.

3.4.2 DIAGNOSIS OF DISEASE

Disease diagnosis is an important part of treatment. ML can increase the ability of disease diagnosis as it undergoes an evaluation of both physiological and environmental aspects accurately. It also develops models for disease diagnosis. Thus, it can also be able to identify the risk factors of a specific disease. Apart from this, signs and symptoms of glaucoma, age-related macular degeneration, and other disorders are currently being identified using ML. SVM, deep learning systems, CNN, and backpropagation networks are some of the ML approaches utilized in disease diagnosis.

The type of data input varies depending on the ailment being diagnosed. Image data is frequently employed in most imaging diagnosis projects. Time series data, which includes a wealth of information such as demographics, patient monitoring data, gene expression, and symptoms, plays a crucial role in diagnosing chronic diseases. ML techniques, including both supervised and unsupervised learning algorithms, are leveraged to learn patterns from this data and enable accurate disease detection.

3.4.3   BEHAVIORAL TREATMENT

As the name implies, it assists in monitoring changes in the behavior of a patient. Behavioral modification is an example of this treatment, which is frequently administered over the patients whose bad habits are contributing to their health problems. ML application over behavioral change is made feasible by the IoT, which allows the collection of massive volumes of data on people. As a result, ML analyzes the individual behavior and suggests appropriate improvements. It provides self-knowledge and recommends solutions for behavioral change in addition to delivering alarms and notifications. ML may also be used to assess behavioral change interferences in order to decide which is the most beneficial for a particular patient. The Bayes network classifier, decision trees, and SVM are some of the ML techniques used in behavioral modification. Feature extraction collects the input data for these methods. IoT devices collect appropriate data such as videos, photos, and records which may be used to characterize human behavior.

3.4.4   CLINICAL TRIALS

Clinical trials are the studies that are conducted to determine the safety and efficiency of surgical and medicinal therapies. Clinical trials frequently involve human beings. It is the last stage in the research process. It must be conducted with care that the participants are not harmed. ML improves the clinical trial process by collecting knowledge about the efficacy of therapies from the previous clinical and biological data sets and other sources. Sensors provide both theoretical and practical proof. Healthcare providers can also use ML algorithms to examine the massive volumes of data to find the efficacy and safety of an intervention. For example, it can be used in clinical trials to develop drugs for COVID-19. In the clinical trial, extracting characteristics from data sets is the first step while implementing ML algorithms. Hence, photos and tables are considered as input data. IoT devices are able to collect data on the clinical trial's variables like weight, heart rate, BP, and blood glucose, which are examples of sensor data and are collected through IoT devices.

3.4.5   SMART ELECTRONIC HEALTH RECORDS

Patient charts have been replaced with electronic health records, which provide fast access to patient information, allowing doctors to provide high-quality care [21]. ML can be used to integrate intelligence into EMRs. Smart electronic health records, for example, may analyze patient data, identify the best treatment, and assist in clinical decision-making. Indeed, it has been demonstrated that combining ML with electronic health information improves ophthalmology. Smart electronic records can also analyze a large volume of data to assess the quality of care provided by the medical people. Linear and logistic regression, ANN, and SVM are examples of ML models which can be integrated into electronic health records. Text, photos, tables, and time series data are collected as input data.

3.4.6 EPIDEMIC OUTBREAK

Predicting emerging and spreading diseases in a community can be disastrous and difficult to control. As a result, stakeholders in the healthcare industry should understand the organization of tools and methods to predict and prepare for epidemic outbreaks. Regulators, administrators, and healthcare personnel can use ML algorithms to anticipate epidemics. ML techniques adopted for disease prediction include

- LSTM
- DNN models.

Text, time series, and other types of data can be fed into ML algorithms. There are two types of data:

- Numerical
- Category.

Time series data is utilized in an ML model to forecast information about the future disease. Apart from this, population density, hotspots, vaccination levels, etc., can be used as an input type of ML. Weather-related data and other sorts of environmental data which can influence the epidemics can also be collected as input to ML. Overall, disease surveillance is important since it aids in the prevention of epidemics and allows stakeholders to plan for potential outbreaks.

3.4.7 HEART DISEASE PREDICTION

In most regions of the world, heart disease is the leading cause of mortality [22]. Heart disease is becoming more common around the world as a result of changing lifestyles and other risk factors. Globally, cardiovascular illnesses claimed the lives of 17.6 million people in 2016, which is about 14.5% higher than the number in 2006. Being able to forecast the disease, adopting appropriate preventative and treatment strategies is the solution for treating heart disease. By utilizing ML, healthcare providers can forecast the occurrence of cardiac disease at the earliest. Patients who are at an elevated risk of cardiac disease may be given the advice to prevent it. To forecast cardiac disease, optimized algorithms (KNN, Naive-Bayes, SVM, etc.,) can also be utilized.

3.4.8 PREDICTION MODELS FOR COVID-19

ML can also be utilized for COVID-19 diagnosis. The goal is to formulate an algorithm that produces a precise result. Temperature, age, lung imaging characteristics, and lymphocyte count are the most commonly reported predictors. ML techniques utilized can analyze a lung image and distinguish between those who are impacted and those who are not impacted. This model can also accept tabular data, text, and time series as input data. A prediction model with eight binary characteristics (age, gender, contact with a corona-affected person, and five early clinical symptoms) predicts COVID-19 with high accuracy. IoT sensor devices used in this ML configuration provide temperature readings and photos of the lungs. Thus, the implementation of ML methods for COVID-19 diagnosis shows an improved accuracy.

3.4.9 PERSONALIZED CARE

Patient-centered care necessitates the provision of individualized services. Patients' care is tailored to their specific requirements, expectations, and beliefs. Personalized care promotes patient happiness and utilization of formal health services in addition to enhancing clinical results. To review each patient's data and generate individualized treatment plans, ML algorithms can be utilized by the healthcare staff. It facilitates personalized care. ML systems make use of the potential of health records to find a person's specific patterns of illness progression by combining with different data sources. This information aids clinical decision-making and healthcare providers to provide more individualized care. ML algorithms can be used to decide the optimal course of therapy by analyzing the data from a patient's medical record [23].

3.5 ROLE OF IOT IN CARDIOMETABOLIC DISEASES TREATMENT

Recent advances in paradigms like medical informatics and eHealth have revolutionized the healthcare industry by enabling the analysis of vast amounts of health data. This data-driven approach empowers healthcare providers to offer better and more efficient treatments to patients, leading to improved patient outcomes and enhanced healthcare services. This type of data analytics not only aids in the development of improved treatment techniques but also aids the discovery of correlations between health parameters, resulting in more accurate disease and risk prediction models. In this industry, both data analytics and IoT play a key role in universal data collection [24]. Cardiovascular disease becomes one of the major causes of death in most of the developed countries. In the USA, about 600,000 people die every year due to this disease and according to the World Health Organization's forecasts, it may increase to 23.6 million by 2030. One of the most significant components of dealing with cardiac disorders is determining their risk in advance using a variety of predictors.

There are numerous ways for determining cardiovascular risks (CVR). Each has their unique sets of benefits and also drawbacks. The FRS, which was devised in 1991 and modified in 2008, is one of the most well-known approaches to detecting CVR. The remote monitoring healthcare system monitors people's health by monitoring their physiological indicators which are measured through IoT devices, as well as visualization of the total therapy based on data analytics. In specific situations, people's cardiometabolic health is monitored and evaluated for deeper insights to illustrate a system. An effective approach to remotely monitoring patients' health and administrating the efficacy of an ongoing treatment would be important in the healthcare system.

3.5.1 DESIGN OUTLINE AND PHYSIOLOGICAL PARAMETERS

An IoT-based eHealth system comprises an eHealth device to examine the physiological data, has a mechanism to communicate, data analysis tools, and end-service delivery [25]. Proactive monitoring, periodic treatment, and chronic disease management are some of the applications of the eHealth system. Data analytics incorporates all the data collected by eHealth devices which are stored in the pool. Clinical research databases can quickly answer questions about risk variables, indicator thresholds, and disease symptoms. IoT makes a significant contribution in this field by improving the efficiency of data collection, storage, and processing. In this type of application, information is gathered mainly from two groups of people and is stored as a separate database. It includes a number of physiological indicators relevant to a person's cardiometabolic profile as shown in Tables 3.1 and 3.2. The details of people shown in the table indicate that they were healthy volunteers.

Medical workers access the databases and observe the entire health history of the persons whose physiological data are collected using eHealth devices. As a result, physiological data must be examined to determine crucial elements such as risk factors for a specific disease/improvement in response to a specific treatment method. Initially, k-means clustering was utilized to detect and separate the clusters in the data sets containing physiological data. Cluster analysis is also illustrated for the separation of clusters. Once the essential parameters in the data sets have been discovered (Tables 3.1 and 3.2), all of the characteristics in each group are linked to cardiovascular risks with the goal of early diagnosis of cardiometabolic disorders.

TABLE 3.1
Data Set I Features [26]

Features	Values
Age	48(± 8)
Sex	Male
BP (systolic)	137(± 19)
BP (diastolic)	88 (± 12)
LDL (mg/dL)	188 (± 38)
HDL (mg/dL)	48 (± 12)
Smoking habitat	39% out of 618 persons
Diabetes	5% out of 618 persons
BMI	26(± 3)
Framingham risk (FR)	0.15 (± 0.09)

TABLE 3.2
Data Set II Features [26]

Features	Values
Age	57 (± 9)
Sex	M:F = 135: 58
BP (systolic)	124(± 13)
BP (diastolic)	73 (± 10)
LDL (mg/dL)	188 (± 38)
HDL (mg/dL)	48(± 12)
Smoking habitat	22% out of 386
Diabetes	7% out of 386
BMI	10.63 (± 2.69)
FR	0.09 (± 0.06)

TABLE 3.3
k-Means Clustering Operation

Cluster	Axes	Values (Approximately)
1	X	135.8
	Y	214
2	X	158.7
	Y	168.6
3	X	125.6
	Y	180
4	X	137.5
	Y	188.1

In addition, this group also indicates the influence of a physiological parameter on a group of people who are involved in CVR. Such analysis is quite useful in assessing the physiological status of persons remotely.

3.5.2 ANALYSIS OF CARDIOMETABOLIC RISK

A collection of physiological parameters-based data matrices (618×8) is created to analyze Cardiometabolic Risk. In this, smoking and diabetes are represented using binary notation. Using k-means clustering, it's clear Low-Density Lipoprotein(LDL) cholesterol can be utilized to convert the data into clusters. When the same clustering technique is repeated for the second data set, LDL cholesterol emerges as the best clustering parameter. In the first data set, three clusters are created based on using the k-means clustering operation as depicted in Table 3.3.

The clusters obtained from the first data set are represented in Figure 3.4) and it depicts the centroid values (X-axis: Systolic BP as 137.3 and Y-axis: LDL as 188.1). As a result, people in the four quadrants have different characteristics, particularly in

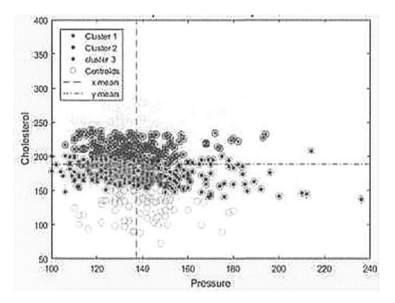

FIGURE 3.4 Cluster distribution.

terms of BP and cholesterol. To infer the impact of these factors over Framingham Risk Score (FRS), the properties of these quadrants (Figure 3.4) are linked with the FR. People in the first quadrant have greater systolic BP and LDL cholesterol than the average. They have a 0.17 FRS on average, with a 0.09 standard deviation (SD) (Figure 3.5). People in the second quadrant have lower systolic BP than the average but greater LDL cholesterol. They exhibited a 0.13 mean FRS with a 0.07 SD in this example.

People in the third quadrant have lower BP and LDL than the average. They had a 0.13 mean FRS with a 0.07 SD. People in the fourth quadrant have systolic BP greater than the average but their LDL cholesterol is lower. They have an SD of 0.10 and a mean FRS of 0.18. As a result, each quadrant represents a distinct risk group with various levels of danger. Since LDL cholesterol has emerged as a significant factor, the data sets are divided into high and low LDL cholesterol groups based on clustering.

Following their separation, the fluctuation of other physiological parameters in relation to LDL is investigated in Tables 3.4 and 3.5. However, the results show a lot of variation in the FR, and hence, based on the FR score, the group is further subdivided into a low, medium, and high risk to gain a better understanding of the parameters' hazards (Table 3.5). Similarly, the data set analyzed with pulse wave velocity is shown in Figure 3.4.

3.5.3 REMOTE HEALTHCARE SYSTEM

The analytics over physiological data provides a holistic perspective of cardiometabolic risks. This system is more useful and supports the medical workers in analyzing

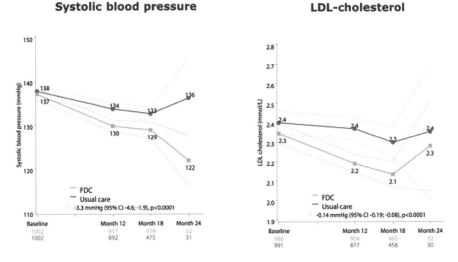

FIGURE 3.5 FR vs SBP and LDL cholesterol (first quadrant).

TABLE 3.4
Risk Analysis over LDL

	Low		High	
Parameters	Mean	SD	Mean	SD
Age (years)	49	8	47	7
BP (systolic)	139	20	135	18
BP (diastolic)	89	12	86	12
LDL	160	20	218	26
HDL	49	14	47	11
BMI	26	4	26	3
FR	0.13	0.07	0.18	0.10

cardiometabolic risks based on their basic physiological data. To promote a remote healthcare platform, eHealth devices are introduced. People's physiological data is measured by IoT-eHealth devices and stored in their respective virtual spaces. The data is accessed by healthcare providers using their unique identities. Additionally, the decision support system aids medical workers in narrowing diagnosis and pre-scribing treatments. This virtual therapy paradigm is especially effective in locations where access to healthcare services is limited.

The main goal of the remote healthcare system is to provide high-quality patient data to physicians for better insights, allowing them to create more personalized and efficient treatments. Intelligent machines have a significant impact on the efficiency of the overall healthcare system since the report generated by a machine can be inferred and easily examined by a machine and, hence, requires minimal human participation.

TABLE 3.5
Group Analysis – 1

Parameters	Low			High		
	Low Risk	Medium Risk	High Risk	Low Risk	Medium Risk	High Risk
Age (years)	44	50	55	11	47	53
BP (systolic)	132	141	153	123	134	146
BP (diastolic)	85	91	96	78	86	93
LDL	155	163	166	214	217	224
HDL	54	47	41	53	47	44
BMI	25	26	28	24	26	26
FR	0.07	0.14	0.28	0.07	0.15	0.13

Initially, the patient's physiological data were clustered and LDL cholesterol emerged as a significant constraint in medical inference. Thus, physiological factors have been evaluated and are examined with the LDL cholesterol and their Framingham risks.

In each case, a complete analysis of the cardiometabolic health, as well as the risks associated with arterial hypertension, high cholesterol, diabetes, and obesity, is observed. The physiological parameters (such as BP, cholesterol, weight, and height) of the groups were perceived via IoT devices and then stored in a pool. This contains detailed data of all parameters, which includes Body Mass Index (BMI). Then, this data set identifies the essential parameters, allowing for the classification of a large number of people into many groups and a detailed analysis of each of them. This in turn results in time consumption. It assists a medical expert to monitor a patient's health status remotely. This can considerably improve the quality of life of older people by making immediate requirements accessible.

Performing a treatment on-site comes at a high cost. These expenditures might be greatly reduced if the assessment could be done automatically at home. As a result, a support system with logical decisions could help medical practitioners regarding treatment plans for their patients. Thus, the IoT eHealth system combined with data analytics forms a new frontier in medical examination and remote healthcare and thus allows an effective detection and treatment in the early stage.

3.6   MOBILE IOMT DEVICE FOR EYE EXAMINATION

A visit to an ophthalmologist on a regular basis is essential for keeping track of our vision. It may become difficult due to many reasons such as personal location or exceptional instances, like COVID-19 pandemic, etc. Thus, for remote inspection of the eye's corneal surface, loop telemedicine topology between an ophthalmologist and patient has been developed. Mobile XML (Extensible Markup Language) Message Interface (XMI) has been tested in a telemedicine setup. The preliminary findings suggest that this cloud-based teleophthalmology architecture could be useful for the detection and diagnosis of corneal illnesses in the early stage. Furthermore, the established medical platform allows disabled patients to have their eyes examined remotely.

3.6.1   EYE EXAMINATION DEVICE

3.6.1.1   Design

A three-dimensional (3D) model mobile medical eye inspection gadget is designed to inspect the eye. It is necessary to wear an ergonomic gadget designed by the patients who undergo remote eye examinations. To improve material distribution, the top-ology optimization method is employed. Figure 3.6 depicts the medical eye examination device's design.

As illustrated in Figure 3.7, the Vertical Field Of View (VFOV) varies in accordance with the distance between the anterior section and an eye. The working distance and height of the anterior section determine the VFOV. As a result, a reference point is needed to calculate the camera's operating distance. The IP camera holder was modeled in accordance with the adjustable working distance. The VFOV can be calculated as follows:

$$\text{VFOE} = 2\text{arc tan } h/f \tag{3.1}$$

where f is the focal length between a person and camera.

3.6.1.2   Additive Manufacturing

Additive manufacturing, commonly known as 3D printing, is indeed a groundbreaking manufacturing process that fabricates 3D objects layer by layer. This method has proven to be highly advantageous, especially in the production of prototypes and

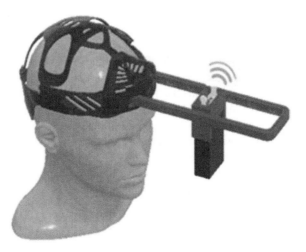

FIGURE 3.6   Wearable medical device for eye.

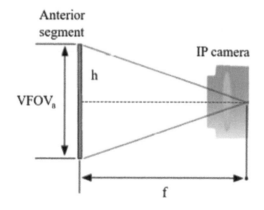

FIGURE 3.7   Optical imaging system with adjustable focal distance.

FIGURE 3.8   Wearable mobile XMI.

medical devices, due to its ability to provide design flexibility, swift prototyping, and the capability to create intricate geometries that might be impractical with traditional manufacturing techniques. Among the various additive manufacturing methods available, the multi-jet fusion technique stands out, particularly when using fine-grained polyamide 12 (nylon 12) with an 80 m layer thickness, which is a specific and effective approach within the realm of additive manufacturing.

There may be additional steps, considerations, and quality control measures involved in the overall development and testing of the biomedical device. Additionally, specific details and technologies may evolve as new advancements are made in the field of biomedical engineering and additive manufacturing. Figure 3.8 depicts the IoMT device prototype's integrated mechanical system.

3.6.2   IoT Platform for Medical Analysis

Early detection of cornea-associated disorders by an ophthalmologist through tele-operation is critical. The ophthalmologist and patient interfaces are two different

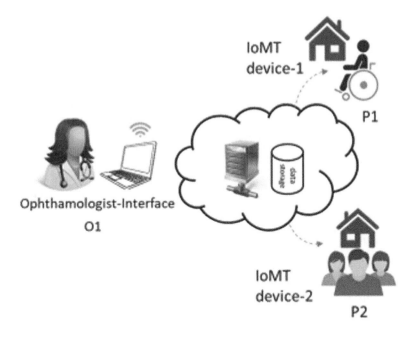

FIGURE 3.9   Remote eye examination (IoMT platform).

types of interfaces on the medical IoT platform. An ophthalmologist in a hospital initiates the remote eye examination procedure. From a remote site to the hospital, the patient wears an IoMT gadget. The approach of the remote testing platform for the eye by employing an IoMT device is shown in Figure 3.9. After connecting to the network, the examination procedure can begin.

3.6.2.1   Device Incorporated for Eye Examination

The IoMT device is connected to a cloud platform and utilizes a wirelessly designed optical instrument to monitor/diagnose cornea-associated disorders and associated symptoms. The corneal surface's streamed picture and video quality have been improved by the integrated lightweight portable device. The changeable focus distance parameter plays a crucial role in calibrating the optical imaging process. Additionally, the adjustable positioning of the IP camera on the head enables precise focusing on the interior section of the eye. Throughout the real-time examination, the testing distance remains fixed. Figure 3.10 provides a comprehensive depiction of the detailed arrangement of the eye's anterior segment, accompanied by an illustrated interface to aid in the examination process.

3.6.2.2   Remote Monitoring of Eye

The remote monitoring of the eye using the cloud includes an ophthalmologist dashboard comprising two camera entries, a choice of individual camera, a photo/ video capture button, and a scrolling system These characteristics are utilized by the

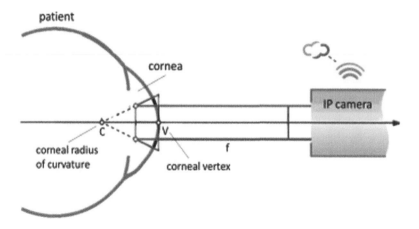

FIGURE 3.10   Eye-cross section – anterior segment.

ophthalmologist during patient monitoring. The cloud-based IoT platform allows fast transfer of the ocular surfaces of the patient to the ophthalmologist.

3.6.3   Cornea Detection Using IoMT

The cornea is the eye's most significant refractive site and outer layer of the globe. Corneal disorders can cause patients' eyesight to fade and distort, leading to blindness. As a result, an eye examination should be done on a regular basis to diagnose early symptoms of the disease. The evaluation of slit-lamp microscopy in the ophthalmology field allows an ophthalmologist to quickly diagnose a corneal illness. Diseases like congenital defects, keratitis, conjunctival malignancies, etc., can affect the cornea. During a routine eye checkup, the regeneration process of the corneal surface can be examined using stem cells also.

3.6.3.1   Regeneration of Corneal Surface

Corneal disorders can cause serious visual deficits and even blindness. Hence, it necessitates appropriate treatment. The regrowth of the cornea by transplanted limbal stem cells has become a subject of numerous studies. Before transplantation, patients should be thoroughly examined. Furthermore, the healing and regeneration procedure using stem cells is time-consuming. During this time, the patient's eye must be examined by an ophthalmologist on a regular basis. As a result, this process becomes more difficult. Thus, the IoMT gadget can be employed to effectively resolve this problem.

3.6.3.2   Anomalies in Cornea

Congenital abnormalities are birth defects that affect the cornea, iris, and pupillary region. The discomposure of neural crest cells and migration is the major cause of these defects, which may occur during embryonic development. Iris hypoplasia, microcornea, and polycoria are some of the examples of these pathological disorders.

Using the IoMT remote eye inspection technology, corneal epithelial lesions can be recognized.

3.6.3.3 Keratitis

Keratitis is a common cause of eye infection. It can be characterized by burning eyes and poor vision. Keratitis, if left untreated, results in permanent visual loss. Once the keratitis-related issues develop, patients should begin proper therapy instantly. It may exist in a variety of forms. Each form of keratitis necessitates a distinct therapy.

3.6.3.4 Corneal Mechanical Injuries

Corneal scarring and vision loss can be caused by small scratches or deeper penetration of the corneal surface and perforating corneal lesions. A patient with an open globe injury is more likely to develop a serious eye infection. As a result, if such a dangerous condition happens, it is essential to consult an ophthalmologist. With the biomicroscopic examination only, it is possible to determine the breadth and depth of the damage. The anterior segment examination with a corneal scleral hole and iris prolapse outside the wound area is shown in Figure 3.11.

3.6.3.5 Conjunctivitis

Infectious conjunctivitis is caused by bacteria, viruses, and fungus. Patients with bacterial conjunctivitis should avoid the crowded area since it is transmittable. Rapid recovery can be seen during the treatment phase. At this stage, it is preferable to examine the condition of patients with IoMT devices.

3.6.3.6 Disorders at the Eyelid

Inflammation, lesion, malignancy, or a mechanical disorder are the most common causes of eyelid illnesses. The cornea is protected by the eyelids, which also aid in the dispersion and removal of eye tears. Ocular discomfort, eye pain, and vision loss are prominent signs of eyelid illness. Closing the eyelids distributes tears across the eye's

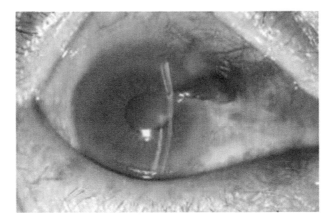

FIGURE 3.11 Anterior segment analysis – eye.

surface. It is because of pumping them into the lacrimal canaliculus through lacrimal puncta. As a result, certain eyelid abnormalities may cause epiphora or tear.

3.6.3.7 Tumors and Benign Growths

Tumors occurring in the conjunctiva of the eye are categorized into three main types: benign, malignant, and those with a pre-malignant potential. Research suggests that about half of these tumors are benign, while approximately 30% are malignant. Another 20% fall into a category with the potential to transform into malignant tumors over time. Given this information, any presence of a mass in the conjunctiva warrants a thorough and careful evaluation to determine its nature and potential risks. Early and accurate assessment of conjunctival tumors is essential to facilitate timely and appropriate medical intervention, ensuring the best possible outcomes for patients. Nevus, atypia, papilloma, and simple cysts are the most frequent benign tumors. Conjunctival degenerations include pinguecula and pterygium. These tumors can be monitored by an ophthalmologist with the help of the IoMT remote gadget.

3.6.4 Preliminary Test Results Observed from the IoMT-Based Remote Device

These types of preliminary tests are being carried out to examine the patient's condition in the loop telemedicine platform. Hence, the ophthalmologist can clearly observe the video of the corneal surface of the patient's eyes.

In the setup for eye examination, an Internet Protocol (IP) camera with a fixed lens (2.8 mm) and a wide oscillatory ventilation angle (110°) is used to capture videos and photographs of the eye at a smooth frame rate of 30 frames per second. The captured media is transmitted using the Real-Time Streaming Protocol (RTSP) and encoded in h.264 format. This data is then processed and streamed through a media server and streaming engine, specifically Wowza. Figure 3.12 displays an image of the patient's eye taken during the preliminary test using this setup.

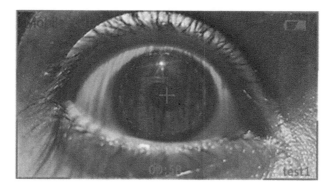

FIGURE 3.12   Post-treatment image.

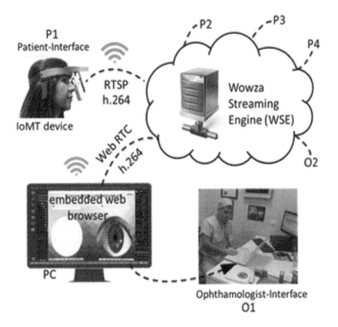

FIGURE 3.13   Eye investigation device based on IoMT.

The real-time streaming capabilities, facilitated by the WebRTC protocol, enable seamless communication between the media server and an ophthalmologist interface. This interface allows the ophthalmologist to remotely view and analyze the eye examination in real time. To implement a scalable and flexible approach, a cloud-based topology is adopted for both the patient and ophthalmologist interfaces, as depicted in Figure 3.13. This cloud-based solution enables efficient resource utilization and the ability to adjust the number of patients per ophthalmologist based on specific requirements. This integrated system brings forth a modern and efficient way to conduct eye examinations remotely, enabling timely consultations and medical evaluations while ensuring convenience and accessibility for both patients and healthcare professionals.

An ophthalmologist can assess the early detection of cornea-associated damages of both chemical and mechanical using the created platform. For typical patients (like individuals with disabilities), it would afford a pleasant remote eye inspection solution. Furthermore, these patients will be able to access the eye examination without any restrictions. 5G Internet topology will enable real-time video transmission using cloud topology.

3.7   CONCLUSION

IoT provides numerous benefits in the healthcare industry. The most important thing is that treatment outcomes can be significantly improved because the data gathered by IoT healthcare technologies is extremely reliable for decision-making. In this, details of patients are approximated instantly and transferred to the healthcare unit through a cloud application. Hence, the misconceptions about data can be reduced. AI-driven algorithms which utilize these IoT devices could also aid in the prediction of understandable findings or recommendations. The cost of IoT-based healthcare is also very low. With the help of IoT-based E-health, remote-based healthcare systems become more effective in a situation like COVID-19 pandemic. Multiple IoT technologies monitor and transmit all the messages to the health department which results in fewer hospital stays and doctor visits. Rapid technology development results in better real-time applications.

REFERENCES

1. Jackson, G. W., Rahman, S. S., Exploring challenges and opportunities in cybersecurity risk and threat communications related to the medical Internet of Things. *International Journal of Network Security & Its Applications,* 11, 75–86, 2019.
2. Bhaskar, K. B., Prasanth, A., Saranya, P., An energy-efficient blockchain approach for secure communication in IoT-enabled electric vehicles. *International Journal of Communication System,* 5189, 1–25, 2022.
3. Alazzam, M. B., Alassery, F., Almulihi, A., A novel smart healthcare monitoring system using machine learning and the Internet of Things. *Wireless Communications and Mobile Computing,* 2021, 1–7, 2021.
4. Abbas, S., An innovative IoT service for medical diagnosis. *International Journal of Electrical & Computer Engineering,* 10, 4918–4927, 2020.
5. AlShorman, O., A review of internet of medical things (IoMT)–based remote health monitoring through wearable sensors: A case study for diabetic patients. *Indonesian Journal of Electrical Engineering and Computer Science,* 20, 414–422, 2020.
6. Rajesh Kumar, D., Lalitha, K., Black-hole attack mitigation in medical sensor networks using the enhanced gravitational search algorithm. *International Journal of Uncertainty, Fuzziness and Knowledge-Based Systems,* 29, 297–315, 2021.
7. Aruchamy, P., Gnanaselvi, S., Sowndarya, D., An artificial intelligence approach for energy-aware intrusion detection and secure routing in internet of things-enabled wireless sensor networks. *Concurrency and Computation: Practice and Experience,* 35, 1–33, 2023.
8. Liaqat, S., SDN orchestration to combat evolving cyber threats in Internet of Medical Things (IoMT). *Computer Communications,* 160, 697–705, 2020.
9. Vineetha, Y., Misra, Y., Krishna Kishore, K., A real time IoT based patient health monitoring system using machine learning algorithms. *European Journal of Molecular & Clinical Medicine,* 7, 2912–2925, 2020.
10. Pandey, H., Prabha, S., Smart health monitoring system using IOT and machine learning techniques. *In 2020 Sixth International Conference on Bio Signals, Images, and Instrumentation,* 1–4, 2020, IEEE.
11. Prasanth, A., Pavalarajan, S., Implementation of efficient intra and inter-zone routing for extending network consistency in wireless sensor networks. *Journal of Circuits, Systems and Computers,* 29, 1–23, 2020.
12. Reddy, S., Reddy, S. A., Shettar, R., IoT based health monitoring system using machine learning. *International Journal of Advance Research and Innovative Ideas in Education,* 5, 381–386, 2019.

13. Prasanth A., Pavalarajan S., Particle swarm optimization algorithm based zone head selection in wireless sensor networks. *International Journal of Scientific & Technology Research*, 8, 1–9, 2018.

14. Saravanakumar, P., Sundararajan, T., Dhanaraj, V. P., Lamport certificateless sign cryption deep neural networks for data aggregation security in WSN. *Intelligent Automation & Soft Computing*, 33, 1835–1847, 2022.

15. Wong, T. K., Real-time machine health monitoring system using machine learning with IoT technology. *In MATEC Web of Conferences,* EDP Sciences, 335, 02–05, 2021.

16. Khan, S., Akhunzada, A., A hybrid DL-driven intelligent SDN-enabled malware detection framework for Internet of Medical Things (IoMT). *Computer Communications*, 170, 209–216, 2021.

17. Aasha M. J., Mary Anita, E. M., Survey on machine learning integrated with IOT. *Recent Trends in Information Technology and Its Application*, 3(2), 1–7, 2020.

18. Jayachitra, S., Prasanth, A., Rafi, S., Hierarchical-based binary moth flame optimization for feature extraction in biomedical application. *International Conference on Machine Learning, Image Processing, Network Security and Data Sciences*, 27–38, 2022.

19. Ahmed, I., Piccialli, F., A deep-learning-based smart healthcare system for patient's discomfort detection at the edge of Internet of Things. *IEEE Internet of Things Journal*, 8, 10318–10326, 2021.

20. D. Lakshmi, D., Srinivas, R. G., Manideep, K., A comparative study on breast cancer tissues using conventional and modern machine learning models. In: Satapathy, S. C., Bhateja, V., Favorskaya, M. N., Adilakshmi, T. (eds.), Smart Computing Techniques and Applications, *Smart Innovation, Systems and Technologies,* Springer, Singapore, 225, 693–699, 2021.

21. Abbas, S., Cyber-medicine service for medical diagnosis based on IoT and cloud infrastructure. *The International Conference on Artificial Intelligent and Computer Vision*, 1153, 617–627, 2020.

22. Kumar, P. M., Cloud and IoT based disease prediction and diagnosis system for health care using fuzzy neural classifier. *Future Generation Computer Systems*, 86, 527–534, 2018.

23. Vinayakumar, R., Alazab, M., Srinivasan, S., Simran, K., A visualized botnet detection system based deep learning for the internet of things networks of smart cities. *IEEE Transactions on Industry Applications.* 75, 1–15, 2020.

24. Rairikar, A., Kulkarni, V., Sabale, V., Lamgunde, A., Heart disease prediction using data mining techniques. In *2017 International Conference on Intelligent Computing and Control,* 1–8, 2017.

25. Ananth, S., Sathya, P., Madhan Mohan, P., Smart health monitoring system through IOT. *In 2019 International Conference on Communication and Signal Processing,* 1–5, 2019.

26. Chatterjee, P., Armentano, R., Internet of Things and decision support system for eHealth–Applied to cardiometabolic diseases. *Proceedings in IEEE International Conference on Machine learning and Data Science*, 75–79, 2017.

4 Secure Healthcare Systems

Recent and Future Applications

K. Umapathy,[1-4] T. Dineshkumar,[1-4]
M. A. Archana,[1-4] S. Omkumar,[1-4] and
W. Boonsong[5]
[1,2,3,4]Department of Electronics and Communication
Engineering, SCSVMV Deemed University, Kanchipuram,
Tamil Nadu, India
[5]Department of Electrical Education, Faculty of Industrial
Education and Technology, Rajamangala University of
Technology Srivijaya, Songkhla, Thailand

4.1 INTRODUCTION

Various researchers across the globe have contributed many innovative systems for diagnosis and treatment of diseases. The health complications are generally linked with variations in parameters such as pulse rate, level of oxygen, temperature of body, etc., inside the physique. In hospitals, they used to check the variations in the above parameters and the positivity or negativity of health complications will be determined. If offset in these parameters varies more from the values of normal, then the complications will amount to death in the majority of patients [1]. However, in many situations, patients may not be able to go to the hospital due to reasons such as insufficient time, illness cost factors, and non-availability of specialist doctors. Hence, health monitoring devices are very much required for these kinds of people to trace symptoms of diseases and go for help in case of abnormal situations [2–6]. These types of health monitoring devices have a good place in the current market [7–10].

Steps have been taken to provide details of the patient at a remote place with no need for visiting the hospital due to rapid development in Internet of Things (IoT) [11]. With this approach, treatment becomes easier for the specialists to determine the nature of action to be taken. The life of the patient will be affected while transiting him in a critical state [12]. Hence, new methods of innovation have been found for the storage and computation of data with the concept of cloud [13, 14]. Cloud is used for processing and storage of patient details, thereby monitoring their symptoms on the basis of real time. The various advantages of the above are reliability, sophistication, reasonable cost, etc. [15, 16].

DOI: 10.1201/9781003405450-4

The scope and applications of cloud computing with respect to the healthcare sector have been addressed by many scientists across the world [17–19]. Despite this, the storage and processing of patient details did arrive in a proper shape to maintain the privacy of patients [20]. It was presented about threats to security with respect to the transmission of patient data via public channels [21]. Hence, a methodology is required for the transition of patient details to respective providers of healthcare, thereby maintaining the privacy of patients. Due to advancements in IoT, there has been more contribution in various domains of challenge, specifically in the medical field. This approach provides accuracy, adaptability, and reliability, thereby bridging the gap between patients, physicians, and service personnel. Thus, doctors and service personnel are enabled to execute their work in an active manner with appropriate effort and smartness.

4.2 SYSTEM FOR RECENT APPLICATIONS

Figure 4.1 shows the system with respect to recent applications. A Raspberry Pi controller is used for the complete processing of the system. The patient and IoT are included in a separate layer called the patient layer. The IoT module receives information from various sensors connected to the patient body. The typical sensors used are a pulse sensor, heart sensor, Digital Humidity and Temperature (DHT)sensor, ECG sensor, etc. It does the process of encryption and transmits data to the database of the cloud. This module includes a set of sensors biomedical in nature which are

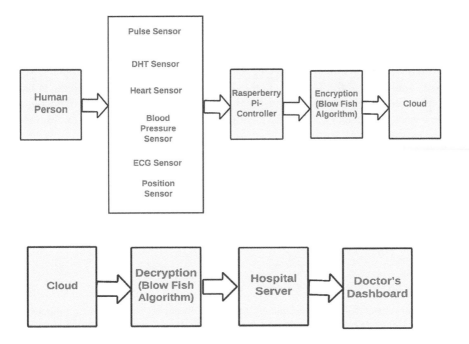

FIGURE 4.1   System for recent applications.

used to determine vital parameters such as the heart rate, oxygen level in the blood, body temperature, etc.

A Raspberry controller (Pi3) connected to Wi-Fi will process the above data, perform encryption using the Blowfish algorithm, and transmit it to the cloud without the requirement for an additional server or mobile application. This methodology is executed automatically without dealing with patients, which makes it comfortable especially for the elderly patients. Encryption is a process by which plain information is converted to secured information so as to provide appropriate security in transmitting data from sender to receiver in the communication link. The concept of the cloud is incorporated for a transition of data between the sender and the receiver. Decryption is a process by which the secured data is converted into plain data which is available on the hospital server for the access of doctors.

4.2.1 RASPBERRY PI CONTROLLER

Raspberry Pi is a microcontroller that can be interfaced with all sorts of I/O devices like keyboard, mouse, etc. It acts as a minicomputer whose size is similar to that of a credit card. It reflects the arrangement of a complete personal computer at a low price. In spite of the usage of computers becoming common everywhere, they are not widely used in a lot of countries. The imbalance between accessing the computer and the technique of programming paved the way for the innovation of the Raspberry controller. It is a single and small onboard computer that gives a lot of sophistication for the people to learn and compute. It is an extended version of the motherboard invented by a foundation of a Raspberry Pi. This computer can be interfaced with any sort of hardware device. The Secure Digital (SD)card of the controller will have the operating system which will boot the computer initially. These controllers are easily compatible with the Linux operating system.

Figure 4.2 shows the Raspberry Pi controller. There are six models available with these controllers: Pi0, Pi1, Pi2B, Pi3, Pi4B, and Pi400. These models differ in their configurations and features with respect to processing speed, frequency of operation, the capacity of memory, and other facilities like Ethernet connection. The following are key features of Raspberry:

- Central Processing Unit
- HDMI Port
- Graphic Processing Unit
- Memory (RAM)
- Ethernet Port
- SD Card Slot

4.2.2 HEART RATE SENSOR

A digital output will be generated by keeping a finger on the sensor to indicate the measurement of the heartbeat. The blood streams will compute the heartbeat by means of fingers. The sensor absorbs shots for each heartbeat with the regulation of light. The heartbeat count is provided by the generation of a flat beat with the regulation

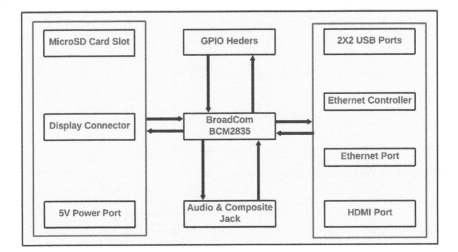

FIGURE 4.2   Raspberry Pi controller.

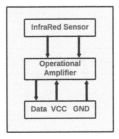

FIGURE 4.3   Pulse sensor.

of light. A pulse sensor integrated with an operational amplifier is employed for the measurement of heartbeats.

Figure 4.3 illustrates the module of the pulse sensor. This type of sensor has a direct link with the Raspberry controller for the manipulation of beats per minute. The standard specification for heart rate is 60–100 beats per minute.

4.2.3   PULSE OXIMETER

A pulse oximeter of high sensitivity – MAX30100 – is used to determine the heart rate and oxygen level in the blood of a patient by means of his fingertip. This sensor is interfaced with a microcontroller which is meant for processing and controlling of all activities. ESP 8266 is used for the purpose of compactness, economy, and speed and includes a built-in module for Wi-Fi with the ability to execute different applications.

Figure 4.4 shows a pulse oximeter with a heart sensor. The library of Node Micro-Controller Unit (MCU)will provide the implementation of Advanced Encryption

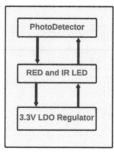

FIGURE 4.4 Pulse oximeter with heart sensor.

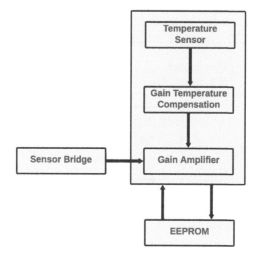

FIGURE 4.5 Blood pressure sensor.

Standard (AES) for the given module. The encryption of data is done by the Cipher Block Chaining (CBC) method and encoding with the format of Base 64. Then it is transmitted to the cloud.

4.2.4 BLOOD PRESSURE SENSOR

A transducer is employed to measure the blood pressure. A pulse signal is transformed into a mechanical signal using the transducer. A pressure sensor belonging to the series of AG3 is used here, which includes a chip for sensing pressure and conditioning the respective circuit. There is no provision for analog to digital and digital to analog conversions in this amplifier. Hence, a complete analog signal is amplified and the output is compensated with temperature. Figure 4.5 indicates the blood pressure sensor.

Additionally, the circuit of amplification is constructed to provide an output with a level of noise. The series of AG3 has a stand-alone function used for the detection of single-point pressure. The comparator internally available will compare analog output and a reference voltage and provide an output in the form of digital. Gain is amplified by the signal conditioning part. The expansion and contraction of arteries are called systolic and diastolic blood pressure, respectively. Their standard values of range are 120–140 mm Hg and 80–90 mm Hg, respectively [22].

4.2.5 TEMPERATURE SENSOR

DHT11 is a sensor used to measure the temperature of a human body, and it is of low cost. This sensor includes two components: a capacitor and a thermistor. It comprises a chip for the conversion of analog to digital and gives the value of temperature in digital form.

Figure 4.6 shows the DHT sensor for measurement of the sensor. The value of temperature in digital form is very convenient for reading with microcontrollers having data bits up to 12. Moreover, the consumption of power is significantly low. New values will be generated for every one second. The reference range values for the temperature of the human body are from 97° F to 99° F and conditions of abnormality are outside this range [23].

4.2.6 ECG SENSOR

This type of sensor will reflect the electrical activity of the heart. The term "activation" indicates the contraction of muscles of the heart. The muscles of the heart will contract at two different instants: relaxation and depolarization appropriately. The analysis of ECG includes the following key activities:

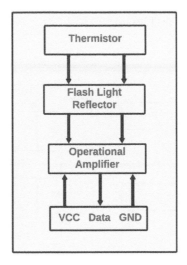

FIGURE 4.6 DHT sensor.

- Obtain the sensor signals
- Process of filtering signals
- Complete signal analysis

Initially, signals from the sensor are converted into a digital format to provide it an input to an Infinite impulse response (IIR) filter. Then this signal output of the IIR filter is analyzed by means of a system algorithm. Figure 4.7 shows the ECG sensor (AD8232).

The following is the methodology for interfacing ECG sensors and observing the electrical rhythm of the heart:

- A Heart Rate Observer having a single lead named AD8232 is employed to measure the electrical rhythm of the heart. It is a cost-effective monitor.
- The record of the electrical rhythm of the heart is called an ECG which also shows the output in analog form.
- The heart monitor behaves like an operational amplifier to get a noise-free signal from respective intervals.
- Aimed to remove, amplify, and sort out small signals with appropriate noise immunity by means of electrode placement at remote.
- Nine connections are available from the Integrated Circuit (IC) .
- From the IC, supply pins, input, and output pins are used for the interfacing monitor with the Arduino microcontroller.
- Other pins such as right arm (RA), left arm (LA), etc., can be used for custom purposes.
- The electrical activity of the heart is matched with an LED lamp for pulsating.
- Appropriate pads and cables for the sensor are needed for the use of a heart monitor.
- Biomedical sensor pads and sensor cables are needed for a heart monitor. The electrodes are interfaced with the sensor. The standard range from the measurement goes up to 120 ms [24].

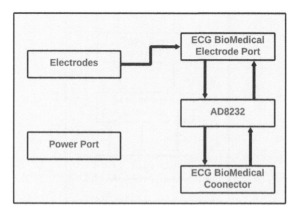

FIGURE 4.7   AD8232-based ECG sensor.

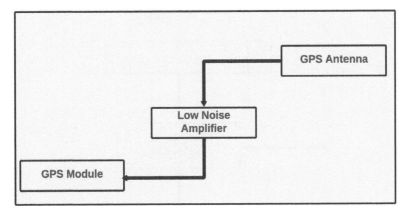

FIGURE 4.8   LS20033 GPS sensor.

4.2.7 POSITION SENSOR

The usage of devices like Global Positioning System (GPS) has evolved in a rapid manner in the past 10 years and still the demand keeps on increasing. Some of the typical examples are finding directions and locations outdoors and communicating using handheld devices. The key features of this facility are direction finding, location finding, and communicating with other people. But this facility can be extended to track too. By this technique, spatiotemporal information can be collected, thereby monitoring the movement of people [25].

Figure 4.8 depicts the GPS Sensor of series LS20033. These products include an antenna and a receiver circuit meant for specific applications of Original Equipment Manufacturer (OEM)systems with a wide spectrum of bandwidth. The embedded antenna will handle 66 satellites simultaneously at the maximum and provides both speed transmission and low consumption of power. With this feature, better sensitivity and optimum performance can be achieved even in dense environments also. GPS is a system meant for the determination of location or position in a particular environment. It is also called geo-positioning [26]. The satellite signals can be used to find out position and time in space. The first GPS was invented by the United States using satellite technology. These modules are generally employed for various applications such as navigation, capturing of time, positioning, etc. It receives information on location from satellites [27, 28].

4.3 ENCRYPTION ALGORITHMS

Nowadays, data security is a priority-based requirement in the field of information technology. Billions of money has been spent on the security of information and the management of risks. Among the techniques available, encryption is one form of the methodology used for the security of data that users of the computer can easily understand. Encryption is a process by which information is transformed from readable form to unreadable form by which access to data is allowable for authorized persons

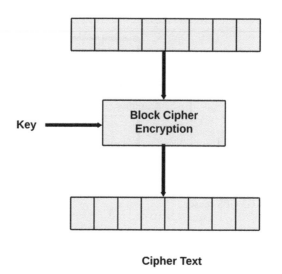

Plain Text

Cipher Text

FIGURE 4.9 Process of encryption.

only. In this process, certain algorithms are employed for a transition of data at both ends by implementing keys given by the sender. By this method, information is made confidential either in stored form or in transit form. The unauthorized form of access will be viewed as an array of bytes in chaotic form. Figure 4.9 shows the process of encryption. The following are the relevant essential terms:

Algorithm: They are norms for the process of encryption. The efficiency of encryption can be determined by various parameters such as the length of keys, features, and relevant functions.

Decryption: The method of transforming unreadable information into a readable format.

Key: A set of bits used for both encryption and decryption of information. Each key belongs to a unique category and keys having longer lengths are difficult to tap. The typical examples are 128 and 256 bits for private and public keys, respectively.

Symmetric Key Systems: In this system, the same key is allocated to all users accessing the information. In order to maintain privacy, the keys used at either end should be kept confidential.

Asymmetric Key Systems: In this system, two keys are employed – one is private and the other is public. The private key must be kept confidential and the public key must be accessible to the needy person. Both keys are integrated into each other in a way that encryption and decryption will be done by public and private keys, respectively.

4.3.1 TYPES OF ENCRYPTION ALGORITHMS

4.3.1.1 Triple DES

The alternative design for Data Encryption Standard (DES) algorithm is the Triple DES algorithm. Sometimes in the past, Triple DES was popular and the most periodically implemented algorithm in the industry. Three separate keys each of 56 bits in length are used here. Due to its slow characteristics, it has been replaced by Advanced Encryption Standard (AES).

4.3.1.2 Advanced Encryption Standard

The Government of the United States and a number of institutions across the world have trust in another algorithm named AES. Generally, it uses a standard form of 128 bits for encryption. Keys having the length of 192 bits and 256 bits are also used in AES for the purpose of heavy applications.

4.3.1.3 RSA Security

It is an algorithm based on a public key used for encryption. This is used on the Internet for secured transmission of data. It is a popular method employed for Pretty Good Privacy (PGP) programs. Because of its pair of keys used, it belongs to a category of asymmetric algorithms. Moreover, the hackers will consume a lot of time to break this algorithm due to its complexity.

4.3.1.4 Blowfish

One more alternative algorithm for DES is Blowfish. Here messages are decomposed into blocks of 64 bits each and subject to encryption separately. High efficiency and speed are the important features of the Blowfish algorithm. The typical application of this algorithm is the protection of passwords in secure payments used for online transactions. It is a flexible method of encryption.

4.3.1.5 Two Fish

The derivative of the Blowfish algorithm is two fish algorithms. It is a symmetric algorithm having a single key of length 256 bits at the maximum. It is a speedy algorithm employed for both software and hardware applications. It is an open source-based algorithm available to all.

4.4 BLOWFISH ALGORITHM

The security of information is an important requirement for all applications in day-to-day lives. The information has to be protected from hackers under all circumstances. Hence, with applications connected to the Internet, there is a crucial requirement for security methods to be implemented for the protection of data. The permitted users can communicate with each other with help of networks. The transmission or reception of data has to be reliable and accessible only to authorized users of the network. The trust of data must be available within a computer as well as during transmission over the network. Blowfish algorithm is implemented for the encryption of medical data which can be sent to the place where diagnostics are carried out. It is a feistel cipher that employs a length of 448 bits at the maximum against the keys and implements S-boxes in a dependent manner. There are 32 bits in each line and four numbers of S-boxes with each having 256 entries and an array having 18 entries. The following are the four steps linked with each round:

- XOR operation of data (left half) with that of P-array.
- XOR input data is used by F-function.
- XOR operation of F-outputs with that of data (right half).
- Swapping of data between left half and right half.

The input data of size 32 bits is decomposed into four numbers of 8-bit quarters which are in turn forwarded to S-boxes. The S-boxes will provide an output of size 32 bits which are subjected to modulo and XOR operations to obtain the final output. The decryption and encryption are similar to each other with the need to change the order of P-array in the other order [29]. The medical information can be viewed by many persons such as physicians, nurses, relatives, and diagnostic personnel from the concerned hospital. The above medical data is totally accessible only to the persons having authorization as per the policy of cipher text followed at the center [30]. In this policy, the key parameters of public type and respective messages are subject to the encryption process. The corresponding private keys are linked with a set of parameters that are used to indicate the authorization of respective users. These users have the right to decryption of a message. The following are the steps associated with the Ciphertext Policy-Attribute Based Encryption (CP-ABE) algorithm [31]:

- **Establishment:** The algorithm integrates a parameter for security and another for description so that output, secret key, and public parameters are generated.
- **Encryption**: This step integrates public parameters, collection of attributes, and message as respective inputs and generates an output (cipher text) accordingly.
- **Generation of Keys**: In this step, the access structure and secret key are taken as inputs and a private key will be generated accordingly.
- **Decryption:** In this step, cipher text with respective attributes and private keys are taken as inputs, and a message is generated as output.

Figure 4.10 presents the block diagram of the Blowfish algorithm for applications.

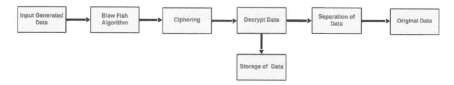

FIGURE 4.10   Blowfish algorithm.

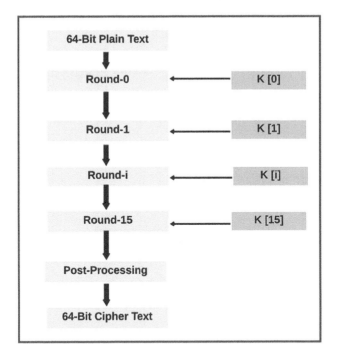

FIGURE 4.11   Blowfish algorithm – encryption process.

Different types of access policies will be followed with respect to the nature of the user. For example, the medical data is completely accessible by doctors, partially by service personnel and relatives of patients. The Blowfish algorithm is very suitable for processors and controllers having large memory. Figure 4.11 shows the encryption process with the Blowfish algorithm.

The medical information collected is accessible only to the users having authorization and not to anyone else [32]. The medical data are available only to the authorized users and the unauthorized users cannot access the data. Figure 4.12 shows the process of decryption with the Blowfish algorithm.

4.5   SYSTEM FOR FUTURE APPLICATIONS: INEXPENSIVE CARDIAC ARRHYTHMIA MANAGEMENT SYSTEM (ICARMA)

Nowadays, a number of IoT devices are available in the market for implementing healthcare such as BP monitors, glucose monitors, oximeters, etc [33]. The healthcare solutions based on IoT can support the patients suffering from different health complications like diabetes, hypotension, heart disease, etc., in the remote place. Arrhythmia is a disease by which electrical signals are generated abnormally by the heart and increases the probability of cardiac arrest. If this is not treated properly, it can pave the way to death. ICARMA is a method used for monitoring heart diseases that differentiates the conditions of the heart by employing Photoplethysmogram (PPG) signals obtained from sensors or cameras.

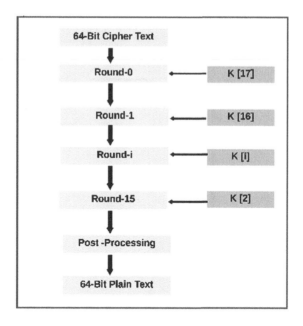

FIGURE 4.12   Blowfish algorithm – decryption process.

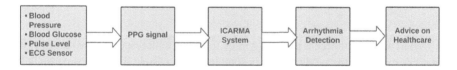

FIGURE 4.13   Architecture for ICARMA.

Typical examples of abnormal conditions of the heart are bradycardia, tachycardia, asystole, etc. But heart diseases can be totally prevented and loss of life can be avoided by timely detection. It is very difficult and more expensive for treating a patient with some extrinsic symptoms in an emergency. However, the same patient can be treated appropriately when he comes across preventive and timely detection. ICARMA seems to be an exploding engine on the side of the host. The camera available at the host site will be used to capture video of blood flow from which PPG signals are extracted. Smartphones can be used for the purpose of cameras and mobility. Figure 4.13 shows the architecture of the ICARMA system.

The concept of de-noising employed for the detection of PPG will provide an effective rate of detection and classification of arrhythmia conditions. These can be achieved by using two parameters: one is the extraction of heart rate and the other is statistical analysis. But current works on the detection of arrhythmia are dependent on an analysis of ECG signals. The analysis and the process of decision-making with ICARMA are generally carried out by using PPG signals only. To achieve a good rate of detection with ICARMA, there are a certain number of constraints to

TABLE 4.1
Conditions for Arrhythmia

Arrhythmia	Condition
Bradycardia (extreme)	Low heart rate (40 bpm) for five consecutive beats
Tachycardia (extreme)	High heart rate (140 bpm) for 17 consecutive beats
Tachycardia (ventricular)	More ventricular beats with higher heart rate (100 bpm)
Ventricular flutter/fibrillation	Fibrillatory/flutter waveform for at least 4 seconds
Asystole	No ECG-QRS for at least 4 seconds

be overcome. Generally, false positive suggestions may lead to crucial conditions for both physicians and patients, and respective alert messages are desensitized. On the other hand, false negative suggestions may lead to fatal conditions, and thereby heart anomalies are not detected. The purpose of this implementation is to minimize and optimize false negative and false positive suggestions, respectively, thereby improving the quality of healthcare service. Table 4.1 shows the various conditions for arrhythmia.

Figure 4.14 and Figure 4.15 depict the functions of the ICARMA system. Table 4.1 indicates an increase in the number of false suggestions. This may be due to an indication of symptoms for arrhythmia when the heart rate and conditions of arrhythmia are close to each other.

Inspired by heart rate (HR) data indications about conditions of arrhythmia, patients are found still to have the disease with appropriate symptoms. The problem is approached by means of conducting a morphological test to determine a deviation of cardio parameters toward the types of alarms. Generally, there are six types of alarms – one normal condition and five types of arrhythmias. The detection of abnormality is done by using PPG signals. The abnormal PPG and normal PPG are mobile and anti-persistent, respectively. In ICARMA, the number of false negatives is found to be less, which indicates the number of conditions undetected. The objective of this system is to minimize and optimize the count of false negatives and false positives, respectively. The opinion of the expert will be different in the case of asystole and detection of ventricular fibrillation as they are subjective. Since the above conditions of arrhythmia are fatal, the objective of the system is fairly satisfied.

The ICARMA aims to prevent the intensity of crucial heart diseases such as bradycardia, tachycardia, and asystole by means of detection carried out in time. PPG signals have the capability to decrease the false rate of detection. The essential requirement of IoT systems is the provision of healthcare in an affordable manner [34]. The patient information obtained by the sensors is transmitted over wireless networks which are more vulnerable when compared to wire networks. The public key algorithms do have more complexity and are inappropriate for transmitting short messages. Hence, symmetric algorithms are taken into consideration. Among these algorithms, Blowfish is found to be better comparatively for the process of encryption. The CP-ABE is employed for authorization of data usage with control

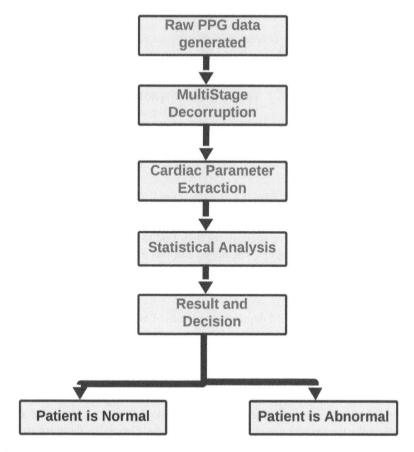

FIGURE 4.14   Functional flow of ICARMA system.

options. The integration of the above two algorithms is appropriate for applications of healthcare since they offer secured and fast transmission of data when compared to other systems [35, 36].

4.6   ADVANTAGES OF REMOTE HEALTHCARE

Three key advancements are persisting currently with respect to remote healthcare. The first among advancements is the availability of flexible, convenient, and cost-effective services of care. The next facility is providing care services at homes rather than providing them at respective hospitals, thus implementing the method of remote monitoring. The third advancement is extending care services for the patients from the state of acute conditions to the state of chronic conditions. Keeping certain future constraints, telehealth must be promoted as a means of support for the patients after corona disease pandemic due to the availability of appropriate shreds of evidence. Due to remote healthcare, there has been significant improvement in accessing services of

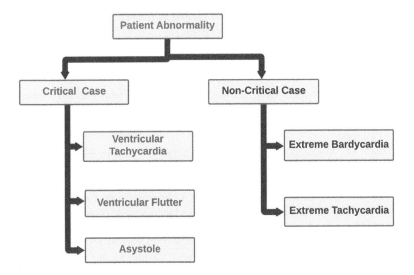

FIGURE 4.15   Functional flow of ICARMA system (continued).

healthcare, thereby promoting the interaction between patients and health personnel. However, appropriate importance must be given to the quality of care in services.

The blend of IoT and medical services can provide a lot of indispensable benefits to the patients. Hence, telehealth is an effective and useful methodology in providing services of healthcare for the people as quality, safety, and engagement are appropriately maintained. Despite many constraints, it presents a means of improving the services of healthcare. Hence, healthcare systems have a provision of implementing the concept of telehealth even after the COVID-19 pandemic. In this context, a lot of surveys indicate the long-term and short-term perspectives of telehealth toward building optimum solutions for improvement in a consistent manner [37].

4.7   CONCLUSION

Currently, there is an indispensable requirement for secure and smart healthcare systems among the patients, elderly people, and physicians for the detection of abnormal human body conditions, especially in remote places. The recent and future applications of those systems with the advent of IoT and cloud computing are enunciated in detail. The system related to recent applications focuses on monitoring and tracking of essential medical parameters, such as pulse rate, oxygen level, body temperature, etc. A Raspberry Pi controller is employed for tracing and processing of these signals along with necessary interfacing components. Then the Blowfish algorithm is implemented for the encryption of data and forwarded to the doctor's dashboard employing a cloud server. Then the authorized doctors will be able to view the measured values after the decryption process at the receiving end. Ultimately, the health status of the patient is monitored periodically at the remote place. The chapter also throws light on a future application named ICARMA for providing healthcare services in remote places in a detailed manner.

REFERENCES

1. Sajadieh, A., Nielsen, O.W., Rasmussne, V., Increased heart rate and reduced heart-rate variability are associated with subclinical inflammation in middle-aged and elderly subjects with no apparent heart disease. *European Heart Journal*, 25(5), 363–370, 2004.
2. Adil, M., Almaayah, M., Omar, A., Almomani, O., an anonymous channel categorization scheme of edge nodes to detect jamming attacks in wireless sensor networks. *Sensors*, 20(8), 2311–2315, 2020.
3. Doulamis, A., Doulamis, N., Angeli, A., A non-invasive photonics-based device for monitoring of diabetic foot ulcers: Architectural/sensorial components and technical specifications. *Inventions*, 6(2), 27–32, 2021.
4. Sedik, A., Hammad, M., Gupta, B., Efficient deep learning approach for augmented detection of corona virus disease. *Neural Computing and Applications*, 3, 1–18, 2021.
5. Hammad, M., Illiyasu, M.A., Subasi, A., A multi-tier deep learning model for arrhythmia detection. *IEEE Transactions on Instrumentation and Measurement*, 70, 1–9, 2020.
6. Jayachitra, S., Prasanth, A., Rafi, S., Hierarchical-based binary moth flame optimization for feature extraction in biomedical application. *International Conference on Machine Learning, Image Processing, Network Security and Data Sciences*, 27–38, 2022.
7. Adil, M., Khan, R., Ali, J., An energy proficient load balancing routing scheme for wireless sensor networks to maximize their lifespan in an operational environment. *IEEE Access,* 8, 163209–163224, 2020.
8. Sekar, J., Aruchamy, P., Haleem, A., An efficient clinical support system for heart disease prediction using TANFIS classifier. *Computational Intelligence*, 38, 610–640, 2022.
9. Dagtas, S., Pekhteryev, G., Cam, H., Real-time and secure wireless health monitoring. *International Journal of Telemedicine and Applications*, 5, 1–10, 2008.
10. Almaiah, M. A., Al-Khasawneh, A., Investigating the main determinants of mobile cloud computing adoption in university campus. *Education and Information Technologies*, 25(4), 3087–3107, 2020.
11. Aruchamy, P., Gnanaselvi, S., Sowndarya, D., An artificial intelligence approach for energy-aware intrusion detection and secure routing in internet of things-enabled wireless sensor networks. *Concurrency and Computation: Practice and Experience*, 35, 1–33, 2023.
12. Esposito, C., Tort, G., Chang, H., Blockchain: a panacea for healthcare cloud based data security and privacy. *IEEE Cloud Computing*, 5(1), 31–37, 2018.
13. Ali Siam, I.A., Khobby, H.E., Abd Elkader, H.A., Enhanced data security model for cloud computing platform. *International Journal of Scientific Research in Science, Engineering, and Technology*, 1(4), 450–460, 2015.
14. Nafea, R.A., Amin Almaiah, M., Cyber security threats in cloud: Literature review. In *Proceedings of 2021 International Conference on Information Technology (ICIT)*, Amman, Jordan, 779–786, 2021.

15. Casola, V., Castiglione, A., Esposito, C., Healthcare-related data in the cloud: Challenges and opportunities. *IEEE Cloud Computing*, 3(6), 10–14, 2016.
16. Ali, O., Shrestha, A., Soar, J., Cloud computing-enabled healthcare opportunities, issues, and applications: A systematic review. *International Journal of Information Management*, 43, 146–158, 2018.
17. Ahmad Al, H., Almaayah, M., Almomani, O., Classification of cyber security threats on mobile devices and applications. *Studies in Big Data*, 90, 107–123, 2021.
18. Yi, X., Athman, B., Song, A., Privacy protection for wireless medical sensor data. *IEEE Transactions on Dependable and Secure Computing*, 13(3), 369–380, 2016.
19. Baker, S. B., Xiang, W., Atkinson, I., Internet of Things for smart healthcare: Technologies, challenges, and opportunities, *IEEE Access*, 5, 26521–26544, 2017.
20. Naveen, Sharma, R. K., Nair, A. R., IoT-based secure healthcare monitoring system. In *2019 IEEE International Conference on Electrical, Computer and Communication Technologies (ICECCT)*, Coimbatore, India, 1–6, 2019.
21. Jaiswal, K., Srichandan, S., Kumar, M. B., IoT-Cloud based framework for patient's data collection in smart healthcare system using Raspberry PI. In *International Conference on Electrical and Computing Technologies and Applications (ICECTA)*, UAE, 12–17, 2018.
22. Shoval, N., Tracking technologies and urban analysis. *Cities*, 25, 21–28, 2008.
23. Raper, J., Gatner, G., Karimi, H., A critical evaluation of location based services and their potential. *Journal of Location Based Services*, 1(2), 35–45, 2007.
24. Yang, C. C. and Hsu, Y. L., A review of accelerometer-based wearable motion detectors for physical activity monitoring, *Sensors*, 10, 7772–7788, 2010.
25. Patel, S., Park, S., Bonato, H. P., A review of wearable sensors and systems with application in rehabilitation. *Journal of Neuro Engineering and Rehabilitation*, 9, 1–17, 2012.
26. Van der Spek, S., Van Schaick, J., De Bois, P., Sensing human activity: GPS tracking. *Sensors (Basel)* 9(4), 3033–3055, 2009.
27. Stephanie Baker, B., Xiang, W., Atkinson, I., Internet of Things for smart healthcare: Technologies, challenges, and opportunities. *IEEE Access*, 5, 26521–26544, 2017.
28. Daemen, J., Rijmen, V., The design of Rijndael: AES the Advanced Encryption Standard. *Springer Science and Business Media*, Berlin, Germany, 26–30, 2013.
29. Schneier, B., *Applied Cryptography*. Second Edition. John Wiley & Sons, 1996.
30. Qiao, Z., Liang, S., Davis, S., Survey of attribute-Based encryption, *Proceedings of 15th IEEE/ACIS International Conference on Software Engineering, Artificial Intelligence, Networking and Parallel/Distributed Computing (SNPD)*, Las Vegas, NV, USA, 1–6, 2014.
31. Hohenberger, S., Waters, B., Attribute-based encryption with fast decryption, public-key cryptography. *Lecture Notes in Computer Science*, 162–179, 2013.
32. Bouabida, K., Lebouche, B., Pomey, M.P., Telehealth and COVID-19 pandemic: An overview of the Telehealth use, advantages, challenges, and opportunities during COVID-19 pandemic. *Healthcare*, 10, 2293–2297, 2022.
33. Chetanya, P., Ukil, A., Bandyopadhyay, S., iCarMa: Inexpensive cardiac arrhythmia management–An IoT healthcare analytics solution. *IoT of Health*, 45–51, 2016.
34. Sathya., Kumar, P.G., Secured remote health monitoring system, healthcare technology. *Letters*, 4(6), 228–232, 2017.
35. Muthukumaran, D., Umapathy, K., Omkumar, S., Health cloud–health care as a service. *Lecture Notes in Networks and Systems*, Springer Nature, 489–497, 2021.

36. Muthukumaran, D., Umapathy, K., Boonsong, W., Real time data based smart hitech classroom using IOT. *Intelligent Systems and Reference Library,* Springer, 221, 85–92, 2022.

37. Umapathy, K. Wireless technique based vehicle speed control system. *AIP Conference Proceedings,* 2519, 050022-1 to 050022-5, 2022.

5 Transforming Healthcare Management

Combining Blockchain, P2P Networks, and Digital Platforms

Janhvi Rajyaguru[1] and Lakshmi D[2]*
[1,2]School of Computing Science and Engineering,
VIT Bhopal University, Madhya Pradesh, India
[1]Email: janhvi.rajyaguru2022@gmail.com
*Corresponding Author: Lakshmi D (Email: lakshmi.
lifefordivine@gmail.com)

5.1 INTRODUCTION

The healthcare industry is currently facing numerous challenges such as interoperability, data privacy, and security issues. To address these challenges, a new approach is needed to manage and secure medical data. The integration of blockchain technology with patient-centric digital platforms and multilayer peer-to-peer (P2P) networks can provide a secure and interoperable solution for healthcare data management. The potential for blockchain technology to improve patient-centric care is immense [1].

Patient data is currently centrally managed and stored, often in a manner that lacks interoperability and security. With blockchain technology, patient records can be securely stored and managed on a distributed database that is decentralized, secure, and accessible by authorized users in real time from any location [2]. Patients can request access to their records at any time, which can improve compliance and accuracy of treatment and improve the overall quality of care. Blockchain-enabled smart contracts can also improve efficiency by automating many of the manual processes currently required for healthcare delivery, including payment verifications, authorizations, claims submissions, and other administrative functions. This has the potential to significantly reduce the administrative burden on providers and lower operating costs for payers and other healthcare system stakeholders [3].

In addition to improving efficiency and security, blockchain technology can also be used to streamline access to medical devices and patient therapies. By enabling patients and healthcare providers to share health data with devices securely and in real time, blockchain technologies have the potential to make digital health products more affordable and accessible by reducing or eliminating friction in the supply chain

DOI: 10.1201/9781003405450-5

[4]. Many devices – including hearing aids, insulin pumps, and wearable biometric monitors – could benefit from blockchain-based authentication solutions [5]. Lastly, blockchain applications can also provide valuable data for medical research and clinical innovation. By capturing and analyzing data on the use and health impact of medical products and other healthcare services, blockchains could enable the development of new treatment options and personalized patient interventions that more effectively meet their needs.

To take full advantage of these benefits, however, it is essential that healthcare organizations fully integrate blockchain technology into their operations and adopt new systems architectures that support this new technology [6]. As with most new technologies, it will take time to develop the necessary competencies and expertise to fully leverage the power of blockchain to improve health outcomes and reduce costs across the healthcare industry. Blockchain technology is an attractive option for storing and processing healthcare data because of its scalability, security, and ease of implementation. In addition, its decentralized nature reduces the risk of data breaches and eliminates the need for intermediaries to oversee transactions and validate data, which could increase transparency and cut costs across the entire health system [7]. However, despite these potential benefits, the current pace of adoption by healthcare providers remains slow due to concerns about cost and complexity.

Because blockchain is a relatively young technology that is not fully understood by many healthcare leaders, it can be challenging for organizations to implement these systems in a standardized way. This challenges the interoperability of current health systems and may require organizations to develop entirely new strategies for managing and storing patient data on these platforms. Despite these hurdles, the potential of blockchain technology to transform the way health care is delivered is undeniable. When used appropriately, it has the potential to provide significant benefits for the healthcare system by helping to reduce costs and eliminate inefficiencies in the system.

5.1.1 INTRODUCTION TO PATIENT-CENTRIC HEALTHCARE

This chapter begins by discussing the importance of patient-centric healthcare and the potential benefits of using blockchain, multilayer P2P networks, and digital platforms in this context. Patient-centric blockchains are a novel approach to utilizing blockchain technology in the healthcare industry to put patients at the center of their health data management [8]. Patients have little ownership and control over their health information in traditional healthcare systems, which frequently entail fragmented and centralized data storage. By utilizing the decentralized and immutable properties of blockchain to provide patients more control, security, and privacy over their health data, patient-centric blockchains seek to revolutionize this paradigm.

Each patient in a patient-centric blockchain has a blockchain-based digital identity that serves as a distinctive identifier for their medical records. A patient's blockchain can be used to securely store data about them, including electronic health records (EHRs), medical histories, lab results, and prescription histories. By authorizing specific healthcare professionals or researchers to access their health data, patients can manage access while preserving their privacy and ownership rights.

Blockchains focused on healthcare also provide strong privacy and security features. Patient data is made tamper-proof and verifiable through the use of cryptographic algorithms, lowering the possibility of data breaches and unauthorized access. To increase confidence and responsibility in the healthcare ecosystem, patients can also have more visibility and transparency into who has access to their health data.

Multilayer P2P networks are a type of distributed network architecture where peers, or individual nodes, collaborate to share resources such as files, data, or services without relying on a central server. In multilayer P2P networks, there are multiple layers or levels of peers that interact with each other to facilitate resource sharing [9]. Overlay networks, which are virtual networks constructed on top of the underlying physical network infrastructure, are often how multilayer P2P networks are organized. These overlay networks, which can be organized or unstructured, are generated dynamically by peers entering and departing the network. The presence of several sorts of peers with varying roles and responsibilities is one feature shared by multilayer P2P networks [10].

Applications like file sharing, content distribution, messaging, and collaborative computing can all be done via multilayer P2P networks. Although they provide benefits like scalability, fault tolerance, and decentralized control, they also present difficulties in terms of effectiveness, dependability, and security. Multilayer P2P network research and development are still in progress, with ongoing work being done to enhance the networks' robustness, performance, and security. These networks continue to be heavily utilized in a variety of distributed applications and play an important role in computer networking and distributed computing [11].

5.1.2 Patient-Centric Blockchains

Patient-centric blockchains are blockchain-based systems that prioritize the needs of patients. A type of blockchain technology known as "patient-centric blockchains" is intended to put patients' demands, privacy, and control over their personal health information (PHI) first. The patient is at the center of the healthcare data ecosystem in a patient-centric blockchain, with the power to manage access to their PHI, give or revoke rights, and take part in the decision-making process for their health data [12]. By granting consumers more ownership and control over their health data, patient-centric blockchains seek to empower patients while also improving data privacy and security. The idea is to use blockchain technology to build a patient-centric, decentralized, transparent, and immutable ledger for securely storing health data.

Some key characteristics of patient-centric blockchains include the following and are shown in Figure 5.1:

1. **Patient control:** Patients have control over their own health information, including the ability to specify who has access to it, which permissions to grant or remove, and how their information will be used.

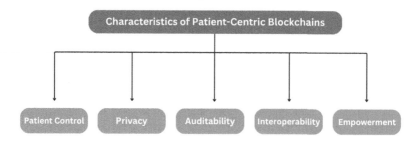

FIGURE 5.1 Characteristics of patient-centric blockchain.

2. **Privacy and security:** Patient-centric blockchains preserve the confidentiality and integrity of health data via encryption and other security measures, ensuring that information is stored safely and exchanged only with authorized parties.
3. **Transparency and auditability:** Patient-centric blockchains offer transparency by keeping an immutable, transparent record of all transactions and modifications to health data, which can be audited and validated by pertinent parties.
4. **Interoperability:** By facilitating smooth and safe data sharing between various healthcare stakeholders, systems, and providers while respecting patient preferences and rights, patient-centric blockchains promote interoperability.
5. **Patient empowerment:** In order to have better patient participation and outcomes, patient-centric blockchains strive to empower patients by granting them more authority, responsibility, and input over their own healthcare decisions.

5.1.3 ADVANTAGES AND DISADVANTAGES OF USING BLOCKCHAIN IN HEALTHCARE

Table 5.1 shows the advantages and disadvantages of using blockchain in the healthcare sector.

Furthermore, patient-centric blockchains could also help to facilitate the growth of personalized medicine and precision health. By providing patients with greater control over their healthcare data, and by enabling more efficient sharing of this data between different stakeholders, patient-centric blockchains could help to advance the development of more targeted and effective treatments for various conditions [13]. However, for these potential applications to become a reality, there are still several challenges that need to be addressed, such as regulatory barriers, technical challenges, and issues around interoperability and data privacy.

5.2 MULTILAYER P2P NETWORKS

Multilayer P2P networks are distributed computer networks where peers (i.e., individual nodes or devices) collaborate to share resources or perform tasks across multiple layers or levels of abstraction. These networks frequently feature

TABLE 5.1
Advantages and Disadvantages of Blockchain in the Healthcare Sector

Advantages	Disadvantages
Blockchain provides a highly secure and tamper-proof way to store and share data, which can help protect patient privacy and ensure the confidentiality, integrity, and authenticity of healthcare data.	This technology still faces challenges in scalability, as the growing size of the blockchain and the associated computational overhead can impact the speed and efficiency of transactions, which may not be suitable for certain healthcare use cases with high transaction volumes.
It can enable interoperability by providing a decentralized and standardized platform for different healthcare entities to securely share and access data, improving data exchange and communication between different stakeholders in the healthcare ecosystem.	It is complex and requires specialized technical expertise for implementation and maintenance, which may pose challenges for healthcare organizations with limited resources or technical capabilities.
It uses consensus mechanisms and cryptographic algorithms to validate and verify data, ensuring the accuracy and consistency of data across the network, which can help reduce data errors and discrepancies.	Achieving interoperability among different blockchain networks or integrating blockchain with existing healthcare systems can be challenging, requiring standardized protocols and interoperability frameworks.
It can enhance the traceability and transparency of the pharmaceutical supply chain, reducing counterfeit drugs, ensuring the authenticity of medications, and improving drug safety.	Implementing and maintaining a network can be costly, including the expenses associated with hardware, software, network infrastructure, and maintenance, which may impact the affordability and feasibility of adoption for some healthcare organizations.

several functional layers or levels, each of which serves a distinct function and aids in the smooth running of the network as a whole. Distinct levels of a multi-layer P2P network could be in charge of distinct functions including routing, data storage, resource discovery, or application-level services [14]. Depending on their roles and capacities, network peers can take part in one or more of these layers. Peers can provide resources (such as computer power, storage, or bandwidth) or consume resources from the network, and they can join or leave the network dynamically.

The P2P network model is a decentralized network architecture where nodes communicate and share resources directly with each other, rather than through a central server. In the context of patient-centric blockchains in healthcare, a P2P network can be used to store and share patient data securely and efficiently. The multilayer P2P network architecture consists of four layers as shown in Figure 5.2.

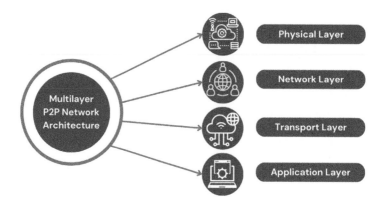

FIGURE 5.2   Multilayer P2P network architecture.

1. Physical Layer: This layer deals with the physical components of the network, such as the hardware and cabling used to connect nodes. The physical layer provides the foundation for the network and ensures that nodes can communicate with each other.
2. Network Layer: This layer is responsible for managing the network topology, routing, and addressing. The network layer ensures that data packets are sent to the correct destination node by using IP addresses and routing algorithms.
3. Transport Layer: This layer is responsible for ensuring reliable and efficient communication between nodes. The transport layer uses protocols such as TCP and UDP to establish connections between nodes and transfer data packets.
4. Application Layer: This layer is responsible for managing the applications and services that run on the network. In the context of patient-centric blockchains, the application layer would manage the blockchain nodes and the healthcare applications that use the blockchain.

By using a multilayer P2P network architecture, patient-centric blockchains can benefit from increased security, improved scalability, and greater decentralization. Each layer of the network provides a specific set of functions and services that help to ensure that data is transferred securely and efficiently between nodes. Moreover, the use of P2P networks can help to reduce the risk of data breaches and ensure that patients have greater control over their healthcare data.

Some of the advantages of using a P2P network model in healthcare include increased security, improved scalability, and greater decentralization. By using a P2P network model, healthcare data can be stored and shared across multiple nodes in the network, rather than being centralized in a single location. This helps to reduce the risk of data breaches and ensures that patients have greater control over their data.

- One of the primary advantages of using a P2P network model in healthcare is increased security. Traditional client-server models rely on a central server to store and manage data, which makes them vulnerable to cyberattacks and data breaches. In contrast, a P2P network model distributes data across multiple nodes, making it more difficult for cybercriminals to compromise the network [15]. Each node in the network acts as a data store, which can help to improve data redundancy and fault tolerance.

- Another advantage of P2P networks in healthcare is improved scalability. Traditional client-server models can struggle to cope with the large amounts of data generated in healthcare, leading to slow data processing times and decreased efficiency. In contrast, P2P networks can scale more easily by adding more nodes to the network as needed. This helps to ensure that the network can handle the increasing volumes of data generated by healthcare applications and services.
- A P2P network model also offers greater decentralization, which can empower patients to take a more active role in their healthcare. By storing healthcare data on a decentralized network, patients can have greater control over who can access their data, and can also grant access to healthcare providers as needed. This can help to improve patient engagement and lead to better healthcare outcomes [16].

Using a P2P network model in healthcare can provide numerous benefits, including increased security, improved scalability, and greater decentralization. By leveraging these advantages, patient-centric blockchains can help to improve healthcare data management, enhance data security and privacy, and empower patients to take a more active role in their healthcare [17].

5.3   DIGITAL PLATFORMS IN HEALTHCARE

The EHR platform is one of the important platforms that is covered. EHRs are computerized patient health records that may be shared and viewed by healthcare professionals. Data security, privacy, and interoperability in healthcare can be greatly enhanced by the integration of EHRs with patient-centric blockchains and multilayer P2P networks [17]. Patients may maintain ownership of their data, and healthcare professionals can securely and effectively access and share it. Health Information Exchange (HIE) is an essential and crucial platform. The interchange of health information across various healthcare organizations and providers is made possible through HIEs. HIEs can offer a secure and decentralized platform for data exchange with the integration of patient-centric blockchains and multilayer P2P networks, enabling patients to share their data across various healthcare providers and organizations without compromising privacy [18].

Patient-centric healthcare is made possible via patient engagement platforms, which are equally essential. These platforms give patients access to their medical records and let them take an active role in their care. Patient engagement platforms can enhance the accuracy and completeness of patient data, enabling more individualized care, by using patient-centric blockchains and multilayer P2P networks [19]. Another significant digital platform that can support patient-centric blockchains and multi-layer P2P networks in healthcare is blockchain technology. To maintain the confidentiality and integrity of patient data, blockchain technology offers a secure and decentralized platform for data storage and sharing [20]. Patients may own their data and grant healthcare professionals access to it by using blockchain technology.

The security, privacy, interoperability, and effectiveness of healthcare data management can be considerably increased by combining these digital platforms with patient-centric blockchains and multilayer P2P networks. Let's clarify the numerous digital infrastructures that can support patient-centric blockchains and multilayer P2P networks in the healthcare industry. Possible subjects include the following.

5.3.1 Healthcare Data Management Platforms

Large amounts of healthcare data must be managed, analyzed, and shared by healthcare organizations with the use of these platforms. They offer a centralized platform for storing and managing healthcare data, which healthcare professionals, researchers, and other stakeholders can access and analyze. By giving healthcare data sharing a safe and convenient platform, healthcare data management platforms can help patient-centric blockchains.

Healthcare providers, academics, and other stakeholders can access and analyze the data more easily due to healthcare data management platforms, which offer a centralized location for storing and managing healthcare data. Additionally, they provide a high level of security and privacy, all of which are essential when working with private health data. They can be used to assist the secure and effective sharing of healthcare data in the context of patient-centric blockchains and multilayer P2P networks in healthcare [21]. These platforms can serve as a data source for patient-centric blockchains by offering a centralized area for storing and managing healthcare data, making it simpler for users to share their data with healthcare practitioners and researchers.

The fact that healthcare data management platforms offer a secure and standardized platform for handling healthcare data is one of the main advantages of using them to enable patient-centric blockchains and multilayer P2P networks. In the context of patient care and research, it is crucial to ensure that the data being provided is accurate and up-to-date [20]. Utilizing healthcare data management platforms has the additional benefit of assisting in enhancing the effectiveness and scalability of patient-centric blockchains and multilayer P2P networks. These platforms can assist to decrease the quantity of redundant data being shared and increase the network efficiency by offering a centralized platform for handling healthcare data.

5.3.2 EHR Platforms

EHR platforms are made to facilitate the management and storage of EHRs. They offer a digital copy of a patient's medical records so that medical professionals can access and update them as required. EHR systems can help patient-centric blockchains by giving patients a safe and convenient platform to exchange their medical records with doctors and researchers [22]. The ability of EHR platforms to allow patient-centric blockchains to assist verifying the dependability and validity of patient data is one of their main advantages. A uniform and secure method of gathering and storing patient data is offered by EHR platforms, and this data can be used to verify the veracity of the data in the blockchain. Utilizing EHR systems also has the benefit of enhancing the general effectiveness of patient-centric blockchains and multilayer P2P networks [23].

The use of EHR platforms as a centralized location for managing and storing patient data can reduce the amount of repetitive information that is exchanged. This can lead to improved efficiency within the network and a lower probability of mistakes or the duplication of data. EHR platforms can also enhance patient empowerment and participation. Patients can control who gets access to their health records and can view their records on EHR platforms. This can inspire patients to participate actively in their healthcare and promote patient-centered treatment.

5.3.3 HEALTH INFORMATION EXCHANGE PLATFORMS

HIE platforms are designed to facilitate the exchange of healthcare data between different organizations and systems. They use standardized protocols to ensure inter-operability between different systems, and can be used to support patient-centric blockchains by providing a secure and standardized platform for sharing healthcare data between patients, providers, and researchers [24]. The ability to transmit health information between various entities in a secure and effective manner is one of the main benefits of adopting HIE platforms. It can be connected with P2P networks and blockchains focused on patients to make it easier for nodes to exchange healthcare data. This may contribute to increasing the network's overall accuracy and complete-ness of healthcare data while also raising the standard of care for patients.

HIE platforms also offer a centralized location for managing and storing healthcare data, which is another benefit of employing them [25]. By doing so, it's possible to lower the chance of errors and data duplication while also guaranteeing the con-sistency and accuracy of patient data throughout the network's many entities. HIE platforms can also aid in the interoperability of various healthcare apps and systems, which can boost patient outcomes and increase the network's overall effectiveness. HIE platforms can also support patient empowerment and involvement. On HIE platforms, patients may view their medical records and manage who has access to them. This can inspire patients to participate actively in their healthcare and promote patient-centered treatment.

5.3.4 PATIENT ENGAGEMENT PLATFORMS

Platforms for patient engagement are created to assist patients in controlling their healthcare more actively. They offer materials and tools that patients can use to monitor their health, create goals, and interact with their healthcare professionals. By giving patients a platform to safely access and exchange their medical data, patient engagement platforms can help patient-centric blockchains [26].

The ability of patient engagement platforms to support patient engagement and empowerment is one of their major benefits. On these platforms, patients can access their medical records, contact healthcare professionals, and get personalized health information. This can assist individuals in taking an active role in their treatment and in making wise health decisions. By promoting communication and collaboration between patients and healthcare providers, patient engagement platforms can also help to improve patient outcomes. To help physicians modify their care plans and enhance patient outcomes, patients can offer feedback on their treatment and report any problems they may be having [27]. Additionally, patient engagement platforms can support the interoperability of various healthcare applications and systems. These platforms enable the sharing of healthcare data between nodes by integrating with patient-centric blockchains and P2P networks. This could better patient outcomes and increase the network's general efficiency [1].

5.3.5 BLOCKCHAIN PLATFORMS

Blockchain platforms are digital ledgers that can be used to record and manage transactions since they are decentralized and secure. By offering a safe and transparent platform for handling healthcare data and transactions, blockchain platforms in the healthcare industry can be utilized to promote patient-centric blockchains. Ethereum, Hyperledger Fabric, and Corda are a few blockchain technologies that are intended primarily for usage in the healthcare industry.

Data security and privacy are two major benefits of employing blockchain platforms in the healthcare industry. Due to the decentralized nature of blockchain technology, it is virtually hard for hackers or unauthorized users to access sensitive patient data because it is stored on a distributed network of nodes [18]. Additionally, blockchain technology employs sophisticated cryptographic methods to guarantee that data is secure and private even as it is transferred between several network nodes. Utilizing is also advantageous since it enables efficient and safe data sharing. Healthcare data can be kept on a distributed ledger using blockchain technology, making it safe and effective for authorized parties to access. Giving healthcare practitioners access to timely and reliable patient data, can assist to streamline healthcare operations and enhance patient outcomes [24]. Additionally, blockchain platforms can aid in fostering interoperability between various healthcare applications and systems. Blockchain technology can help to ensure that healthcare data is available across various healthcare systems and apps by offering a safe and decentralized platform for exchange, increasing the overall efficiency and efficacy of the healthcare system.

5.4 CONNECTING PATIENT-CENTRIC BLOCKCHAINS WITH MULTILAYER P2P NETWORKS

The administration of medical records is one of the most potential use cases for patient-centric blockchains. Healthcare providers can guarantee that patient data is safe, unchangeable, and accessible by keeping patient medical records on a blockchain. By lowering the possibility of medical mistakes and empowering healthcare professionals to make more informed decisions about patient care, this could enhance patient outcomes. Clinical trials are another possible application for patient-centric blockchains [28]. Researchers can run clinical studies that are more effective and accurate by using blockchain technology to securely store and share patient data, thereby hastening the discovery of novel treatments and therapies.

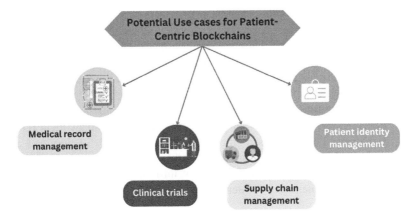

FIGURE 5.3 Potential use cases of patient-centric blockchains.

Blockchains focused on patients have potential in the field of managing the supply chain for medical supplies. The risk of counterfeit goods entering the supply chain is decreased by utilizing blockchain technology to track the flow of drugs and medical devices [29]. This allows providers to confirm that the products are genuine and have not been tampered with. Blockchains that are focused on patients may also be utilized to enhance healthcare payment systems. Providers and payers can save money on administrative expenses and increase the precision and transparency of payment processes by adopting blockchain technology to securely manage payments and refunds. Figure 5.3 shows the potential use cases for patient-centric blockchains in healthcare.

1. **Medical record management**: Blockchains focused on the needs of the patient might be utilized to provide a safe, decentralized platform for keeping track of medical records. Every patient might have their own blockchain, which would store all of their test results, medical records, and other pertinent data. The patient would be in charge of who has access to their blockchain and might grant healthcare providers access as needed. As a result, people would have more control over their medical information, and healthcare professionals would be able to share that information more quickly and securely.

2. **Clinical trials**: Clinical trials may be facilitated by the use of patient-centric blockchains. Researchers might guarantee that all data is secure and unchangeable by building a blockchain expressly for a clinical trial, and they could also give patients power over their own data. Patients had the option of choosing to take part in the experiment and give researchers access to their data, and they were free to cancel that access at any moment. This could help allay worries about data security and privacy in clinical studies, and it might also make research more productive and successful.

3. **Supply chain management**: Blockchains that are centered on patients may also be used to trace the origins of pharmaceuticals, medical equipment, and

other healthcare supplies. Healthcare providers might guarantee that products are genuine, have not been tampered with, and are given to the right patient by developing a blockchain that follows the transfer of these products from producer to patient. Particularly in the case of expensive pharmaceuticals or medical devices, this could aid in lowering fraud and enhancing patient safety [30].

4. **Patient identity management**: In the context of international healthcare, patient-centric blockchains might also be utilized to handle patient IDs [28]. Healthcare professionals might authenticate a patient's identity and access their medical records from anywhere in the world by developing a blockchain that contains all of a patient's identity information. Patients who regularly travel may benefit from better access to healthcare, and it may also lessen identity fraud.

These are just a few potential use cases for patient-centric blockchains in healthcare. By using blockchain technology to create secure, decentralized platforms for managing medical data, patient-centric blockchains could help to address a range of challenges in healthcare, from data privacy and security to supply chain management and patient identity.

5.4.1 CHALLENGES AND CONSIDERATIONS

While patient-centric blockchains, multilayer P2P networks, and digital platforms have a lot of potential for the healthcare industry, there are many obstacles and things to keep in mind. For instance, privacy issues must be properly addressed to guarantee patient confidence and trust. To ensure that these technologies can be broadly embraced and used efficiently, technical difficulties like interoperability and standardization must also be solved [18].

While patient-centric blockchains, multilayer P2P networks, and digital platforms have the potential to transform the healthcare industry, they also face several challenges and considerations. Some of these challenges include:

1. Data privacy and security: The use of patient data in these technologies raises concerns about data privacy and security. Healthcare providers and technology companies must take steps to ensure that patient data is protected and secure.
2. Interoperability: The healthcare industry is notoriously fragmented, with data stored in multiple systems and formats. Interoperability is a critical challenge to the widespread adoption of these technologies, as data must be able to flow freely between systems.
3. Regulation: Healthcare is a heavily regulated industry, and the use of these technologies may be subject to various regulatory requirements. Companies must ensure that they comply with relevant laws and regulations, including Health Insurance Portability and Accountability Act (HIPAA), General Data Protection Regulation (GDPR), and others.

4. Adoption: Widespread adoption of these technologies will require buy-in from healthcare providers, patients, and other stakeholders. Education and awareness campaigns will be needed to help people understand the potential benefits of these technologies.

5. Technical challenges: Implementing patient-centric blockchains, multilayer P2P networks, and digital platforms requires significant technical expertise. Companies must have the resources and expertise to design, build, and maintain these complex systems.

6. Cost: The implementation and maintenance of these technologies can be expensive, particularly for smaller healthcare providers or those with limited resources.

The healthcare industry must carefully consider these challenges and considerations as they explore the use of patient-centric blockchains, multilayer P2P networks, and digital platforms. By addressing these challenges, however, the industry can unlock the potential of these technologies to improve patient outcomes, enhance care coordination, and reduce healthcare costs.

5.4.2 Connecting Patient-Centric Blockchains with Digital Platforms

The combination of these technologies with machine learning (ML) and artificial intelligence (AI) algorithms represents one possible avenue for growth. Healthcare professionals and researchers could more readily access enormous volumes of patient data to train ML algorithms and enhance diagnoses and treatment plans by leveraging patient-centric blockchain systems and P2P networks to securely share data. These technologies allow for the real-time collection of patient data, which decreases the requirement for in-person visits to clinical trial locations while potentially raising participation rates. P2P networks and patient-centric blockchains have the potential to enhance healthcare system interoperability and make data sharing across various providers and organizations easier.

Some potential future developments of these technologies include:

1. Greater adoption: While these technologies are still in their early stages, it is likely that they will become more widely adopted in the coming years. As healthcare providers and patients become more comfortable with these technologies, we may see a significant increase in their use.

2. Integration with other technologies: Patient-centric blockchains, multilayer P2P networks, and digital platforms may be integrated with other emerging technologies, such as AI, ML, and the Internet of Things. This integration may lead to new opportunities for healthcare providers to improve patient outcomes and reduce healthcare costs.

3. Improved data sharing and collaboration: By utilizing these technologies, healthcare providers may be able to share data more easily and collaborate more effectively. This could lead to improved care coordination, more efficient healthcare delivery, and better outcomes for patients.

4. Personalized medicine: These technologies have the potential to support the development of personalized medicine, where treatments are tailored to individual patients based on their unique characteristics and needs. This could lead to more effective treatments and improved patient outcomes.
5. Increased patient empowerment: By giving patients more control over their health data, these technologies may increase patient engagement and empowerment. Patients may be able to use their data to make more informed healthcare decisions and better manage their health.

5.5 FUTURE DIRECTIONS

Let us finally talk about how crucial it is to keep this field developing, especially in terms of interoperability, security, and privacy. Additionally, it is important to investigate the potential applications of these technologies in brand-new fields of healthcare, such as telemedicine, genomics, and personalized medicine. For patient-centric blockchains, multilayer P2P networks, and digital platforms in healthcare to fully realize their promise, healthcare practitioners, researchers, and technology developers must collaborate, which this chapter's conclusion emphasizes. It also emphasizes how critical it is to keep innovating and using these technologies to enhance patient outcomes across the globe.

5.5.1 ADVANCES IN BLOCKCHAIN TECHNOLOGY

Blockchain technology advancements have created new opportunities for patient-centered healthcare systems. The rise of permissioned blockchains, which enable the system to incorporate access control and data protection features, is one of the most important developments. Healthcare providers will find it simpler to adhere to legal standards and safeguard patient data as a result. The creation of smart contracts, which are self-executing contracts with the terms of the agreement expressed in code, is another significant breakthrough. Automation and trustless transactions made possible by smart contracts allow both the management of clinical trials and the processing of insurance claims to be streamlined. Additionally, advances in blockchain scalability have made it feasible to more effectively handle massive amounts of data. This problem is being addressed, and layer 2 solutions like sidechains and state channels are being created to enhance the functionality of blockchain systems.

5.5.2 GROWTH OF INTEROPERABILITY

The seamless interchange and use of data by various healthcare systems, appliances, and applications is referred to as the evolution of interoperability. The development of standards and protocols that enable interoperability and the use of technologies that support data transmission, such as application programming interfaces (APIs) and HIE platforms, have received increased attention in recent years.

Healthcare interoperability is essential because it allows healthcare professionals to access patient data from many sources, coordinate patient care among various providers, and ultimately give patients better, more effective care. It also permits the development of new technologies and services that can use health data to enhance health outcomes and gives people more control over their own health data. The adoption of EHRs and other digital health technologies, as well as regulatory mandates like the 21st Century Cures Act in the United States (US), which requires healthcare providers to make patient data available through APIs, has all contributed to the growth of interoperability.

5.5.3 Artificial Intelligence and Machine Learning

The fields of AI and ML in healthcare are expanding quickly and have the potential to revolutionize patient care and research. The term "AI" refers to the creation of computer systems that are capable of carrying out activities that ordinarily call for human intelligence, such as picture recognition or natural language processing. A branch of AI called ML uses algorithms that can learn from data and get better over time. AI and ML may be used to analyze vast volumes of healthcare data and find patterns and insights that help guide clinical decision-making and enhance patient outcomes in the context of patient-centric blockchains and multilayer P2P networks.

For instance, using ML algorithms to forecast patient outcomes based on their medical background and demographic data can assist healthcare professionals in tailoring treatment strategies for their patients. Additionally, patient data stored on blockchains, and P2P networks can benefit from increased security and privacy due to AI and ML. For instance, by examining network traffic for unusual activity, AI algorithms can be used to identify and stop data breaches. Additionally, ML models can be trained to identify anomalies in patient data, which can help detect fraudulent activity or errors in medical records.

5.5.4 Expansion of Telehealth

Telehealth is the practice of providing medical care and information to patients remotely via the use of telecommunications technology. Patients are no longer obliged to physically visit their doctors for routine checkups, follow-ups, or other health concerns due to the development of telehealth. People who reside in distant or disadvantaged locations or who might have mobility challenges now have increased access to healthcare.

The development of communication technologies, such as video conferencing, secure texting, and remote monitoring equipment, has aided the growth of telehealth. Regardless of their location, these tools allow healthcare professionals to interact with patients and give care in real time. Additionally, telehealth has shown promise in enhancing patient outcomes, decreasing hospital readmissions, and bringing down healthcare costs. The COVID-19 epidemic has also sped up the implementation of telehealth services because it offered a secure and practical approach to delivering care while maintaining social segregation practices. Telehealth has been essential in giving patients care while halting the spread of the virus.

5.5.5 REGULATORY CHALLENGES

The use of patient-centric blockchains, multilayer P2P networks, and digital platforms in healthcare is subject to a variety of regulatory difficulties, as is the case with any nascent technology. These issues include worries about data security and privacy, the necessity for interoperability between various platforms and systems, and the requirement for unambiguous standards and guidelines to guarantee the safe and efficient use of these technologies.

Ensuring compliance with current healthcare standards, such as the Health Insurance Portability and Accountability Act in the US, is a significant regulatory burden. Any new technology employed in the healthcare sector must abide by these standards in order to be regarded as secure and compliant and to ensure the privacy and security of patients' personal health information [31].

Ensuring interoperability between various systems and platforms is another difficulty. Patients may use a variety of healthcare providers and services, therefore it's critical that these systems can connect to one another seamlessly and securely. In addition to the integration of various technologies and platforms, this calls for the creation of precise standards and protocols for data sharing.

5.6 CONCLUSION

A patient-focused blockchain system has been developed by a local healthcare provider, remote Healthcare, and is linked to a multilayer P2P network and digital platform. The system gives people access to, and control over, their own health information while also making it available to healthcare professionals and other key stakeholders. Healthcare now has a secure, effective, and patient-centric healthcare data management system due to the adoption of a blockchain system that is centered on the patient and is connected to a multilayer P2P network and digital platform. Technology has increased productivity, security, and patient engagement while also improving data management. Other healthcare organizations seeking to deploy comparable solutions can learn from the success of implementation.

REFERENCES

1. Cao, T., Yu, Decouchant, Luo, X., Verissimo, P. Exploring the monero peer-to-peer network. *In Financial Cryptography and Data Security: 24th International Conference*, Malaysia, 578–594, 2020.
2. Chen, H. S., Jarrell, J., Carpenter, K.,, Cohen, D. S., & Huang, X. Blockchain in healthcare: A patient-centered model. *Biomedical Journal of Scientific & Technical Research*, 20, 15017, 1–12, 2019.
3. Moro-Visconti R., Connecting patient-centric blockchains with multilayer P2P networks and digital platforms. In Malaya B, Roberto V, Ganesh C. *Blockchain in Digital Healthcare*, Chapman and Hall/CRC, 93–112, 2021.
4. Poongodi, C., Lalitha, K., Dhanaraj, R. K. The role of blockchains for medical electronics security. In Kavita S, Pethuru C, Deepak S. *Essential Enterprise Blockchain Concepts and Applications*, 231–262, 2021.

5. Ghosh, P. K., Chakraborty, A., Hasan, M., Siddique, A. H. Blockchain application in healthcare systems: A review. *Systems*, 11, 38, 2023.
6. Bhaskar, K. B, Prasanth, A., Saranya, P, An energy-efficient blockchain approach for secure communication in IoT-enabled electric vehicles. *International Journal of Communication Systems*, 35, 1–30, 2022.
7. Garon, J. M., Legal implications of a ubiquitous metaverse and a Web3 future. *Marquette Law Review.*, 106, 163, 2022.
8. Takeuchi, H., Contribution of particle design research to the development of patient-centric dosage forms. *KONA Powder and Particle Journal*, 39, 150–175, 2022.
9. Maxwell, E., Open standards, open source, and open innovation: Harnessing the benefits of openness. *Innovations: Technology, Governance, Globalization,* 1, 119–176, 2006.
10. Schollmeier, R., A definition of peer-to-peer networking for the classification of peer-to-peer architectures and applications. In *Proceedings of the First International Conference on Peer-to-Peer Computing*, 2001, 101–102.
11. Al Amin, K., Suryanto, Y. Blockchain web application design for legal companies in Indonesia, *EasyChair,* No. 9047, 2022.
12. Singh, A. P., Pradhan, N. R., Luhach, A. K., Agnihotri. A novel patient-centric architectural framework for blockchain-enabled healthcare applications. *IEEE Transactions on Industrial Informatics*, 17, 5779–5789, 2020.
13. Kordestani, H., Barkaoui, K., Zahran, W. HapiChain: A blockchain-based framework for patient-centric telemedicine. *IEEE 8th International Conference on Serious Games and Applications for Health (SeGAH)*, 2020, 1–6.
14. Liu, Y., Obaidat, M. S., Kumar, N., Khan, M., Choo, K. K. R. Blockchain-based identity management systems: A review. *Journal of Network and Computer Applications*, 166, 102731, 2020.
15. Abadin, Z. U., Syed, M. H. A pattern for proof of work consensus algorithm in blockchain. In *EuroPLoP,* 2021, 1–20.
16. Shneidman, J., Parkes, D. C. Rationality and self-interest in peer to peer networks. In *IPTPS*, 2735, 139–148, 2003.
17. Ismail, L., Materwala, H., Khan, M. A. Performance evaluation of a patient-centric blockchain-based healthcare records management framework. In *Proceedings of the 2nd International Electronics Communication Conference,* 2020, 39–50.
18. Tene, O., What Google knows: Privacy and internet search engines. *Utah L. Rev.,* 1433, 1–72, 2008.
19. Liso, N. D. ICTs and the digital division of labour. In *Dynamic Capabilities between Firm Organisation and Local Systems of Production.* Vandana S, Balamurugan B, Joshua T and Godlin A. Routledge, 364–392, 2007.
20. Pushpalatha, N., Sudha M., Sivaranjani, S. 5 Enterprise data. *Data Fabric Architectures: Web-Driven Applications,* 2023, 1–23.
21. Seligman J., The rise and fall of cryptocurrency: The three paths forward. *Washington University in St. Louis Legal Studies Research Paper,* 22–06, 2022.
22. Thang, P., Trang, T., Tai, B. Multimedia privacy, security, and protection within the bockchain: A review. *2022 5th International Conference on Contemporary Computing and Informatics (IC3I)*, 31171–31176, 2022.
23. Papautsky, E. L., Patterson, E. S. Patients are knowledge workers in the clinical information space. *Applied Clinical Informatics*, 12, 133–140, 2021.
24. Dubovits,kaya, A., Baig, F., Xu, Z., Shukla, R., Zambani, P. ACTION-EHR: Patient-centric blockchain-based electronic health record data management for cancer care. *Journal of Medical Internet Research*, 1–17, 22, 2020.

25. Chandrasekar, V., Wisetsri, W., Ullah, I. URR blockchain and distributed ledger technology (DLT): The future of accounting. *Psychology and Education Journal*, 58, 320–323, 2021.

26. Bailey, K. L., Sayles, H., Campbell, J., Khalid, N., Anglim, M. COVID-19 patients with documented alcohol use disorder or alcohol-related complications are more likely to be hospitalized and have higher all-cause mortality. *Alcoholism: Clinical and Experimental Research*, 46, 1023–1035, 2022.

27. Pourebrahimi, B., Bertels, K., Vassiliadis, S. A survey of peer-to-peer networks. In *Proceedings of the 16th Annual Workshop on Circuits, Systems and Signal Processing*, 2005, 570–577.

28. Jabarulla, M. Y., Lee, H. N. A blockchain and artificial intelligence-based, patient-centric healthcare system for combating the COVID-19 pandemic: Opportunities and applications. *Healthcare*, 9, 1–21, 1019, 2021.

29. Antonopoulos, N., Exarchakos, G., Li, M., Liotta, A. A survey of peer-to-peer architectures for service-oriented computing. In *Handbook of Research on P2P and Grid Systems for Service-Oriented Computing: Models, Methodologies and Applications*, IGI Global, 2010, 1–19.

30. Manjunath, Y. S. K., Kashef, R. F. Distributed clustering using multi-tier hierarchical overlay super-peer peer-to-peer network architecture for efficient customer segmentation. *Electronic Commerce Research and Applications*, 47, 101040, 2021.

31. Naresh, V. S., Reddi, S., Allavarpu, V. D. Blockchain-based patient-centric health care communication system. *International Journal of Communication Systems*, 34, 1–16, 2021.

6 Convergence of IoMT and Blockchain for Emerging Personalized Healthcare System
Challenges and Use Cases

Nguyen Tien Dung,[1] Pham Chien Thang,[2]*
Ta Thi Nguyet Trang,[3] and A. Prasanth[4]
[1]Thai Nguyen University of Medicine and Pharmacy,
Thai Nguyen, Vietnam
[2]TNU-University of Sciences, Thai Nguyen, Vietnam
[3]International School, Thai Nguyen University,
Thai Nguyen, Vietnam
[4]Department of Computer Science and Engineering,
Vel Tech Rangarajan Dr. Sagunthala R&D Institute of
Science and Technology, Chennai, India
*Corresponding Author: Pham Chien Thang
(Email: thangpc@tnus.edu.vn)

6.1 INTRODUCTION

The Internet of Medical Things (IoMT) and blockchain technology can transform the healthcare industry by providing a more efficient, cost-effective, and secure personalized healthcare system. By employing connected devices and blockchain, healthcare companies may collect and analyze data from many sources to offer more tailored and effective treatment regimens. However, there are several challenges with a personalized healthcare system based on merging IoMT and blockchain technology [1–3]. The application of blockchain and IoMT in healthcare is examined in this chapter. It also discusses some challenges individuals and healthcare organizations may encounter when utilizing this cutting-edge technology.

IoMT refers to integrating connected devices and sensors in the healthcare industry. These devices are used to gather and transmit data, such as vital signs, medical histories, and treatment progress, to healthcare providers and other relevant parties. The IoMT includes many wearable devices, diagnostic equipment, and electronic health records systems [4–5]. The use of IoMT in healthcare has numerous benefits, including improved patient care, enhanced communication, and reduced costs.

DOI: 10.1201/9781003405450-6

Blockchain technology is a decentralized and secure digital ledger that can record transactions and other data. It comprises data-linked and secured blocks using cryptography [6]. Blockchain in healthcare has numerous benefits, including improved security, enhanced transparency, and increased efficiency [7].

The convergence of IoMT and blockchain technology has the potential to create a new personalized healthcare system that is more efficient, secure, and effective. By combining the capabilities of connected devices and the security and transparency of blockchain, healthcare providers can gather and analyze data from various sources to provide more personalized and effective treatment for patients [8]. Some potential use cases for the convergence of IoMT and blockchain in healthcare include electronic health records and clinical trials.

6.2   CHALLENGES IN THE ADOPTION OF IOMT IN HEALTHCARE

One of the main challenges in adopting IoMT in healthcare is the high cost of implementing the technology. Implementing an IoMT system can be quite expensive, especially for small healthcare organizations that do not have the financial resources to invest in the necessary hardware and software. Another challenge is the lack of standardization in the IoMT industry. Many different types of devices and sensors are available in the market, and each has its proprietary protocols and standards. This makes it difficult for healthcare organizations to choose the right devices and integrate them into their existing systems. Additionally, privacy and security concerns surround the use of IoMT in healthcare. The personal and sensitive health data collected by IoMT devices can be vulnerable to cyberattacks if proper security measures are not implemented. Several challenges can hinder the adoption of the IoMT in the healthcare industry (see Figure 6.1).

- *Security and Privacy Concerns*: IoMT devices generate and transmit large amounts of sensitive data, making them vulnerable to cyberattacks and data breaches. This can lead to concerns about the confidentiality, integrity, and availability of data, as well as the potential for unauthorized access or misuse of patient information [9].
- *Cost and Affordability*: Implementing IoMT systems can be expensive, particularly for smaller hospitals or clinics that may not have the budget to invest in new technology. The cost of purchasing, installing, and maintaining IoMT devices and systems can also be a barrier to adoption [10].
- *Integration with Existing Systems*: IoMT devices may need to be integrated with existing healthcare systems and processes, which can be complex and time-consuming. There may also be challenges in integrating devices from different manufacturers, as they may use different protocols or standards [11].
- *Lack of Standardization*: The IoMT industry is still in its early stages, and there is a lack of standardization in terms of protocols, interoperability, and data formats. This can make integrating different devices and systems difficult and limit the ability to share data across different platforms [12].

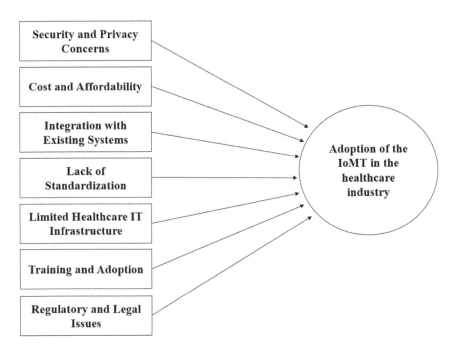

FIGURE 6.1 Challenges to the adoption of the IoMT in the healthcare industry.

- *Limited Healthcare IT Infrastructure*: Many healthcare providers may not have the information technology (IT) infrastructure to support the deployment and use of IoMT devices. This includes the need for robust wireless networks, data storage, and computing resources [13].
- *Training and Adoption*: The successful adoption of IoMT requires healthcare providers to be trained in using new technologies and devices. This can be challenging, particularly for smaller organizations with limited resources [14].
- *Regulatory and Legal Issues*: The healthcare industry is heavily regulated, and there may be legal and regulatory challenges related to using IoMT devices. These include issues around data privacy, security, and liability [15].

Adopting IoMT in the healthcare industry requires a significant investment in time, resources, and infrastructure and addressing various challenges related to security, cost, integration, standardization, and regulatory issues.

6.3 CHALLENGES IN THE ADOPTION OF BLOCKCHAIN TECHNOLOGY IN HEALTHCARE

The adoption of blockchain technology in healthcare is also facing several challenges (see Figure 6.2). One of the main challenges is the lack of understanding and awareness about technology among healthcare professionals. Many healthcare professionals are not familiar with the technical details of blockchain and how it works, which makes

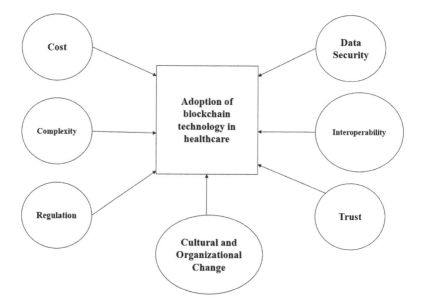

FIGURE 6.2 Challenges in the adoption of blockchain technology in healthcare.

it difficult for them to see its potential benefits. Another challenge is the lack of regulatory frameworks for using blockchain in healthcare. There are currently no clear guidelines on how blockchain should be used in the healthcare industry, which makes it difficult for healthcare organizations to adopt the technology [16–17].

Additionally, there are concerns about the scalability of blockchain technology in healthcare. Blockchain technology's decentralized nature requires many nodes to validate transactions, which can be a challenge for large healthcare organizations with a high volume of transactions. There are several challenges in the adoption of blockchain technology in healthcare [18–20]:

- *Cost*: Implementing blockchain technology requires significant financial investment, which can be a barrier for many healthcare organizations.
- *Complexity*: The technology behind blockchain is complex and requires specialized knowledge and skills to implement and maintain. This can be a challenge for healthcare organizations that may not have the necessary resources or expertise.
- *Regulation*: Healthcare is a heavily regulated industry, and blockchain technology is still evolving. This can create uncertainty and complexity for organizations looking to adopt the technology.
- *Data Security*: One of the main benefits of blockchain technology is its ability to store and transfer data securely. However, there are concerns about the potential for hacking and data breaches, which can be a barrier to adoption.
- *Interoperability*: One of the main goals of blockchain in healthcare is to improve interoperability between different systems and organizations. However, this

requires the participation of multiple stakeholders and integrating various systems, which can be challenging.

- *Trust*: Blockchain technology relies on trust and consensus among participants, which can be difficult to establish in the healthcare industry. There may be concerns about the reliability and credibility of the information stored on the blockchain.
- *Cultural and Organizational Change*: Adopting blockchain technology requires significant cultural and organizational change, which can be difficult for many healthcare organizations. This includes changes to processes and systems, as well as the need to educate and train staff on the use of the technology.

6.4 USE CASES FOR CONVERGING BLOCKCHAIN TECHNOLOGY WITH IOMT IN PERSONALIZED HEALTHCARE SYSTEMS

- *Secure and Transparent Data Exchange*

The convergence of IoMT and blockchain technologies has been acknowledged as critical enablers of personalized healthcare systems to provide a secure and reliable mechanism for storing and sending data [4]. When data is sent between healthcare professionals and patients and stored in different systems, these technologies can be utilized to improve its security. Wearables, biosensors, and medical equipment are just a few examples of the many linked devices that make up the IoMT and can potentially increase data collection accuracy while lowering the danger of data breaches. As each data set is encrypted and maintained in an immutable distributed ledger, blockchain technology can help ensure that data is securely stored, communicated, and utilized to verify the authenticity of data [21]. This could lessen the danger of unauthorized access to or manipulating data by ensuring that only authorized personnel can access it. By enabling the safe exchange of data between systems, combining IoMT and blockchain technology may help increase interoperability between healthcare providers. In conclusion, the fusion of blockchain and IoMT technologies may offer a trustworthy and safe method for data transfer and storage, enhancing the security and interoperability of systems for personalized healthcare. This makes it possible to perform clinical research, monitor the effectiveness of a treatment, and make data-driven healthcare decisions.

- *Identity and Access Management*

Blockchain technology can potentially significantly improve identification and access management in the healthcare sector. Blockchain can help with safe patient data storage and increase accuracy, transparency, accountability, and security in healthcare data management, according to a study by Pandey and Litoriya [8]. Additionally, it can save expenses, enhance data interoperability, and guard against illegal access to private information [22]. According to Attaran [1], blockchain technology can provide a secure and decentralized way to manage identities and medical records, preventing unauthorized access to sensitive health information and ensuring that only authorized people have access to medical records. This is true despite the complexity of integrating blockchain solutions with current IT infrastructure and processes.

- *Supply Chain Management*

By guaranteeing the quality, safety, and integrity of medical items, IoMT, and blockchain technology can potentially transform supply chain management in the medical industry. Blockchain can track the location and quality of medical supplies, streamline payment processing, and provide a secure and tamper-proof record of all transactions within the supply chain [23–24]. This can lower expenses, increase the overall quality of healthcare, and dramatically improve the security of medical products. From the manufacturer to the point of care, the movement of medical products can be tracked using blockchain. This can lessen the likelihood of product fraud and help maintain the items' integrity and safety [25]. By verifying the quality and safety of medical items worldwide, blockchain in supply chain management can play a crucial role in protecting healthcare consumers and providers.

- *Clinical Trial Management*

IoMT and blockchain technology have many benefits for clinical trial management, including better data security and accuracy, quicker data processing, and higher patient privacy. Clinical trial management with blockchain technology is a challenging procedure with several prospects. Increased security, better data quality and openness, and more effective data sharing are all possible advantages of blockchain technology. By enhancing the confidentiality and privacy of the data collected, decreasing the amount of paperwork and the cost of data storage and maintenance, and enhancing the accuracy and dependability of clinical trial results, blockchain technology can considerably improve clinical trial outcomes [26–27]. More research is necessary to understand further the difficulties and possibilities of using blockchain technology in clinical trial management.

- *Payment Processing*

Blockchain technology has become more widely used in the healthcare industry. According to Roman-Belmonte et al. [28], it can aid in payment processing, lower payment processing costs, and lessen the risk of fraud and mistakes. Also, it can increase the efficiency and speed of payment processing, freeing up time and resources for healthcare organizations. Moreover, blockchain technology can offer a higher level of security for processing payments, preventing the compromise of patient data. The use of blockchain technology for payment processing in the healthcare industry has some essential factors to consider, including protecting data security and privacy, integrating current IT infrastructure, and complying with regulations. Healthcare businesses should adequately address these issues to deploy blockchain technology for payment processing [29]. Blockchain technology can significantly boost payment accuracy, decrease the time it takes insurance companies and providers to resolve claims, and promote transparency in healthcare reimbursement and insurance settlement processes [30]. Overall, blockchain technology has the potential to significantly increase the speed, accuracy, and security of insurance settlement and healthcare reimbursement, but implementation problems must be overcome.

6.5 CHALLENGES IN THE IMPLEMENTATION OF A PERSONALIZED HEALTHCARE SYSTEM BASED ON THE CONVERGENCE OF IOMT AND BLOCKCHAIN TECHNOLOGY

The convergence of IoMT and blockchain technology may enable personalized healthcare, but implementing such a system presents difficulties, including integrating the two technologies into existing healthcare systems, ensuring interoperability between different IoMT and blockchain systems, and safeguarding the security and privacy of patient data. Although personalized healthcare aims to provide each patient with a unique treatment plan, developing a system based on the convergence of IoMT and blockchain technology necessitates addressing a number of challenges [31]. These challenges include the following:

- *Data Privacy and Security*

Integrating IoMT and blockchain technology in personalized healthcare systems presents opportunities and challenges. Keeping sensitive and private patient data private and secure is one of the significant issues [32]. Although there are still concerns regarding the security of these systems, blockchain technology can offer a decentralized, distributed database that can store and safeguard data against alteration or unauthorized access. When sharing data with other parties, consent management systems and privacy-preserving technology can aid in ensuring data security and privacy. IoMT and blockchain technology have risks, including data breaches and potential data misuse, particularly regarding international data transfers [33]. Consent-based data collection and sharing models, solid legal and regulatory frameworks, and rigorous security measures and policies can all be used to reduce these dangers. De-identification methods can help safeguard privacy while enabling data use for research and other purposes. It is necessary to address any data bias to avoid unfair treatment or discrimination in patient care and treatment decisions.

- *Data Interoperability*

The healthcare sector can benefit from better data interoperability by utilizing IoMT and blockchain technologies. But the information from many sources is frequently compartmentalized, which can make it harder for healthcare professionals to give individualized care. The IoMT devices, such as wearable fitness trackers and remote monitoring tools, produce copious amounts of data that can be utilized to monitor health indicators. However, because private systems are segregated, other healthcare practitioners or systems frequently do not have easy access to this data [34]. The potential advantages these devices could offer are constrained by the lack of interoperability, making it challenging for healthcare practitioners to access and use this data in a meaningful way.

When implementing blockchain technology to increase data interoperability in the IoMT, there are a number of difficulties that must be overcome, including the problem of scalability. Several blockchain networks may not be able to handle the massive amounts of data produced by IoMT devices due to their present limitations in capacity [35]. Machine learning algorithms and artificial intelligence (AI) can help standardize and analyze data from many sources to get around this problem.

- *Regulatory Issues*

IoMT and blockchain technology in healthcare can offer safe and effective patient data storage and access. Yet, some regulatory difficulties must be resolved to guarantee patient security and privacy. Data privacy and security are two primary challenges that require stringent regulations for gathering, storing, and accessing data and using secure protocols and encryption techniques [36]. Another problem is interoperability, which can be resolved by defining protocols for data transmission between various electronic health record systems and standardizing platforms. The usage of IoMT devices and the data they gather are also subject to regulatory concerns, such as those relating to data governance for maintaining and observing data quality and integrity, as well as defined rules for data use, access, and protection [37]. The usage of blockchain technology in healthcare also creates new issues with data governance and regulation, which might be resolved by creating regulatory frameworks with industry-specific specifications for rules and requirements.

- *Cost and Resource Constraints*

IoMT and blockchain technology can enhance healthcare systems' efficiency, accuracy, and security, but it comes with high costs and resource constraints [38]. These costs cover employing qualified staff, adhering to changing legislation, and integrating these technologies with current healthcare systems, in addition to the initial investment in equipment and infrastructure. Healthcare institutions can collaborate with tech firms, leverage open-source tools, and access cloud-based services to reduce these expenses. Notwithstanding these difficulties, the advantages of new technologies should be taken into account because they may improve patient outcomes while lowering costs for both patients and healthcare professionals. Healthcare organizations will likely find it easier to implement these technologies as they become less expensive and less resource-restrictive as they advance.

- *Ethical and Social Concerns*

Blockchain and IoMT technologies can completely transform the healthcare industry but raise several moral and societal issues. Since the IoMT entails gathering and exchanging sensitive personal data, privacy is a top ethical concern. Many different parties have access to this data, which raises significant privacy concerns if it is utilized without the subject's knowledge or consent [39]. As a result, the IoMT requires that individuals and organizations have access to and control over their data.

Other challenges include the possibility of technology abuse or misuse and social concerns. For instance, wearable technology can be used to track employee productivity and health, raising questions about the right of businesses to track their workers. These devices must only be used for appropriate medical purposes and not to track or monitor people in other situations. The IoMT needs to be guided by defined ethical norms and guidelines [39–40]. All stakeholders, particularly marginalized groups, must have their needs and concerns considered during the creation and implementation of the IoMT. Finally, the IoMT must be integrated into current healthcare systems to encourage social support and interaction to overcome the risk that it will lead to the development of new types of social isolation.

6.6   CONCLUSION

In conclusion, the convergence of the IoMT and blockchain technology has the potential to revolutionize personalized healthcare systems. Several challenges need to be addressed before this can be fully realized. These challenges include data privacy and security, interoperability, and regulatory compliance. Despite these challenges, there are already several use cases where the IoMT and blockchain have been successfully implemented in the healthcare industry. These include electronic health records, supply chain management, and clinical trial management. Overall, the combination of the IoMT and blockchain has the potential to revolutionize personalized healthcare and improve patient outcomes. However, further research and development are needed to address the challenges and fully realize this potential.

REFERENCES

1. Attaran, M., Blockchain technology in healthcare: Challenges and opportunities. *International Journal of Healthcare Management*, 15(1), 70–83, 2022.
2. Gürkaynak, G., Yılm\az, I., Yeşilaltay, B., Bengi, B., Intellectual property law and practice in the blockchain realm. *Computer Law & Security Review*, 34(4), 847–862, 2018.
3. Joyia, G. J., Liaqat, R. M., Farooq, A., Rehman, S., Internet of medical things (IoMT): Applications, benefits and future challenges in healthcare domain. *Journal of Communication.*, 12(4), 240–247, 2017.
4. Jan, M. A., Cai, J., Gao, X. C., Khan, F., Mastorakis, S., Usman, M., Alazab, M., Watters, P., Security and blockchain convergence with internet of multimedia things: Current trends, research challenges and future directions. *Journal of Network and Computer Applications*, 175, 102918, 2021.
5. Avinashiappan, A., Mayilsamy, B., Internet of medical things: Security threats, security challenges, and potential solutions. *Internet of Medical Things: Remote Healthcare Systems and Applications*, 1–16, 2021.
6. Thang, P., Trang, T., Tai, B., Multimedia privacy, security, and protection within the blockchain: A review. *2022 5th International Conference on Contemporary Computing and Informatics (IC3I)*, 31171–31176, 2022.

7. Wang, H., Chen, K., Xu, D., A maturity model for blockchain adoption. *Financial Innovation*, 2, 1–5, 2016.

8. Pandey, P., Litoriya, R., Implementing healthcare services on a large scale: Challenges and remedies based on blockchain technology. *Health Policy and Technology*, 9(1), 69–78, 2020.

9. Fazeldehkordi, E., Owe, O., Noll, J., Security and privacy in IoT systems: A case study of healthcare products. In *2019 13th International Symposium on Medical Information and Communication Technology (ISMICT)*, 1–8, IEEE, 2019.

10. Desingh, V., Internet of Things adoption barriers in the Indian healthcare supply chain: An ISM-fuzzy MICMAC approach. *The International Journal of Health Planning and Management*, 37(1), 318–351, 2022.

11. Jain, S., Nehra, M., Kumar, R., Dilbaghi, N., Hu, T., Kumar, S., Kaushik, A., Li, C. Z., Internet of medical things (IoMT)-integrated biosensors for point-of-care testing of infectious diseases. *Biosensors and Bioelectronics*, 179, 113074, 2021.

12. Malamas, V., Chantzis, F., Dasaklis, T. K., Stergiopoulos, G., Kotzanikolaou, P., Douligeris, C., Risk assessment methodologies for the internet of medical things: A survey and comparative appraisal. *IEEE Access*, 9, 40049–40075, 2021.

13. Yaacoub, J. P. A., Noura, M., Noura, H. N., Salman, O., Yaacoub, E., Couturier, R., Chehab, A., Securing internet of medical things systems: Limitations, issues and recommendations, *Future Generation Computer Systems*, 105, 581–606, 2020.

14. Elias, A. A., Nanda, S., Adoption of internet of medical things: A Systems Thinking Approach. *Journal of Global Information Technology Management*, 26(1), 9–24, 2023.

15. Alsubaei, F., Abuhussein, A., Shandilya, V., Shiva, S., IoMT-SAF: Internet of medical things security assessment framework. *Internet of Things*, 8, 100123, 2019.

16. Massaro, M., Digital transformation in the healthcare sector through blockchain technology. Insights from academic research and business developments. *Technovation*, 102386, 2021.

17. Patel, V., A framework for secure and decentralized sharing of medical imaging data via blockchain consensus. *Health Informatics Journal*, 25(4), 1398–1411, 2019.

18. Mackey, T., Bekki, H., Matsuzaki, T., Mizushima, H., Examining the potential of blockchain technology to meet the needs of 21st-century Japanese health care: Viewpoint on use cases and policy. *Journal of Medical Internet Research*, 22(1), e13649, 2020.

19. Dimitrov, D. V., Blockchain applications for healthcare data management. *Healthcare Informatics Research*, 25(1), 51–56, 2019.

20. Tang, P. C., Ash, J. S., Bates, D. W., Overhage, J. M., & Sands, D. Z., Personal health records: Definitions, benefits, and strategies for overcoming barriers to adoption. *Journal of the American Medical Informatics Association*, 13(2), 121–126, 2006.

21. Awasthi, M. V., Karande, N., Bhattacharjee, S., Convergence of blockchain, IoMT, AI for healthcare platform framework. *International Journal of Engineering Research & Management. (IJERM)*, 9, 1–7, 2022.

22. Mikula, T., Jacobsen, R. H., Identity and access management with blockchain in electronic healthcare records. In *2018 21st Euromicro Conference on Digital System Design (DSD)*, 699–706, IEEE, 2018.

23. Clauson, K. A., Breeden, E. A., Davidson, C., Mackey, T. K., Leveraging blockchain technology to enhance supply chain management in healthcare: An exploration of challenges and opportunities in the health supply chain. *Blockchain in Healthcare Today*, 1(1–11), 2018.

24 Pisa, M., Reassessing expectations for blockchain and development. *Innovations: Technology, Governance, Globalization*, 12(1–2), 80–88, 2018.

25. Baruffaldi, G., Sternberg, H., Chains in chains-logic and challenges of blockchains in supply chains. In *Proceedings of the 51st Hawaii International Conference on System Sciences*, 3936–3943, 2018.
26. Maslove, D. M., Klein, J., Brohman, K., Martin, P., Using blockchain technology to manage clinical trials data: A proof-of-concept study. *JMIR Medical Informatics*, 6(4), e11949, 2018.
27. Omar, I. A., Jayaraman, R., Salah, K., Yaqoob, I., Ellahham, S., Applications of blockchain technology in clinical trials: Review and open challenges, *Arabian Journal for Science and Engineering*, 46, 3001–3015, 2021.
28. Roman-Belmonte, J. M., De la Corte-Rodriguez, H., Rodriguez-Merchan, E. C., How blockchain technology can change medicine. *Postgraduate Medicine*, 130(4), 420–427, 2018.
29. Akram, S. V., Malik, P. K., Singh, R., Anita, G., Tanwar, S., Adoption of blockchain technology in various realms: Opportunities and challenges, *Security and Privacy*, 3(5), e109, 2020.
30. Ahmad, R. W., Salah, K., Jayaraman, R., Yaqoob, I., Ellahham, S., Omar, M., The role of blockchain technology in telehealth and telemedicine. *International Journal of Medical Informatics*, 148, 104399, 2021.
31. Prasanth, A., Lakshmi, D., Rajesh, D., *Cognitive Computing for Internet of Medical Things*. CRC Press, 1–272, 2022.
32. Wang, Y., Zhang, A., Zhang, P., Qu, Y., Yu, S., Security-aware and privacy-preserving personal health record sharing using consortium blockchain. *IEEE Internet of Things Journal*, 9(14), 12014–12028, 2021.
33. Rawat, R., A systematic review of blockchain technology use in e-supply chain in internet of medical things (IoMT). *International Journal of Computations, Information and Manufacturing (IJCIM)*, 2(2), 2022.
34. Tan, T. F., Li, Y., Lim, J. S., Gunasekeran, D. V., Teo, Z. L., Ng, W. Y., Ting, D. S., Metaverse and virtual health care in ophthalmology: Opportunities and challenges. *The Asia-Pacific Journal of Ophthalmology*, 11(3), 237–246, 2022.
35. Pushpalatha, N, Sudha M, Sivaranjani, S, 5 Enterprise data. *Data Fabric Architectures: Web-Driven Applications,* 2023, 1–23.
36. Olaronke, I., Oluwaseun, O., Big data in healthcare: Prospects, challenges and resolutions. In *2016 Future Technologies Conference (FTC)*, 1152–1157, IEEE, 2016.
37. De Prieëlle, F., De Reuver, M., & Rezaei, J., The role of ecosystem data governance in adoption of data platforms by Internet-of-Things data providers: Case of Dutch horticulture industry, *IEEE Transactions on Engineering Management*, 69(4), 940–950, 2020.
38. Soltanisehat, L., Alizadeh, R., Hao, H., & Choo, K. K. R., Technical, temporal, and spatial research challenges and opportunities in blockchain-based healthcare: A systematic literature review. *IEEE Transactions on Engineering Management,* 2020.
39. Rothstein, M. A., Ethical issues in big data health research. *Journal of Law, Medicine & Ethics*, 43(2), 425–429, 2015.
40. Mbunge, E., Fashoto, S. G., Akinnuwesi, B., Metfula, A., Simelane, S., Ndumiso, N., Ethics for integrating emerging technologies to contain COVID-19 in Zimbabwe. *Human Behavior and Emerging Technologies*, 3(5), 876–890, 2021.

7 Role of Access Control Mechanism for Blockchain-Enabled IoMT in Personalized Healthcare

Shreya Kakkar,¹ Lakshmi D,¹* and Ranju Yadav²
¹School of Computing Science and Engineering, VIT Bhopal University, Madhya Pradesh, India
²School of Applied Science and Language, VIT Bhopal University, Madhya Pradesh, India
*Corresponding Author: Lakshmi D (Email: lakshmi. lifefordivine@gmail.com)

7.1 INTRODUCTION

Access control mechanisms preserve the confidentiality, safety, and accuracy of medical information in personalized healthcare powered by blockchain-enabled Internet of Medical Things (IoMT). The emergence of IoMT has made it possible for healthcare providers to monitor and analyze patients' health individually. Nonetheless, this technological progress also gives rise to apprehensions regarding protecting patients' data.

The current access control mechanisms for IoT-enabled devices have several limitations in securing medical data from unauthorized access. One of the limitations is the centralized nature of the access control systems (ACS), which renders them susceptible to a single point of failure. In addition, the current access control mechanisms rely on usernames and passwords, which can be easily compromised by hackers. Moreover, there is a lack of accountability and transparency in the current access control mechanisms, making it challenging to identify the source of any unauthorized access to medical data [1].

With blockchain technology, only registered users can access patients' data, ensuring that medical information remains confidential and secure. This enables healthcare providers to deliver personalized care while prioritizing the privacy and security of patients' data. Incorporating blockchain technology in the security systems of IoMT-enabled devices can improve the reliability and openness of access control mechanisms, guaranteeing that any unauthorized attempt to access medical information can be promptly detected and dealt with.

DOI: 10.1201/9781003405450-7

Mainly, access control mechanisms for blockchain-enabled IoMT in personalized healthcare serve the purpose of establishing a secure and transparent platform for managing medical data. However, if you are new to this domain, worry not! We will discuss each of these in detail starting from IoMT, personalized healthcare, present ACS, the limitations of the current access control mechanisms for IoT-enabled devices, and how blockchain technology can overcome these limitations.

We will also delve into the role of blockchain technology in ensuring privacy and security in the era of IoMT-enabled personalized healthcare and provide a detailed analysis of the benefits of integrating blockchain technology into novel security systems for IoMT-enabled devices and the potential for further research and development in this area [2].

7.1.1 What Is IoMT?

The IoMT comprises devices like sensors and other connected technologies that are specifically engineered to gather, archive, and distribute healthcare data via the Internet. IoMT is a component of the broader concept of the Internet of Things (IoT) which denotes the interconnectivity of appliances, devices, and sensors with software via the Internet, helping them to communicate [3].

The spectrum of devices encompassed by IoMT is vast, including wearable sensors that monitor health signals like heart rate and blood pressure, intelligent inhalers that improve medication compliance in patients with respiratory ailments, and remote monitoring systems that enable healthcare providers to monitor patient health data beyond the confines of a hospital setting. Typically, IoMT devices use wireless communication technologies like Bluetooth or Wi-Fi to connect to other devices and send data to a central database or healthcare provider. This data can be analyzed to monitor patient health, track treatment outcomes, and inform clinical decision-making.

Incorporating IoMT in healthcare can transform the industry by delivering precise and timely data to healthcare providers, facilitating customized care, and enhancing patient outcomes [4]. However, it also raises concerns about data privacy and security, which must be addressed through robust access control mechanisms and other security measures.

7.2 PERSONALIZED HEALTHCARE

Personalized healthcare is an approach to medical treatment that tailors care to each individual's unique needs, preferences, and characteristics. Rather than using a one-size-fits-all approach, personalized healthcare takes into account a patient's genetics, lifestyle, medical history, and other factors to develop a treatment plan that is customized for them.

For example, in cancer treatment, personalized healthcare involves the DNA of a patient's tumor being examined to detect particular genetic mutations that could be the cause of cancer. This data is subsequently utilized to design tailored treatments that combat cancer cells while minimizing the adverse effects of therapy [5].

In cardiology, personalized healthcare uses wearable technology to monitor the patient's heart rate, blood pressure, and other critical signs. This data can help recognize possible cardiovascular issues in the early stages and create an individualized treatment strategy that incorporates lifestyle adjustments, medications, and other interventions.

It can also help to reduce healthcare costs by improving the efficiency of medical care. By tailoring treatment plans to the specific needs of each patient, unnecessary medical tests and procedures can be avoided, reducing healthcare spending and improving patient outcomes. It indicates a departure from the conventional approach of providing uniform medical care to a more patient-centric approach that acknowledges the distinct requirements and inclinations of every individual. With the rise of digital technologies such as IoMT, personalized healthcare is becoming increasingly accessible and effective [6].

7.2.1 KEY COMPONENTS OF PERSONALIZED HEALTHCARE

Personalized healthcare [7] is an emerging field that uses a combination of various emerging technologies such as IoMT, artificial intelligence, big data, and blockchain. However, it mainly revolves around some major components which make the whole process efficient. They include

Personalized diagnosis: Using data and technology to understand the underlying causes of a patient's condition and develop targeted and personalized treatment plans.

Personalized treatment: Using data and technology to understand each patient's unique biology and preferences, and to develop treatment plans that are most likely effective for that patient.

Personalized monitoring: Using data and technology to monitor a patient's health over time, and to adjust treatment plans as needed.

Personalized engagement: Using data and technology to engage patients in their healthcare, and to empower them to actively participate in their health and well-being.

7.3   ROLE OF IOMT IN PERSONALIZED HEALTHCARE

The role of IoMT in personalized healthcare is becoming progressively more significant by enabling the collection and analysis of patient data in real time. IoMT devices can collect data on a patient's vital signs, physical activity, medication adherence, and other health-related information, which can be used to personalize their treatment plan.

It has revolutionized personalized healthcare to a great extent by providing more accurate and timely data, enabling personalized treatment plans, improving patient engagement, and ultimately leading to better health outcomes. However, it is important to address concerns about data privacy and security through robust access control mechanisms and other security measures [8].

As an illustration, an individual with a long-term ailment like diabetes can utilize an IoMT-based glucose monitoring device that persistently assesses their blood sugar levels and instantaneously sends the data to their healthcare provider. Subsequently, the provider can use this data to modify the patient's treatment regimen as necessary, possibly mitigating the likelihood of complications and enhancing their general health results. In addition to improving the accuracy of treatment plans, IoMT can also help to increase patient engagement and adherence to treatment. Patients can use IoMT-enabled devices to track their progress toward health goals, receive reminders about medication schedules, and communicate with their healthcare provider more easily.

7.3.1   IoMT-Based Healthcare Monitoring Systems

Have you ever wondered how health monitoring systems work? Well, IoMT-based health monitoring systems usually consist of three domains: perception, network, and cloud. Let's break it down!

The perception domain acts as the eyes and ears of the system and comprises devices that monitor a patient's health signs (such as heart rate, blood pressure, and blood sugar) and that collect information regarding the patient's surroundings (such as air pressure, humidity, and sound). It also includes actuators that provide immediate medical treatment. The primary objectives of this domain are to link tangible objects to the IoMT edge network and to obtain and manage data from these objects through IoMT sensors. Afterward, the information is conveyed to the upper domain through the gateway [9].

The network domain is responsible for transmitting the data gathered by the perception domain. This domain acts as a mediator in the system and utilizes various communication technologies, such as Wi-Fi, 4G/5G, and the Internet, to send the data to the cloud domain via integrated networks. Lastly, we have the cloud domain, located at the top of the architecture, which receives the data from the network domain and uses it to deliver personalized cloud-based services to the patient, healthcare providers, and authorized individuals, such as family members. This system has the potential to enhance patient care and establish a more interconnected healthcare ecosystem [10].

7.3.2   Advantages of Integrating IoMT with Personalized Healthcare

Integrating IoMT can offer several benefits, such as enabling the collection of data from multiple medical devices, sensors, and wearables. This data can provide valuable insights into a patient's health and help create tailored treatment plans that are more likely to be effective, thereby improving the overall healthcare system [11]. Figure 7.1 lists all the advantages of integrating IoMT with personalized healthcare.

- **Improved patient outcomes:** IoMT enables remote monitoring of patients, which can lead to early detection of potential health problems and prompt intervention.
- **Increased patient engagement:** IoMT enables patients to take an active role in their own healthcare, and to monitor their health. This can increase patient engagement, and improve patient satisfaction.

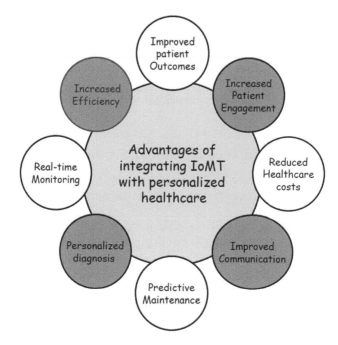

FIGURE 7.1 Advantages of integrating IoMT with personalized healthcare.

- **Reduced healthcare costs:** The integration of IoMT can lead to a decrease in healthcare expenses by facilitating the prompt detection and prevention of potential health issues, and by minimizing the requirement for hospital visits.
- **Improved communication between healthcare providers:** IoMT can help to improve communication between healthcare providers, and to streamline the sharing of patient data between different providers. By facilitating more effective and efficient healthcare delivery, the integration of IoMT can lead to an improvement in the overall quality of healthcare.
- **Predictive maintenance:** IoMT can be used to closely monitor and analyze the health of patients and predict potential problems, allowing healthcare providers to take preventative measures before an issue becomes critical.
- **Personalized diagnosis and treatment:** IoMT data can be used to understand each patient's unique biology, environment, and lifestyle. Using this information, personalized treatment plans can be created that are tailored to the patient's specific needs and are more likely to be effective.
- **Real-time monitoring:** Real-time monitoring of patients using IoMT devices can facilitate rapid response by healthcare providers to any changes in the patient's condition.
- **Increases efficiency:** Automation and integration of data can help healthcare providers to make more informed decisions and reduce errors.

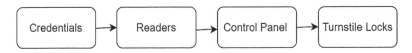

FIGURE 7.2   How do access control systems work?

7.4   ACCESS CONTROL SYSTEMS

Before diving into the world of blockchain you must understand ACS. They are security mechanisms that control access to physical or digital environments based on predefined rules and policies. These systems ensure that only authorized individuals are granted access to a building, room, or computer network, and prevent unauthorized access or breaches.

Let's understand this with some examples.

A hospital may use ACS to regulate entry to secure areas such as patient rooms, labs, and medication storage areas. The hospital's ACS may use biometric identification such as fingerprint or facial recognition scanners, keycard readers, or PIN codes to verify the identity of authorized personnel and grant them access. The system may also record access attempts and activities for auditing purposes.

In corporate offices, ACS are used to manage access to different floors or rooms within the building based on an employee's job responsibilities or clearance level. The system may use keycard readers or PIN codes to grant access, and may automatically revoke access if an employee leaves the company or is terminated. The working of these systems is shown in Figure 7.2.

Data centers can utilize these systems to ensure that access to servers and other network equipment is restricted to authorized personnel only. The system may use biometric identification or digital certificates to authenticate users and implement encryption to protect data in transit. Overall, they are essential tools for enhancing security in various settings such as government buildings, hospitals, data centers, and other high-security environments. By implementing ACS, organizations can protect sensitive information, prevent security breaches, and ensure that only authorized personnel can access resources [12].

7.4.1   Existing ACS

ACS are of various types, each offering its distinct features and advantages, which can be used to control access to physical and digital resources. We will now examine some of the most prevalent kinds of ACS in greater detail [13]. Physical Access Control Systems (PACS), Logical Access Control Systems (LACS), Role-Based Access Control (RBAC), and Attribute-Based Access Control (ABAC) are just a few examples of the many ACS that can be implemented to enhance security in various settings.

- **Physical Access Control Systems**: PACS are designed to control physical access to buildings, rooms, and other tangible spaces. These systems may use a variety of technical controls such as keycard readers, PIN codes, biometric identification, and physical barriers such as fences, gates, and turnstiles.

For example, a university campus may use PACS to control access to residence halls, academic buildings, and other areas of the campus. The system may use keycard readers or PIN codes to grant access to authorized personnel, and may also include security guards to monitor activity in high-risk areas.

- **Discretionary Access Control Systems** (DAC): DACs are systems that provide the owner of a resource with complete control over who can access it and the level of access they have. This type of access control works on the identity of the user and the source they are trying to access.

  An example of a DAC access control system is a file or folder on a computer. The owner of the file or folder has complete control over who can access it and what level of access they have. The owner can set permissions for individual users or groups of users, such as read-only access, full access, or revoked access as well.

- **Logical Access Control Systems:** LACS manage access to digital resources such as computer networks and databases. These systems may use authentication and authorization mechanisms such as usernames, passwords, digital certificates, and encryption to control access to sensitive data [14].

  For instance, a financial institution might use LACS to control access to information and other sensitive financial data in the customer's account. The system may require users to enter a username and password to gain access to the network, and may also use digital certificates as well to ensure that only registered devices are allowed to connect.

- **Role-Based Access Control** (RBAC): RBAC is an ACS that provides access to users based on their role in the organization. It is commonly implemented in larger organizations that have numerous roles and responsibilities [15].

  For example, a hospital may use RBAC to control access to patient records and other sensitive information. The system may grant access to doctors, nurses, and other healthcare professionals based on their role within the organization, and may also include different levels of access based on the sensitivity of the information.

- **Attribute-Based Access Control**: ABAC systems provide access to resources based on attributes such as user behavior, location, and time of day. This approach is often used in high-security environments where access needs to be carefully managed and controlled.

  For instance, a government agency may use ABAC to control access to classified information. The system may grant access based on a user's security clearance, location, and other attributes, and may also monitor user behavior to detect potential security threats.

7.4.2 DRAWBACKS OF THE EXISTING ACS

Although ACS has improved the security of systems to a great extent, still there exist certain problems. They are pretty complex, difficult to scale, create a frustrating user experience, may not integrate well with other systems, and can be expensive to implement and maintain. Let us discuss them in detail.

- **Insecurity:** Existing ACS may not provide adequate security, making it easy for unauthorized users to access resources. For example, if a patient's personal health information (PHI) is stored on a centralized server, it may be vulnerable to hacking or other forms of unauthorized access.
- **Lack of tamper-proof records:** Existing ACS may not provide a tamper-proof record of access attempts and data access, making it difficult to detect and prevent unauthorized access and data breaches. For example, if a hospital's access control system does not provide a tamper-proof record of access attempts, it is hard to detect and prevent unauthorized permissions to patients' data.
- **Manual access control:** ACS that rely on manual processes can be time-consuming and error-prone. For instance, if a hospital's access control system is based on paper records, it may result in delays in patient care and increase the risk of data breaches.
- **Lack of data privacy**: Existing ACS may not provide adequate privacy protection, making it easy for unauthorized parties to access patient data. For example, unauthorized access to a patient's PHI could potentially result in fraudulent activities if proper protective measures are not in place.
- **Difficulty in compliance and regulatory requirements**: Existing ACS may not provide a complete audit trail of all access attempts and data access, making it difficult to meet compliance and regulatory requirements. For example, if a hospital's ACS does not provide a complete audit trail of all access attempts and data access, it can be difficult to meet the regulatory requirements of the Health Insurance Portability and Accountability Act (HIPAA).
- **Limited transparency**: Existing ACS may lack transparency, making it difficult for healthcare providers and patients to understand and control access to their data. For example, if a hospital's ACS lacks transparency, it can be difficult for patients to understand and control access to their data.

Since these drawbacks majorly affect the security and data privacy of systems and hinder personalized healthcare to reach its full potential, it's essential to integrate it with a stronger structure like blockchain that helps to overcome these drawbacks [16].

7.5 BLOCKCHAIN TECHNOLOGY

Blockchain [17] is a digital ledger that records transactions securely and transparently. It allows multiple parties to have a copy of the same database, which is constantly updated and verified by a network of computers.

In simpler terms, think of a blockchain as a digital spreadsheet that everyone can access and edit, but no one can delete or modify any previous entries. Each entry, or "block," is linked to the previous one in a chain, hence the name "blockchain."

Figure 7.3 shows how a blockchain works [18]. The most well-known example of blockchain technology is Bitcoin, the digital currency that uses blockchain to record

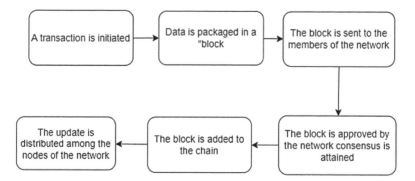

FIGURE 7.3   Flowchart: how does blockchain work?

transactions. Whenever someone buys or sells Bitcoin, the transaction is added to the blockchain, which is verified and stored permanently. However, blockchain has many other potential uses beyond cryptocurrencies. It can facilitate the creation of smart contracts that are triggered by specific conditions or allows tracking of asset ownership and transfers, such as real estate or intellectual property. Finally, blockchain technology functions as a distributed ledger and relies on three primary interconnected components to ensure secure communication. The components are (1) hash function, the purpose of which is to identify the block, (2) public–private key pair, and (3) digital signature, which is used for the authenticity of the transaction [19]. Now that we know what a blockchain is, let us understand why we should consider integrating it as a solution.

7.5.1   BLOCKCHAIN AS A CONSIDERABLE SOLUTION

Figure 7.4 shows several reasons as to why we should consider blockchain as a solution and integrate it into access control mechanisms for blockchain-enabled IoMT in personalized healthcare. Let's understand them in detail.

- **Security**: Blockchain technology is inherently secure due to its decentralized and distributed nature, which makes it difficult for hackers to tamper with the data. This makes it an ideal solution for the healthcare industry, where data security is of utmost importance.
- **Transparency:** Blockchain technology offers a permanent and transparent record of transactions that cannot be altered. This makes it easy to track the flow of data and guarantees the accuracy of the data. This is particularly important in the healthcare industry, where accurate and timely data is crucial for making informed decisions.
- **Interoperability:** Blockchain technology can facilitate interoperability between different healthcare systems by providing a common platform for data sharing and exchange – thus improving the efficiency of healthcare service delivery.

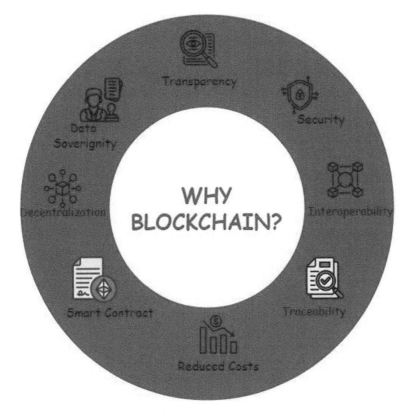

FIGURE 7.4   How blockchain is influential?

- **Data sovereignty:** Blockchain technology can ensure that patients have control over their data, which can help to protect patient privacy and enable them to share their data with healthcare providers on their terms.
- **Decentralization:** Blockchain technology can enable the decentralization of healthcare data, which can help to reduce the dependence on centralized systems and improve data accessibility.
- **Smart contract:** Blockchain technology can enable the use of smart contracts, which can automate various processes, such as the management of medical records and the tracking of medication adherence.
- **Traceability:** The use of blockchain technology can guarantee a secure and unalterable record of transactions, which can facilitate the tracking of medical products such as drugs and medical devices to ensure their traceability.
- **Cost-effective:** Blockchain technology can help to reduce costs by enabling the automation of various processes, such as the management of medical records, and by reducing the need for intermediaries [20].

7.6   BLOCKCHAIN SECURITY SYSTEMS

IoT edge networks have seen various blockchain-based security mechanism proposals, but there is a lack of specifically tailored solutions for IoMT edge networks. Therefore, there is a need to develop security mechanisms for these networks using blockchain technology. Before this, it is essential to distinguish between two types of blockchain-based security mechanisms: (a) those customized for IoMT edge networks and (b) those designed for other IoT networks that have similar capabilities and technical features, which can be adapted for use in IoMT edge networks.

7.6.1   PROPOSED ARCHITECTURES

Several blockchain architectures have been proposed ever since these issues came into existence and a lot of research has been done in this domain.

In the research [21], there is a proposal for an architecture for a smart home model that utilizes blockchain technology. The architecture proposed by the researchers encompasses a network overlay that comprises smart homes, service providers, cloud storage, and personal computers. The concepts of a local blockchain and a local miner are introduced. Although their research is based on a blockchain that uses a miner, they have eliminated the need for proof of work and coins for the blockchain to operate.

In [22], the fundamental ideas of the consensus protocols were discussed. It refers to a collection of regulations that are employed by the nodes in a blockchain network to reach an accord on the current state of the data and verify the legitimacy of a transaction. This guarantees that all participants maintain a shared record of transactions. The two widely adopted types of consensus algorithms are known as proof of work and proof of stake.

Smart contracts on the Ethereum blockchain have the potential to enhance the security and efficiency of transmitting and processing medical data, particularly concerning coronavirus disease 2019 (COVID-19). They can facilitate the continuous updating of all parties involved in the network concerning requirements, medical information, and test updates, thereby establishing trust and minimizing the risk of fraudulent transactions or certificates. This application can prove to be a useful solution for better management of confidential medical data [23].

The article "Managing Keys in an IoMT Patient Monitoring System" brings forth an architecture for managing keys in an IoMT patient monitoring system. It is composed of two layers: a platform key management layer that allows us to establish secure channels between multiple devices in the IoMT system, and a data key management layer for encrypting patient data from end to end. While the integration of IoMT into healthcare offers many benefits, it also poses challenges related to the collection, storage, and processing of sensitive medical information in compliance with regulations such as General Data Protection Regulation (GDPR) . To address these challenges, the article proposes a comprehensive key management framework that includes a solution for obtaining GDPR compliance consent integrated into the technology. This is the first time such a solution has been suggested in the technology industry. By implementing this framework, healthcare providers can ensure the secure collection, storage, and processing of patient data while meeting all regulatory requirements.

Because of inadequate secure communication protocols among the parties involved in the IoMT, a malicious actor could potentially manipulate confidential health-related information. This could involve not only intercepting messages, but also modifying, deleting, or inserting harmful messages during communication. To address this significant concern, a new protocol called BAKMP-IoMT has been developed. The use of blockchain technology in this protocol enables the secure management of keys between implantable medical devices, personal servers, and cloud servers. This reduces the risk of security breaches in the IoMT environments [24].

The authors in [25] suggest a mechanism that utilizes blockchain technology to connect the worldwide healthcare system. Their proposal includes an international framework in response to the increasing need for a global healthcare system, which has become more apparent due to the COVID-19 pandemic. The authors outline the advantages of this architecture and also address the challenges that may arise during its implementation.

7.6.2　Hyperledger Fabric

Unlike other blockchains that follow an order-execute model, Hyperledger Fabric adopts an execute-order-validate architecture. Here, the transaction process can be broken down into three distinct steps, which are illustrated in Figure 7.5.

Executing and verifying the correctness of the transaction: A predefined endorsement policy is used to send transactions to peers for endorsement in Hyperledger Fabric. The peers execute and validate the transaction, which completes the endorsement process. This step is comparable to the transaction validation phase observed in other blockchains.

Ordering the transactions using a consensus protocol: Hyperledger Fabric utilizes a pluggable consensus protocol to determine the order in which transactions are grouped into blocks, irrespective of their characteristics.

Validating **the transactions based on trust assumptions:** In the last step, the ordered results of the transactions are distributed to the peers, who then validate them in a consistent manner and in the same order they were received.

7.6.2.1　Hyperledger-Based Architectures

A permissioned blockchain specifically designed for IoT applications has adopted Hyperledger Fabric as its underlying technology. In the proposed architecture,

FIGURE 7.5　Steps for the transaction process in Hyperledger Fabric.

Hyperledger Fabric's different features, including the Certification Authority (CA) and a local peer operating as an endorser or validator, are integrated.

The suggested blockchain implementation architecture for IoT is a multi-layer network that utilizes Hyperledger Fabric. It comprises a local blockchain (LB) mechanism that connects IoT system gateways to base stations as well as a global blockchain (GB) that serves as a bridge network between them. To assess its efficiency, this architecture was implemented on both a Raspberry Pi and a virtual machine [26].

7.6.3   BLOCKCHAIN-BASED ARCHITECTURES

The suggested architecture involves combining two blockchain networks: a local network, which is a single blockchain integrated into the IoT edge network, and a global network that connects each perception domain to a blockchain. This enables the accurate transfer and maintenance of data across perception domains. The main objective is to create a flexible architecture that can be easily integrated with other blockchain systems, such as a healthcare provider blockchain network or a health information management system.

In a healthcare ecosystem that involves IoT devices and multiple perception domains, it is crucial to ensure the security and integrity of the transactions that take place between different entities. To achieve this, two types of blockchain technologies are used: LB and GB.

A. LB – single node blockchain
B. GB – multiple node blockchain

The LB is a decentralized ledger utilized to enhance the security of transactions occurring within the perception domain's IoT network. It maintains records of all transactions and is verified and validated by the nodes present in the network. This ensures high security and that the data remains immutable and tamper-proof. On the other hand, the GB is used to manage the transactions that take place between multiple perception domains and participating healthcare providers. It is deployed across various entities and provides a platform for secure and efficient transaction processing. The GB also ensures that all transactions are executed in a transparent and auditable manner.

By using both LB and GB, healthcare organizations can ensure the security and integrity of their transactions while also enabling seamless and efficient communication between different entities within the ecosystem [27].

7.6.4   USE CASES: IoMT-BASED BLOCKCHAIN ACCESS CONTROL MECHANISMS

Blockchain-based ACS has proven to enhance the security, privacy, and reliability of transmitting, sharing, and storing medical data in the IoMT. There are various ways to implement IoMT-based blockchain access control mechanisms, which may vary depending on the specific use case and requirements. The popular access control protocols are shown in Table 7.1

TABLE 7.1
IoMT-Based Blockchain Access Control Mechanisms

Types of Access Control	Description
Public-key cryptography	This approach utilizes digital certificates and public–private key pairs to verify and grant permission for accessing the system. Each user is assigned a distinct digital certificate containing their public key, while their private key is kept confidential. When a user attempts to access the system, the authenticity and integrity of their digital certificate are validated to ensure that it has not been compromised [28].
Smart contracts	They are computer programs that run by themselves on a blockchain network. They have the potential to automate access control mechanisms by setting predefined rules and conditions that must be fulfilled before access can be granted. One possible use case for smart contracts is to authenticate a user's identity before granting access to a specific medical record or device [29].
Consensus algorithms	Smart contracts validate the transactions on a blockchain network, ensuring their compliance with network rules. Furthermore, they can impose access control mechanisms by mandating the consensus of multiple nodes before granting access. This can substantially boost the security and dependability of the system, thus minimizing the chances of a single point of failure [30].
Role-based access control (RBAC)	A commonly employed mechanism for access control that allows users to specific roles that come with a predefined set of permissions. By incorporating blockchain technology, this method can be employed to verify that only authorized users can access specific data or devices [31].
Zero-knowledge proofs	A cryptographic method that allows one party to demonstrate to another party their familiarity with particular information, without divulging the information itself. This technique can be utilized for user authentication and authorization of access to the system, without disclosing sensitive data such as personal identification information or medical records [32].
Public blockchain-based access control	This mechanism employs a public blockchain network that is accessible to individuals for participation. Users are allowed to establish accounts on the blockchain network, and their access privileges can be governed by executing smart contracts on the blockchain. Ethereum and Bitcoin are two illustrations of public blockchain networks.
Private blockchain-based access control	This access control mechanism is employed within a closed network that is limited to authorized users. Private blockchain networks are often utilized by corporations to regulate access to sensitive information and resources. Hyperledger Fabric and R3 Corda are some instances of private blockchain networks.

(continued)

TABLE 7.1 (Continued)
IoMT-Based Blockchain Access Control Mechanisms

Types of Access Control	Description
Permissioned blockchain-based access control	This system bears a resemblance with a private blockchain network; however, access rights are governed through a permissioned model. Prospective participants are required to gain authorization before joining the network, and the network administrators are responsible for regulating access privileges.
Hybrid blockchain-based access control	A hybrid system employs both public and private blockchain networks to govern access control. The public blockchain network is utilized for managing user identities and access privileges, whereas the private blockchain network is employed for storing and regulating access to sensitive data and resources.
Decentralized access control	This access control system involves decentralized management of access privileges, with no central entity overseeing access control. Users can establish accounts on the blockchain network, and consensus mechanisms executed on the blockchain regulate access privileges.

7.7   CONCLUSION AND FUTURE WORK

In conclusion, integrating blockchain technology into security systems for IoMT-enabled devices has the potential to transform the healthcare sector by ensuring the confidentiality, security, and accuracy of patients' medical data. Blockchain technology could potentially overcome various limitations in the current access control mechanisms used for IoT-enabled devices. A key limitation is the centralized nature of current ACS, which renders them vulnerable to single points of failure. By using a decentralized network of nodes to verify and authorize access requests, blockchain technology eliminates the necessity for a central authority. This decentralized approach boosts the security of the access control mechanism, as there is no sole point of failure that could compromise the entire system. Another limitation of the current access control mechanisms is the reliance on usernames and passwords, which can be compromised by hackers. With blockchain technology, cryptographic keys are used instead of usernames and passwords to authenticate users, making it challenging for hackers to access the system. This strategy not only amplifies the security of the access control mechanism but also delivers accountability and transparency, since every transaction on the blockchain is documented and can be traced back to its origin. Moreover, blockchain technology ensures the integrity and privacy of medical data by using advanced encryption techniques and protecting the data. The immutable nature of the blockchain also makes it easier to detect any unauthorized changes to the data, ensuring that the data remains accurate and trustworthy.

REFERENCES

1. Almalki, J., Al Shehri, W., Mehmood, R., Enabling blockchain with IoMT devices for healthcare. *Information*, 13(10), 1–448, 2022.
2. Xu R., Blendcac: A blockchain-enabled decentralized capability-based access control for IoTs. *IEEE International Conference on Internet of Things (iThings) and IEEE Green Computing and Communications (GreenCom) and IEEE Cyber, Physical and Social Computing (CPSCom), and IEEE Smart Data (SmartData)*, 1027–1034, 2018.
3. Joyia, G. J., Liaqat, R. M., Farooq, A., Internet of medical things (IoMT): Applications, benefits and future challenges in the healthcare domain. *J. Commun.*, 12(4), 240–247, 2017.
4. Jayachitra, S., Prasanth, A., Hariprasath, S., AI enabled internet of medical things in smart healthcare. *AI Models for Blockchain-Based Intelligent Networks in IoT Systems: Concepts, Methodologies, Tools, and Applications*, 141–161, 2023. Springer.
5. Gray, M., Gray, J., Howick, J., Personalised healthcare and population healthcare. *Journal of the Royal Society of Medicine*, 111(2), 51–56, 2018.
6. Muneeswari, G., Sajithra, S., Ramakrishna, H., Self-diagnosis platform via IOT-based privacy preserving medical data. *Measurement: Sensors*, 25, 1–17, 2023.
7. Visvikis-Siest, S., Theodoridou, D., Kontoe, M. S. Milestones in personalized medicine: from the ancient time to nowadays—the provocation of COVID-19. *Frontiers in Genetics*, *11*, 569175, 2020.
8. Khezr, S., Moniruzzaman, M., Yassine A., Blockchain technology in healthcare: A comprehensive review and directions for future research. *Appl. Sci.*, 9, 1736, 2019.
9. Srivastava, J., Routray, S., Ahmad, S., Internet of medical things (IoMT)-based smart healthcare system: Trends and progress. *Computational Intelligence and Neuroscience*, 2022, 1–23, 2022.
10. Pelekoudas-Oikonomou, F., Zachos, G., Papaioannou, M., Blockchain-based security mechanisms for IoMT Edge networks in IoMT-based healthcare monitoring systems. *Sensors*, 22(7), 2449, 2022.
11. Kavitha, M., Roobini, S., Prasanth, A., Sujaritha, M., Systematic view and impact of artificial intelligence in smart healthcare systems, principles, challenges and applications. *Machine Learning and Artificial Intelligence in Healthcare Systems*, 21, 25–56, 2023.
12. Mohamed, A. K. Y. S., Auer, D., Hofer, D., Küng, J., A systematic literature review for authorization and access control: Definitions, strategies and models. *International Journal of Web Information Systems*, 18(2/3), 156–180, 2022.
13. Gusmeroli S., Piccione S., Rotondi D., A capability-based security approach to managing access control in the Internet of things. *Mathematical and Computer Modelling*, 58, 1189–1205, 2013.
14. Masoumzadeh, A., van der Laan, H., Dercksen, A., BlueSky: Physical access control: Characteristics, challenges, and research Opportunities. In *Proceedings of the 27th ACM on Symposium on Access Control Models and Technologies*, 163–172, 2022. New York.
15. Ferraiolo, D., Cugini, J., Kuhn, D. R., Role-based access control (RBAC): Features and motivations. In *Proceedings of 11th Annual Computer Security Application Conference*, 241–48, 1995.
16. Ouaddah, A., Mousannif, H., Abou Elkalam, A., Access control in the Internet of Things: Big challenges and new opportunities. *Computer Networks*, 112, 237–262, 2017.

17. Bhaskar, K. B., Prasanth, A., Saranya, P., An energy-efficient blockchain approach for secure communication in IoT-enabled electric vehicles. *International Journal of Communication Systems*, 35, 1–30, 2022.

18. Meunier, S., Blockchain 101: What is blockchain and how does this revolutionary technology work? In *Transforming Climate Finance and Green Investment with Blockchains*, 23–34, 2018.

19. Karafiloski, E., Mishev, A., Blockchain solutions for big data challenges: A literature review. In Alastair, M., *IEEE EUROCON 2017-17th International Conference on Smart Technologies*, 763–768, 2017. Elsevier.

20. Conte de Leon, D., Stalick, A. Q., Jillepalli, A, Blockchain: Properties and misconceptions. *Asia Pacific Journal of Innovation and Entrepreneurship*, *11*(3), 286–300, 2017.

21. Dorri, A., Blockchain for IoT security and privacy: The case study of a smart home. *2017 IEEE Int. Conf. Pervasive Comput. Commun. Work. PerCom Work.*, 618–623, 2017.

22. Alzahrani N., Towards true decentralization: A blockchain consensus protocol based on game theory and randomness. In *International Conference on Decision and Game Theory for Security*, 465–485, 2018.

23. Hasan, H. R., Salah, K., Jayaraman, R., Arshad, J., Yaqoob, I., Omar, M., Ellahham, S., Blockchain-based solution for COVID-19 digital medical passports and immunity certificates. *IEEE Access*, 8, 222093–222108, 2020.

24. Garg, N., Wazid, M., Das, A. K., Singh, D. P., Rodrigues, J. J., Park, Y., BAKMP-IoMT: Design of blockchain enabled authenticated key management protocol for internet of medical things deployment. *IEEE Access*, 8, 95956–95977, 2020.

25. Biswas, S., Sharif, K., Li, F., Nour, B., Wang, Y., A scalable blockchain framework for secure transactions in IoT. *IEEE Internet of Things Journal*, 6(3), 4650–4659, 2018.

26. Honar Pajooh, H., Rashid, M., Alam, F., Demidenko, S., Hyperledger fabric blockchain for securing the edge internet of things. *Sensors*, 21(2), 359, 2021.

27. Fotopoulos, F., Malamas, V., Dasaklis, T. K., Kotzanikolaou, P., Douligeris, C., A blockchain-enabled architecture for IoMT device authentication. In *2020 IEEE Eurasia Conference on IoT, Communication and Engineering (ECICE)*, 89–92, 2020.

28. Hellman, M. E., An overview of public key cryptography. *IEEE Communications Magazine*, 40(5), 42–49, 2002.

29. Kolvart, M., Poola, M., Rull, A., Smart contracts. *The Future of Law and Etechnologies*, 133–147, 2016.

30. Nguyen, G. T., Kim, K., A survey about consensus algorithms used in blockchain. *Journal of Information Processing Systems*, *14*(1), 2018.

31. Sandhu, R. S., Role-based access control. In Marvin V, *Advances in Computers*, Elsevier, 46, 237–286, 1998.

32. Fiege, U., Fiat, A., Shamir, A., Zero knowledge proofs of identity. In *Proceedings of the Nineteenth Annual ACM Symposium on Theory of Computing*, 210–217, 1987.

8 Protecting the Privacy of IoT-Based Health Records Using Blockchain Technology

P. Mathivanan,[1] D. MohanaPriya,[1] P. Manjula,[2] and Mariya Ouaissa[3]*
[1]Faculty of KIT-Kalaignarkarunanidhi Institute of Technology, Coimbatore, India [2]Department of Applied Machine Learning, Institute of Computer Science and Engineering, Saveetha School of Engineering, Saveetha Institute of Technical and Medical Sciences, Chennai, India.
[3]Moulay Ismail University, Meknes, Morocco
*Corresponding Author: P. Mathivanan
(Email: mathivanan190688@gmail.com

8.1 INTRODUCTION

The quantity of associated gadgets is expanding with each spent day and considering the persistent addition of associated gadgets, another organizational framework is being arranged and presented. Diverse construction houses have planned one more observation of the Internet. The Internet of Things (IoT) is growing quickly as well as framing itself in the recent decades. The Internet of Medical Things (IoMT) is an assortment of gadgets associated with the web that give well-being-related administrations [1]. Fundamentally, IoMT is an associated framework with well-being frameworks like clinical gadgets, programming applications, and administrations. All the more unequivocally, the association among gadgets and sensors empowers the medical services associations to make their clinical tasks and work process more effective and to observe patient well-being even from far-off areas [2].

The IoT is integrated with the wireless sensor network to sense real-time data. This integration will be used in various smart applications like smart healthcare, smart grid, etc. [3–5]. The association of therapeutically related gadgets will significantly affect patients and clinicians. In "Clinical Error Prevention" the makers analyze the different purposes behind clinical slip-ups, suggesting numerous approaches to thwarting them.

DOI: 10.1201/9781003405450-8

As suggested by the makers, by an unrivaled and more broad usage of information and communication technology (ICT) a couple of decisive or supportive bumbles could be avoided: considering the previously mentioned, unimaginable assistance with canning is given furthermore by the huge show of advances like Electronic Health Record (EHR) to lessen clinical slip-ups and increase patient prosperity [6]. Meanwhile, with the headway of new Health Records, an immense store of more inconspicuous and wearable clinical gadgets and applications, permitting the specific confirmation of various clinical cutoff points at inhabitants' homes or any spot the tenants need, has been made recently. To go through interminable blood tests, it is currently not fundamental to go to an examination office and take a model, yet they should be conceivable at drug stores or at thriving focuses dispersed all through the area. Incredibly more extraordinary assessments, like ultrasound, should be conceivable by experts at the patient's home, with new reduced contraptions.

8.2   OVERVIEW OF BLOCKCHAIN TECHNOLOGY

The blockchain is essential to the transaction being duplicated and distributed to the computer system of the entire network [7]. It is a mutual improvement for appropriate information sharing and registering. Blockchain empowers the obscure gatherings to perform various exchanges in the organization even if they don't confide in one another. It is used to track the data and store the data with a huge number of IoT devices with unified cloud storage. Computerized data was recorded with the combination of information and is cautiously designed for the blockchain.

The digital signature is used for each transaction of the ledger authorized by the owner. That information is highly secure by digital signature. The blockchain system contains some important features such as a highly secure, decentralized system, capability of automation, faster transaction compared to others, etc. [8–10]. It has three leading technologies: the first one is cryptographic keys, the second one is the shared ledger of a peer-to-peer network, and the last one is computing and transaction of stored data of the networks. In blockchain technology, the most important aspect is the identity of secured data with a digital signature. There are four types of blockchain that are utilized in various applications [11]: the first one is a private blockchain, the second one is a public blockchain network, the third one is a permission blockchain network, and the last one is a consortium blockchain. Figure 8.1 illustrates the basic working process of the blockchain network.

8.2.1   BLOCKCHAIN WORKING PROCESS

Step1: System has requested that the transaction be required with the authorized owner.

Step 2: The block containing the required transaction is created with an authorized user.

Step 3: Each block is sent to the node of the network.

Step 4: Each node should be validated and verified with the transaction.

Step5: The proof of work has received the node as a reward.

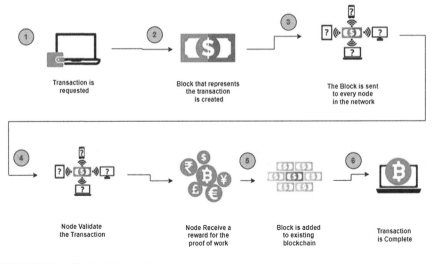

FIGURE 8.1   Block chain working process.

Step 6: That block is added to the previous block with the hash value.

Step 7: The transaction process is completed with the identity digital signature of the authorized owner.

Many creators have examined various answers for secure IoMT. One of the important answers for protected IoMT is in the encryption of sequenced data [12]. Encryption was utilized by the calculations to scramble with normal messages. The public outlet was communicated with the code text to the investor. According to the security perspective, the proposed convention can give solid security highlights just as the shortage of assets. Considering the idea of IoT proposed an answer connected with security and security assurance in current brilliant medical services frameworks. They proposed a model construction in view of a frivolous classified homomorphism estimate as well as with computation of encryption enhanced from data encryption standards [13].

A plan in view of distributed computing utilizing IoT sensors is connected with the advanced mark, timestamp system, and the topsy-turvy innovation to screen the other individual data [14]. This plan is extremely productive in offering clinical types of assistance and using fewer clinical assets. Safety measures and execution investigation portrays that the greater than notice plans are able to deal with the difficulties looked within the clinical consideration framework. One more method for getting IoMT is way in control. The control information framework that was accessed characterizes a few policies and the personality of a client which forestalls an unapproved client to get information [15].

Figure 8.2 depicts the structure of the blockchain and it contains the number of blocks connected with each other with a hash value, that hash value is generated with some cryptographic algorithm such as SHA-256, AES, DES, etc., when the third parties mediate the transaction and the member node of the consensus protocol of

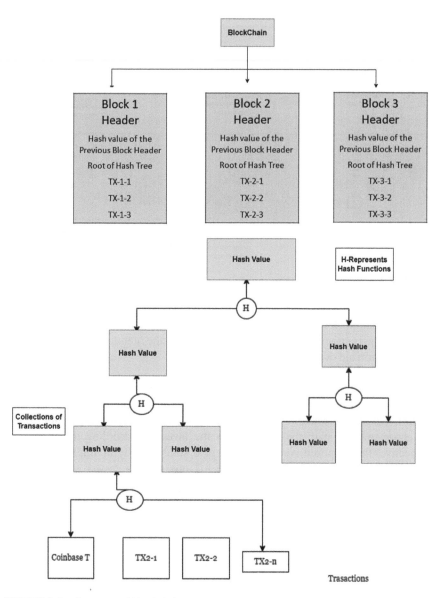

FIGURE 8.2 Structure of blockchain.

blockchain was agreed. The transaction of integrity ensured that the digital signature of ledger content is by using cryptographic hashes [16].

The creators analyze extensive cases in which new kinds of organization are generally helpful, coming to create the frameworks for the meaning of a consortium blockchain, a sort of semi-public chain pertinent in situations where numerous associations have a similar objective and will share the information, accordingly taking out the requirement for an outsider element to manage exchanges for individuals.

There must thus be a system inside the actual organization that ensures the dependability of every exchange and the information contained in that. This unwavering quality is called the agreement, that is, when every individual from the organization settles on the legitimacy of the approaching information. The manner by which the organization carries out the administration of assent, straightforwardly and in a roundabout way, decides its versatility to alter and assault as much with regard to the addition of wrong or inadvertent information. A significant part of the work in this way centers around the review and execution of calculations and conventions that are steady, insignificantly obtrusive, or more generally safe.

8.3   BACKGROUND

The IoMT is an assortment of gadgets associated with the web to give well-being-related administrations [17–20]. Essentially, IoMT is an associated framework of well-being frameworks like clinical gadgets, programming applications, and administrations as displayed in Figure 8.3. All the more unequivocally, the association among gadgets and sensors empowers the medical care associations to make their clinical tasks and work process more productive and to check patient well-being even from far-off areas.

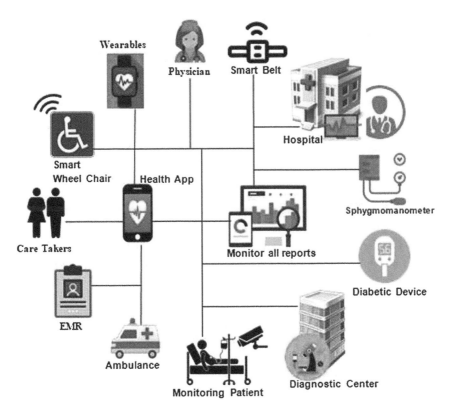

FIGURE 8.3   Internet of Medical Things.

The IoMT coordinates the advanced and actual world mutually toward accelerating course of determination along with medicines with added precision in the direction of patient's work well-being and alters patient conduct with real-time status of information. It shows the IoMT visualization, the clinical preliminary spot of the Personal digital assistant (PDA)of the patient that was imagined as an electronic clinical report (EMR), which is seen by an expert on a high-level cell. These circumstances display a direct machine-to-machine (M2M) correspondence that maintains IoMT [21].

Alongside the quick increment and different nature, tying down IoMT has turned into a colossal test because advanced security issues emerge while previous security issues develop into additional extremes. Storing the secure information was significant and moved information with practically no unapproved admittance to guarantee uprightness, legitimacy, and information protection. The secured information must be recovered by validated clients [22]. Cybercrime hurts gadgets and organizations step by step since unknown clients are speaking with one another. A lot of IoMT information is gathered, moved, and conveyed among various gatherings. The exchanges ought to be done in a protected manner [23–25].

8.3.1 CHALLENGES IN HEALTHCARE

People who went to organized trained professionals or accomplishment frameworks were viewed as solid subjects, experiencing a solitary motivation driving why they went to the informed power. Normally the degree obviously was low and they got no chance of being inquisitive regarding their pathology. A solitary master had been genuinely focusing on them all through for as long as they can recall and, expecting they were hospitalized, a particular social affair had the whole commitment of the ideal way [26].

Advanced clinical practice of the 20th century boast essentially misrepresented properties and necessities of patients. Luckily, pollution with the intention of truly inciting annihilation in an undeniable level of cases can be directed or treated possibly for a really long time or, in any case, for a long time. This refined an improvement in the interaction of the future which was joined by a solid extension in the more setup individuals with fluctuating levels of frustration and an elevated conviction and different pathologies of patients.

The fast digitization of the universe of clinical thought has actuated the formation of gigantic degrees of clinical information; however, much data progress has had the decision to stay aware of the improvement of a continually creating number of tremendous authentic help, it should now challenge an expanding interest for levels of progress for their connection. In the general vision, the standard weights to arise connect with money-related issues and plans: the unconventionality of creating expenses of a clinical foundation that can give magnificent ideas is perseveringly customary, particularly for nations with a high record of making.

The shot at an incredibly joined framework might be beaten by a more decentralized game plan, which can preventively oversee adaptability issues and which can securely allow the affiliations. Focuses on straightforwardness and clear nature ought to likewise be joined into the underpinnings of any clinical thought structure, to permit end clients more immense command over their data. It would in this way be imperative to set up the ground for an obviously massive utilization of these advances. Likewise, the urgent piece of the accomplishment reality ought to be thought of, to be unequivocal the stock chains of game plans, clinical stuff, and their relative association; it is immaterial to expect the most top tier movements assuming that it is absolutely hard to pass on the information they produce. Dealing with this information needs between accommodating endpoints, or the capacity to trade data in a cautious, significant, and brief way [27].

Interoperability, similarly especially like a vital variable in the straightforward-ness and speed of information plan between two contributed individuals, licenses suppliers to safely share a patient's fragile data paying little mind to where they are, in this way extending level headed activity times. This brand name sees basically more significance while thinking that the information is assorted in the environment because they move toward beginning a store as the source of electronic and source of non-electronic data, every so often behind the times and actually sensible with present-day structures. Notwithstanding this epic number of difficulties, blockchain can offer assured help to orchestrate information and secure the catch of clinical things gadgets.

8.4   IOMT-BASED HEALTH RECORD USING BLOCKCHAIN

The health record application provides the consumer data that was built on the inter-face to the probable server-based blockchain [28]. This kind of application can be used to secure various access levels. They provide the security key to interact with the blockchain network. So, it should be a decentralized server where no one can't be mutable and no failure is occurred. Adaptable prosperity applications in light of blockchain-based health records have the normal fill-in as an association point for customers to consume and give critical data to their clinical consideration providers [29]. Blockchain technology provides a secure protocol that IoMT devices work with to transmit data to some applications. Thus, it increases the secure data transmission among the multiple IoMT devices [30].

8.5   PROPOSED METHODOLOGY

IoMT is based on checking the framework that can be utilized in brilliant urban or home areas. Here, the patient's data is connected with embedded sensors, now the patient is ready toward the screen for accurate measurements in an individual manner. IoT is a cutting-edge innovation that guarantees quarantine for all tainted people experiencing this infection. This is gainful for a safe observing framework during isolation. Utilize the network-based association, and all high-hazard patients are effectively observed.

The framework is utilized in favor of estimating biometrics, for example, pulse, and levels of glucose. Information acquired from IoMT gadgets will assist specialists with diagnosing patients with the fitting treatment plan and accomplish the ideal results. Due to the responsiveness of the well-being record, the information should be secured very still and on transmission utilizing cryptographic natives.

The well-being record is traded through an intermediary re-encryption instrument. The encryption keys and other data needed for the validation cycle will then, at that point, be put away on the entryway server intermediary. Well-being documentation metadata resolve is there put away on a confidential blockchain to empower look for and opposition attributes. The well-being record is able to be utilized by additional well-being documentation proprietors, for example, medical care suppliers (e.g., doctors and attendants).

8.5.1 Data Management in IoMT-Based Health Records

Construction data and trades protected and managing their right coordination are basic cutoff points with regard to any data-driven association. As an issue of first significance, the key data are made by the exchanges between the patient and his PCPs/organized subject matter experts. This information contains the anamnesis, advancing anxieties, and additional data of physiology.

Different parts requiring consent to this data should demand it through the electronic record. Beginning there, the proprietor will pick whether or not to recall it. Presently the main issue of interest of the entire association should be visible, which joins an enlightening record, blockchain, and dispersed end. The commitments to the subject reach from review on a high level to really complete executions. Clearly, it is presented as an improvement for cross-locale sharing of pictures. Besides, the blockchain-based improvement to settle data, the trailblazers here presented the issues with the sharing of data in electronic clinical records. Patients are capable of getting to record reports of dissimilar crisis natural surroundings all the way through this construction, in a way getting past clinical data far from being allocated different educational arrangements and they can help centers with discovering a patient's clinical history of information.

Along with the nearly everyone uncommon executions of such an arrangement is the framework shown, which incorporates a data-sharing application considering blockchain: this execution gives a method for controlling and arranging customer data without compromising security and an astonishing strategy for working on the information on progress structures while keeping patient data stowed away. Table 8.1 enumerates the benefits and shortcomings of the several data management methods.

A conceivable utilization of blockchain progresses the same as design that fills the control of controlling affirmation on the way to clinical records and prospering information held inside it as a blueprint. The exchanges inside the squares would contain an identifier of the client no matter what an encoded relationship with this information, all high level with metadata to stimulate reasonability.

8.5.2 Protecting the IoMT

As has been expressed, IoMT frameworks assume an inexorably significant part in the improvement of clinical data frameworks. With this innovation, apparatuses, for

TABLE 8.1
Summary of Strengths and Shortcoming

Methods	Strength	Shortcoming
MedRec	The blockchain contains just information connected with shrewd agreements that empower admittance to the clinical information guaranteeing that main enlisted medical care suppliers are allowed to annex squares to the MedRec blockchain.	It provides various errors while processing the larger information. This could cause issues if there should be an occurrence of a crisis.
	The crude clinical documentation satisfied is in no way put away on the blockchain, yet somewhat reserved in suppliers' current information stockpiling framework.	The utilization of a brought-together referee of a "supplier white list" to decide the legitimacy of every potential sealer goes against the decentralized soul of blockchain innovation.
	Works with surveying, sharing, and posting of new records through an adaptable interface of user flexibility.	Security: To be sure, even with a private blockchain, it is vital to consider the mining centers, which process this fragile metadata.
	Zero in lying on convenience designed for the clinical documentation use case, concealing the intricacy of blockchain-based innovation.	Protection: experimental statistics safekeeping is entrusted toward the provider.
Blockchain and Data Lake	Undeniable degree of versatility because of the data controlled in the blockchain with the aim of addressing a list, a rundown of all the client's well-being account as well as well-being information.	Information lakes should be executed in a public innovation foundation for well-being IT in view of open norms.
	The security of clinical information is ensured on account of the concentrated and secure administration of the information lake.	Concentrated information lake structures might release practical ways for digital assaults. It is important to check the safekeeping level connected with such information holders.
	Biometric character frameworks would be used as they present improved protection.	The arrangement acquires the restrictions of information lakes: a lot of information that by and large are not valuable. Possibly high idleness.

(continued)

TABLE 8.1 (Continued)
Summary of Strengths and Shortcoming

Methods	Strength	Shortcoming
	Unlimited oversight by patients of the administration of access consents to their delicate information.	Information is not secured.
Blockchain consensus used data sharing of medical imaging	Great productivity level, there are no clinical pictures put away on the blockchain.	Consistence with guidelines and protection laws.
	The proposed arrangement fulfills a large number of the prerequisites of an interoperable well-being framework.	Complex client experience.
	The prerequisite picture sharing with the patient-controlled for a central database.	Digital protection isn't outright, as in numerous comparative arrangements.
	Client verification is initiated just when requisite.	The information from the outer source could prompt the proprietor of the imaging information
	Handle nearly everyone's normal arrangements for clinical imaging.	
Medblock	Great security level: Confidential blockchain as well as unique mark innovation. The framework knows how to oppose character camouflage, answer assault and restrict assault.	While dormancy is somewhat better compared to different methodologies, it stays a flimsy part when the quantity of clients develops.
	Validation and access control in light of public–private key pair used to connect movement lying on the organization with a particular member, i.e., patient, substance, or gadget.	
	A distributed organization that guarantees a profoundly defensive trustless base framework among patients and experts eliminating the requirement for outsider middle people.	

example, pulse screens, scan the whole body and some wearable devices can congregate, interact along with offer progressively data during the web. As innovation progresses, suppliers can perform information investigation simultaneously when they are created and share the outcomes with the individuals who approach freedom to the data.

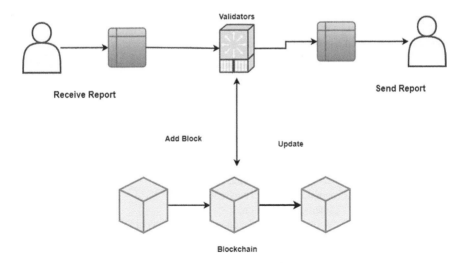

FIGURE 8.4   Wireless Body Area Network (WBAN) pipeline.

The blockchain was executed to the inside of the IoMT permitting the patient to go about as a wellspring, everything being equal, with the extra instrumentation that is regularly in steady activity and consequently creates tremendous measures of information. The produced information will then, at that point, be interceded by keen frameworks that will channel the critical data and add it to the blockchain when fundamental. The outcome is, as alluring, an upward direction incorporated framework that is secure and accessible anytime.

Figure 8.4 illustrates the pipeline process of the wireless body area network. Blockchain has a collection of secure blocks linked with a chain. The entire node has a secure hash value and that hash value is connected with the previous node of each block. Validate module is worked with the blockchain, they only provide authorization to the add and update to the blockchain. Sender A (like a doctor) sends patients' information to the validate module, which they added to the block in the blockchain. The validate module sends a secure report to the patients by using blockchain technology. Table 8.2 exposes the advantages and disadvantages of the proposed system.

8.5.3   BLOCKCHAIN: AN EFFECTIVE SOLUTION

Customary cloud is compromise protection while blockchain is secure and unavoidable sealed computerized record and nobody can adjust the records which build the exactness of records. Cloud gives concentrated information structure, but the blockchain is a decentralized information structure in which there is no focal information center and no outsider approaches. Blockchain gives the audit ability and straightforwardness of disseminated information which overwhelms the cloud as far as security and protection are concerned. Shared exchange is given by blockchain with no mediator and every hub adjusts the exchange rather than the focal center point.

TABLE 8.2
Strengths and Weaknesses of the Proposed System

Techniques	Strengths	Shortcomings
Distributed hash table (DHT)	Join blockchain and off-blockchain capacity will enhance the security of the system. Clients own and control their own information. The client might adjust the arrangement of consents and renounce admittance to recently gathered information.	Appropriate for capacity and arbitrary questions, it isn't extremely proficient for handling information (large information examination).
Blockchain, smart contracts for automated remote patient monitoring	The deliberate information is securely installed within the brilliant agreements shared with the blockchain.	Recognizability of a lot of estimated information could build inactivity and diminish execution on the off chance that request comes from constant applications.
	Security: no affiliations can be made among patients and their information. Straightforwardness: Patients can interface remote checking activities straightforwardly to their clinical records while keeping up with protection and organization. Careful copies of the blockchain on all hubs permit significant degrees of adaptation to non-critical failure.	A huge scope key administration instrument through huge statistics is a requisite. A base number of hubs is needed to guarantee the essential degree of approval signature.
Hybrid blockchain and IoT network	Completely decentralized design.	The framework doesn't think about the normalization of savvy contracts.
	Great effectiveness: close to constant.	Effectiveness if there should arise an occurrence of a public block chain network.
	Interoperability.	A base numeral of web-based hubs is needed meant for checking the square's age and innovative exchanges.
	Unchanging nature.	Weakness because of programmer assaults on the shrewd agreement.
	Adaptability with little work to other application spaces.	-
	Completely decentralized design.	The framework doesn't think about the normalization of savvy contracts.

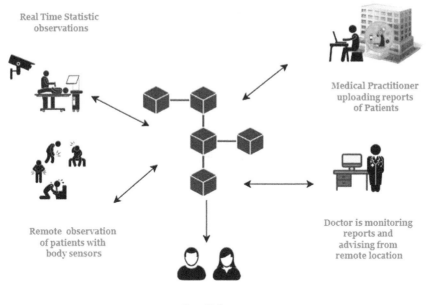

FIGURE 8.5   Blockchain-based IoMT architecture.

History of patient clinical data contains individuals along with sensitive information that attracts people from all areas of civilization, together with aggressors
or any person who needs to retaliate. Some of the data will be alive guaranteed
along with irritability exhibited through conveying. IoMT contraptions have a need
of massive limit with regard to consistent taking care because of the epic propor-
tion of clinical records. As of now, most IoMT associations store the accumulated
clinical data and convey it to the server of applications inside the cloud. Seeing that
referred to previously, the best concern in completing IoMT using the cloud is the
data assurance along with security. Contraptions are offering essential data to each
other and we can't keep the truth from getting data spillage. Blockchain has stood
out from everybody (made famous by the fruitful Bitcoin) because of numerous
different highlights.

We proposed engineering as an answer designed for protected communication
of patient well-being information in light of blockchain innovation toward getting
clinical information. A decentralized blockchain-based philosophy would defeat
a significant number of the issues related to the brought-together approach of the
cloud. .

Figure 8.5 depicts the blockchain-based IoMT architecture with the working
process of the system. This architecture explains how the patient and doctor
communicated with the applications. It has five main components: caretaker, remote
observation, statistics observation, patient medical report, and doctor monitoring
system. Caretaker work is mainly provided to the patient monitoring system with

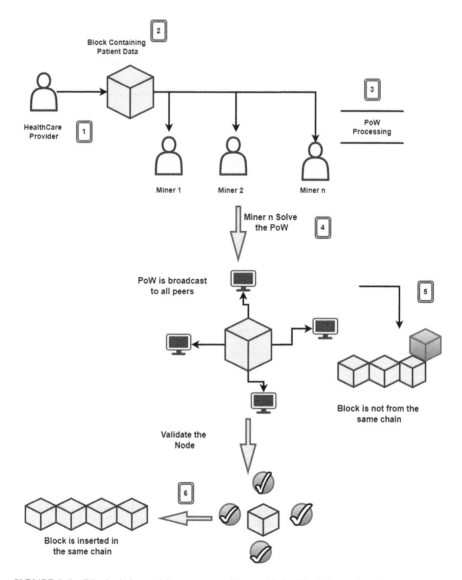

FIGURE 8.6 Block chain working process with an added a block for patient data.

blockchain. All the components are interconnected with the blockchain system because it provides a high-security system.

In this system, the patients are embedded with multiple sensors. These sensors will monitor and collect the data from the patients periodically. The collected information is then sent to the node which is connected with the blockchain environment. Here, the node will be validated and stored the data in the blocks. Doctors are monitoring the patients with a collection of sensor data. Doctor advising the patients from statistical observation of patient's health records using the application with remote

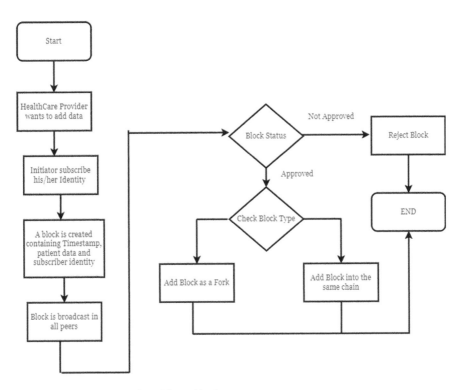

FIGURE 8.7 Flowchart for adding a block.

location system. Then a medical practitioner uploads the patient's report to verify the authenticated doctor and no one is able to modify the patient's record since it was connected with the blockchain system of the decentralized ledger.

Figure 8.6 explains the exhaustive operational standard of healthcare data analysis and data transfer. Initially, the patient's records or data are entered into the database by the healthcare provider, and it contains a complete medical history of each patient. All these medical records are stored in a block to achieve high security; each block contains patients' medical records along with a timestamp to enter and details of healthcare providers for further reference. Here Miner represents the doctor's portentous prescriptions for the meticulous patient further – extracting medical reports from the block and providing supplementary suggestions to improve their health condition. This detail has to be broadcasted in all peer networks of patients to endorse solutions. Finally, the updated medical reports are stored as a chain of the block along with the previous block. When the medical record is forwarded in the opposite direction, then a Fork chain is created (it means stored in the different chain).

Figure 8.7 demonstrates the function of the block added to the blockchain and creates the hash value for each block linked with the previous block and also each node is verified and validated. The routine program runs for creating blocks in the

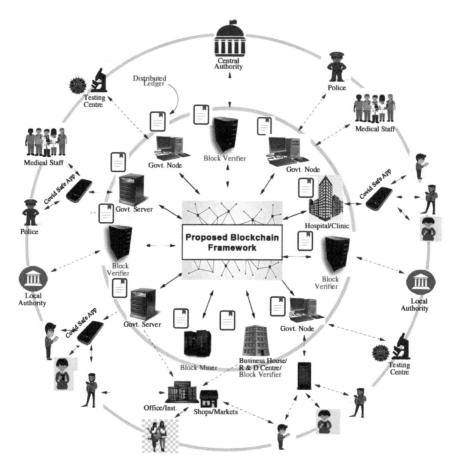

FIGURE 8.8 Proposed framework for privacy of IoT-based health records using blockchain technology.

blockchain and whether the block is validated and verified. It is then validated and verified means added to blockchain; otherwise, it rejects the block in node.

The proposed framework for the privacy of IoT-based health records using blockchain technology is presented in Figure 8.8. It shows the securely provided data from the blockchain system. It has two components: block miner and block verifier; its global collected data is in the form of the ledger and it verifies the node is validated and then the transaction proceeds with the blockchain system.

8.6 CONCLUSION

Blockchain progress is getting significant attention from individuals and connections of coordinated sorts and sizes. The objective is to assist with ensuring various benefits pulled inside the complex connections, for example, applications of the healthcare system should be acquainted with the advantages of the patient, keeping away from what is powerfully occurring. There are by and by unequivocal difficulties to be tended to, for instance, the trading of information across nations.

Security laws are swayed and administrative occasions are broadly long, so normalization and rule issues ought to be settled as quickly as time awards. The different evaluations that ensured the tirelessness of the coalition bit by bit gave up-down. Hence, there is a need to look at creative structures that cultivate completely close to the augmentation in information load. It has promised security and privacy inside the IoMT devices with the holds of blockchain. The main objective of the proposed blockchain-based IoMT architecture is to store the patient's data in the blockchain system. It can't be modifiable and verified with one of the blockchain algorithms of consensus-based digital data with a decentralized ledger generated.

REFERENCES

1. Ali, M., Hossain, G., Muhammad, Sangaiah A.K. An intelligent healthcare system for detection and classification to discriminate vocal fold disorders. *Future Generation Computer Systems*, 85, 19–28, 2018.
2. Dang, L.M., Piran, M.J., Han, D., Moon, H. A survey on internet of things and cloud computing for healthcare. *Electronics*, 8, 768, 2019.
3. Lavanya, S., Prasanth, A., Jayachitra, S. A tuned classification approach for efficient heterogeneous fault diagnosis in IoT-enabled WSN applications. *Measurement*, 183, 109771, 1–22, 2021.
4. Kadhim, K.T. An overview of a patient's health status monitoring system based on internet of things (IoT). *Wireless Personal Communications*, 114, 1–28, 2020.
5. Prasanth, A., Pavalarajan, S. Implementation of efficient intra and inter-zone routing for extending network consistency in wireless sensor networks. *Journal of Circuit Systems and Computers*, 29, 1–23,2020.
6. Zheng, Y. Scalable and secure sharing of personal health records in cloud computing using attribute-based encryption. *IEEE Transactions on Parallel and Distributed Systems*, 24, 131–143, 2013.
7. Bhaskar, K.B., Prasanth, A.P., Saranya, P. An energy-efficient blockchain approach for secure communication in IoT-enabled electric vehicles. *International Journal of Communication System*, e5189, 1–25, 2022.
8. Aras, S.T., Kulkarni, V. Blockchain and its applications–A detailed survey. *International Journal of Computational Application*, 29–35, 180, 2017.
9. Nguyen, G., Kim, K. A survey about consensus algorithms used in blockchain. *Journal of Information Process System*, 14, 101–128, 2018.
10. Thang, P., Trang, T., Tai, B. Multimedia privacy, security, and protection within the blockchain: A review. *2022 5th International Conference on Contemporary Computing and Informatics (IC3I)*, 31171–31176, 2022.
11. Khezr, Moniruzzaman, Yassine, Benlamri, Blockchain technology in healthcare: A comprehensive review and directions for future research. *Journal of Application and Science*, 9, 1736, 2019.
12. Birje, M.N., Hanji, S.S. Internet of things based distributed healthcare systems: A review. *Journal of Data, Information and Management*, 2, 1–9, 2020.
13. Venkatesh, V., Parthasarathi, P. Trusted third party auditing to improve cloud storage security. *Wireless Communication*, 5, 183–187, 2013.

14. Haber, S., Stornetta, W.S. How to time-stamp a digital document. *Journal of Cryptol.* 3, 99–111, 2008.

15. Lounis, A., Hadjidj A., Bouabdallah, A. Healing on the cloud: Secure cloud architecture for medical wireless sensor networks. *Future Generation Computer Systems*, 55, 266–277, 2016.

16. Daraghmi, Y., Daraghmi, E., Yuan, S. MedChain: A design of blockchain-based system for medical records access and permissions management. *IEEE Access*, 7, 164595–164613, 2019.

17. Chichisan I., Costin H., Geman O., Chiuchisan A. Adopting the internet of things technologies in health care systems. *International Conference and Exposition on Electrical and Power Engineering (EPE)*, 16–18, 532–535, 2019.

18. Jo, B.W., Khan, A., Lee Y. Hybrid blockchain and internet-of-things network for underground structure health monitoring. *International Journal of Sensors*, 18, 4268, 2018.

19. Mathivanan, P., IoT based real time healthcare monitoring system and visualization. *IEEE–International Conference on Systems Computation Automation and Networking*, 1109, 1–6, 2020.

20. Priya, D., A real time support system to impart medicine using smart dispenser. *IEEE–International Conference on Systems Computation Automation and Networking*, 1109, 22–28, 2020.

21. Liu, X., Wang, Z., Li, F. A blockchain-based medical data sharing and protection scheme. *IEEE Access*, 7, 1–6, 2019.

22. Liang, X., Zhao, J. Shetty, Li, D. Integrating blockchain for data sharing and collaboration in mobile healthcare applications. *IEEE 28th Annual International Symposium on Personal, Indoor, and Mobile Radio Communications*, 8–13, 2017.

23. Griggs, K.N. Healthcare blockchain system using smart contracts for secure automated remote patient monitoring. *Journal of Medical System,* 42, 130.

24. Zhang, J. Xue, N., Huang, X.. A secure system for pervasive social network-based healthcare. *IEEE Access*, 4, 9239–9250, 2016.

25. Zyskind, G., Nathan, O., Pentland, A. Decentralizing privacy: Using blockchain to protect personal data. *IEEE Security and Privacy Workshops*, 180–184, 2015.

26. Krishnasamy, L., Dhanaraj, R. K., Ganesh Gopal, D. A heuristic angular clustering framework for secured statistical data aggregation in sensor networks. *Sensors*, 20, 1–17, 2020.

27. Mathivanan, P. Intelligent content based image retrieval model using Adadelta optimized residual network. *International Conference on System, Computation, Automation and Networking (ICSCAN)*, 1–5, 2021.

28. Patel, V. A framework for secure and decentralized sharing of medical imaging data via blockchain consensus. *Journal of Health Information System,* 25, 1398–1411, 2018.

29. Fan, K., Wang, S., Ren, Y. MedBlock: Efficient and secure medical data sharing via blockchain. *Journal of Medical System,* 42, 136, 2018.

30. Jayachitra, S., Prasanth, A., Hariprasath, S., AI enabled internet of medical things in smart healthcare. Springer. *AI Models for Blockchain-Based Intelligent Networks in IoT Systems: Concepts, Methodologies, Tools, and Applications*, 141–161, 2023.

9 Securing IoMT Devices to Protect the Future of Healthcare from Rising Cyberattacks

V. Saranya, *T. Devi, and N. Deepa*
Department of Computer Science & Engineering,
Saveetha School of Engineering, Saveetha Institute of
Medical and Technical Sciences, Saveetha University,
Chennai, India
*Corresponding Author: Email: saranyav9069.
sse@saveetha.com

9.1 INTRODUCTION

The Internet of Medical Things (IoMT) devices connect the network of doctors and patients. It enables transferring data in the healthcare sector by wireless communication. IoMT devices are a combination of hardware, software, and medical-based devices that help to connect and store medical information and retrieve this information remotely [1]. It assists the patient with IoMT devices to connect with the authorized doctor in an emergency. The IoMT monitoring device is used to monitor children with attention-deficit hyperactivity disorder (ADHD).

9.1.1 ADHD

An ADHD child has some issues concentrating on one thing, learning attention and listening attention are very low, and they misbehave without thinking of the outcome [2]. The symptoms of ADHD children are shown in Figure 9.1.

The below symptoms are common in ADHD children. There are three different types of ADHD: predominantly inattentive type, predominantly hyperactive-impulsive type, and combined type.

Predominantly Inattentive Type: A child with this type of disorder is not able to follow or continue the specific work, cannot continue the task frequently, not listening to the class and conversations, does not follow the rules and restrictions, and can easily distract from their work. These children also forget what they are doing and move on to the next work without thinking of the outcome.

DOI: 10.1201/9781003405450-9

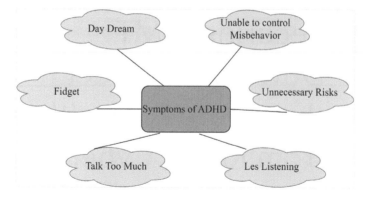

FIGURE 9.1 ADHD symptoms.

Predominantly Hyperactive-Impulsive Type: In this type of disorder, children feel nervous, overthinking, bored, excited, and speak too much. Adults have trouble with their behaviors, they talk at inappropriate times and manners, disturb others continuously, feel very disturbed and restless, and are unpredictable or impulsive. It becomes hard for them to wait for their turn and listen to the instructions. They have more impulsivity, which defines behaving without knowing the risks, accidents, and injuries they have more than others.

Combined Type: In this type of disorder, children have the symptoms of both inattentive and hyperactive-impulsive. These symptoms can affect the disordered people's personal life, work, relationship, and home. It causes restlessness, impulsiveness, hyperactivity, and extreme feelings. These symptoms are more severe when they decide to do work continuously and correctly, feeling too much stress to complete a particular work [3].

9.1.2   IoMT Device for Monitoring ADHD Child

The monitoring device is used to observe ADHD children because they do anything without knowing the output and therefore they should be monitored by parents and healthcare providers. It is a wearable device with a tracker and it connects remotely with the authorized person and healthcare providers. In case of an emergency, this device sends an alert message to the concerned person who is connected to that device.

9.1.2.1   IoMT Device Challenges

The IoMT ecosystem connects the stakeholders like medical device providers, manufacturers, technical providers, integrators, Internet connection providers, and end users. It is a systematic manner, and information on daily activities, health-based data, and monitoring data is stored with the help of an Internet connection. Depending on this Internet usage several challenges are raised. The challenges of the IoMT device are shown in Figure 9.2.

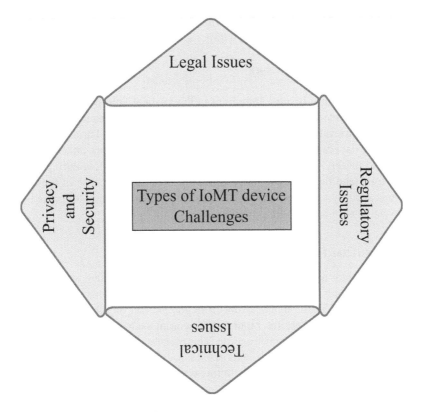

FIGURE 9.2 Types of IoMT devices.

a. Legal Issues

The ecosystem of the IoMT device connects more stakeholders and users. When a message is passed by the device, it is stored by all the stakeholders; and since it is a distributed system, the message can be replicated more times, which complicates the distributed network. An authorized user can only erase the message and until this deletion happens the message can be distributed to different parties.

b. Regulatory Issues

IoMT device stores sensitive medical-based data; these sensitive data are retrieved for future reference also. It also contains rules and regulations for the protection of data and the user. These regulations may not be more protective and secure for some devices. Therefore, regulatory issues may be raised.

c. Technical Issues

IoMT is a distributed system that can communicate safely with every person connecting and using the device. The safety measurements and protocol standards are most important for communication with one another. But the problem is that the system cannot keep the updated data within the dates.

d. Security and Privacy Issues

Data confidentiality is more important in the medical field because the personal data of each patient should be safe and secure. The IoMT devices use the Internet for data storage, retrieval, collection, integration, and transmission. Through this Internet cloud storage data can be stolen and used by unauthorized persons, attackers can steal the data and modify the original data to mislead the entire system during the transmission time, and they can eavesdrop on the medical data because of these issues. Therefore, security and privacy protocols need more concentration to secure the data storage and communication transmission [4].

9.1.3 ARTIFICIAL INTELLIGENCE

The human brain is a complex system to understand. The complete work of the brain is based on sending electrical signals from one neuron and this signal is received by another neuron. These signals differ from one another and it processes different emotions. These signals are the input to the neuron; each carries some information and hands over the data to another neuron. This process is repeated continuously until the information is received by the authorized place of the body. This working mechanism is the basis for AI technology. In this way, this mechanism is used to process the data in AI technology. AI contains a lot of processed data with labels, and these labels help to filter the data easily. Processed data used for the new data can be learned by this and assessed this data to find the pattern or problem-based solutions [5]. These patterns can make predictions.

The learning process has three steps to find the output. The first step is the training process of new data focal points for obtaining the required data and deciding rules to achieve a specific task. The next step is the reasoning process which focuses on selecting the correct algorithm or set of processes to obtain an accurate output. The final step is the correction process, which needs continuous updates of rules and regulations to find the most suitable result for the given input.

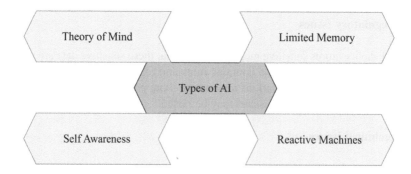

FIGURE 9.3 AI types of systems.

FIGURE 9.4 AI for cybersecurity.

AI has been categorized into four types. In earlier times, task-specific techniques were widely used, which is a work that follows step-by-step regulations [6]. Nowadays sentiment analysis has grown up in this AI field. The types of AI are shown in Figure 9.3.

9.1.3.1   Artificial Intelligence in Cybersecurity

Computers are connected to an open communication environment. This cloud environment has difficulties like data theft, leakage, unauthorized access, malware, virus injection, and denial of services. These difficulties are called cyberattacks. AI technology algorithms enable the control mechanism for these types of attacks and protect data. The AI algorithm contains a preprocessed data set, and it can detect the intrusion of unauthorized access and cyberattacks. Figure 9.4 displays the works of AI in the cybersecurity sector.

Different kinds of AI algorithms for cybersecurity are used, such as supervised, unsupervised, and reinforcement algorithms [7]. These algorithms securely allow an open communication system, interacting online for data transferring, secure data from cyberattacks based on the communication, and data transfer algorithms changed to enhance security.

9.1.4   Blockchain Technology

Blockchain technology is a developed database system that stores the data in blocks, and these blocks are connected with a chain or link. It can share information transparently via an open network. The blockchain idea first appeared in 1991. A research group intended to develop a technique for timestamping digital content. So, they could not be modified or amended. Satoshi Nakamoto later converted and recreated the technique. Nakamoto launched the first cryptocurrency, a blockchain-based project dubbed bitcoin, in 2008. Basically, in blockchain, two main data structures are used. They are pointers and linked lists. The pointer variable will gather information regarding the location of another place. The linked list is a series of blocks, each having its data and linked to the next with the use of a pointer.

Figure 9.5 shows the working progress of blockchain hashing. Blockchain is used as a critical component of the technology that underpins Bitcoin and digital currencies. Generally, cryptocurrencies are digital currencies that may be transferred online, employing cryptographic hashes and message authentication to validate

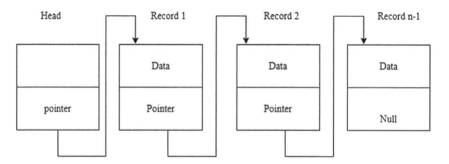

FIGURE 9.5 Blockchain hashing.

transactions and eliminate the token from double-spending. Cryptocurrencies are digital payment systems that operate online and are built on peer-to-peer communication networks and cryptography with public keys. Blockchain systems enable users to trade value in an unreliable environment, payments are moderate and irreversible, and each payment will be monitored in a distributed way, ensuring all the participants should agree that the payment occurred.

Marc Andreessen is well known as a venture capitalist in cryptocurrencies. The bitcoin hypothesis was initially stated in a white paper released under the pseudonym in 2008. Cryptocurrencies are not backed by any government or commodity and there is no central authority. They are based on the notion that value is determined by shortage and the quantity of effort necessary to attain scarce things [8]. The blockchain is essential for making this restriction a reality. The blockchain not only maintains a redundant, global database of all transactions, but also contributes to the creation of value in the particular cryptocurrency [9].

9.1.4.1 Block Architecture of Blockchain Technology

Blockchain architecture is used to serve the following: cost reduction, history of data, data validity, and security.

Cost reduction: A large amount of money is invested in maintaining centrally stored databases current and secure from cybercrime and other unscrupulous purposes.

Data history: in the history of the blockchain, it will check the history of all possible transactions at any time. It will grow the achiever's chart of the specification of the point.

Data validity and security: It takes time to tamper with the data due to the blockchain nature of the data. Blockchain has three cauterized data. They are public blockchain, private blockchain, and consortium blockchain. Figure 9.6 depicts the architecture of IoMT based on blockchain technology.

9.2 RELATED WORKS

Future-generation wireless networks must support strategic and tactical levels and low-latency communications. AI has grown in popularity in recent years as a result of advances in machine learning (ML), particularly deep learning (DL) and supervised

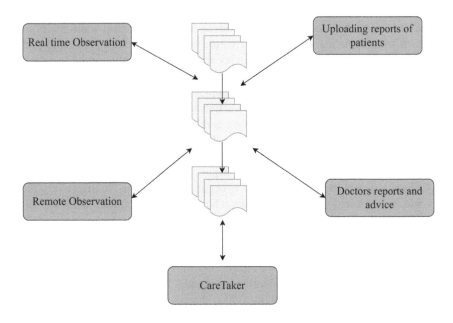

FIGURE 9.6   Blockchain-based IoMT architecture.

learning demonstrating its utility in a broad range of situations in which regression or classification problems play a significant role. The management of Internet of Things (IoT) infrastructures is one of the key applications of next-generation wireless networks. The deployment of wireless networks that enables IoT paradigms is gaining traction among academic and industrial researchers. The complex nature and rapid spread of these systems pose numerous challenges, such as the development and integration of diverse data transmission, evolving ability to adapt to different operating scenarios, and so on. Due to the versatile, inhomogeneous, and scattered nature of this type of system, many professionals and researchers have explored the use of DL methods to make IoT intellect, credible, and slightly elevated.

Fortune magazine anticipated that the IoT company might expand to $457 billion. Smart buildings, microgrids, smart well-being, and manufacturing IoT are the major contributions to this substantial adjustment and growth. The shift referred to as industry makes heavy use of several scattered devices that produce a continuous amount of information. Wireless explanations are critical in this frame of reference as evidenced by the rapid production of 25 industrial components that have assisted in the exact incorporation. Finally, even though IoT devices frequently use restricted computing, information processing, and energy supplies, they increasingly depend on side and central connections to handle methods and interpret information. As a consequence, DL-based corners and fundamental gadgets are essential for the development of smart and efficient raw materials and network planning, in addition to the overall improvement of system performance.

Indeed, careful assessment and enhancement of IoT devices is an essential field of study. Wireless traffic has been growing dramatically with the consistent growth in the number of IoT devices able to produce large short packet transmitters over Wi-Fi. A transformation in the social creature is necessary due to the rapid global climate change. New, creative technologies are needed to continuously monitor the surroundings and act appropriately to solve this problem. Systems can be made reliable and flexible using ML. IoT systems deployed in remote places run on a small amount of battery and are expected to function without interruption for many years. Deep neural network-based methods were employed to effectively gather data from various sensing devices and track the health of electronic device batteries. The attribute mean method was used to process the suggested scheme. It is then converted utilizing the conventional scalar method [10].

Collaboration is the cornerstone of cybersecurity defense. To effectively identify and isolate sneaky malicious actors who conceal their traffic under the guise of legitimate Internet data transmission, a collaborative detection system enables multiple associates or network operators to start sharing their vulnerability information. The main difficulty in designing a collaborative system is protecting collaborators' privacy in a decentralized environment without imposing significant computational and communication overheads. We use the healthcare industry as a case study in this chapter and introduce sharing is caring (SIC) – a framework that permits multiple health organizations to share their containment measures and strike data with the other institution for the teamwork defense against popular attackers without jeopardizing the confidentiality of their configuration options and customer data.

Two fundamental characteristics are guaranteed by the SIC framework: the first one is that it prevents parties from learning how a specific healthcare organization has responded to attacks, suspicious IP addresses, or security incidents and it conducts business in a decentralized manner without relying on a reliable third party. We analyze the privacy and security features of our framework concerning both malicious and benevolent players. The proposed system is prototyped and its efficiency in terms of processing time and network bandwidth is assessed. The SIC approach is a reasonable solution for the private information interaction of sensitive data among the cooperating healthcare organization due to its reasonable computation cost and bandwidth overhead [11].

Ever since the IoMT was founded, cyberattacks have been a threat. Because there is a lack of vital security protection, various threats and attacks could result in catastrophic failures for both the networks and the user. The IoMT organization and protection thus assume a lot of importance. This chapter identifies a method for controlling and protecting the data of the IoMT. To transfer medical data wirelessly, a system needs to be safe through data encryption and password authentication. By first encoding data and then ciphering it with a reshuffled key before being used to transmit over the networks, a new encrypted communication system is demonstrated. Using his login information and cryptographically signed, the doctor aims to restore the secure information. Utilizing inexpensive hardware and effective software, the proposed system was implemented and demonstrated that data can be transmitted. [12]. Table 9.1 describes the details of challenges faced by IoMT devices.

TABLE 9.1
The IoMT Is Experiencing Challenges

Challenges	Problem Recognition
Protection	The biggest problem facing the IoT is security, which is a key component of the Internet. Due to the flaws in their design, smart devices could have security vulnerabilities. These devices are in charge of sending and receiving data, which means that if any of them has security flaws, the system is in danger because the data could be altered or intercepted.
Isolation	The IoT faces several privacy-related challenges because the need for information should be protected and treated confidentially.
Prevailing	The absence of a standard can cause interoperability issues.
Standard regulation	IoT legal and regulatory issues required thoughtful investigation. Data controversy between civil liberties and the rules, data confinement and breakdown policies, privacy barfing, and breach of security are massive problems in IoT devices.

    I.   Algorithm for authenticating and encoding sensor data

Obtain the patient's vital information, such as their temperature. The client-side run length scripting method is used to encode information, then use the Advanced Encryption Standard (AES) technique to encrypt the information using a pivoting passcode instead of the synchronizer key. The client-side uses the esp2866 Wi-Fi module to send encrypted information to local Wi-Fi. Local Wi-Fi transmits secure data to the online decoder server.

    II.   Algorithm for authentication method decoding and decryption of sensor data

Data received from the patient side is encrypted by the doctor's server using a rotated key. Using the run length decrypting technique, the doctor server decrypts the received data to retrieve the original statement. Information is posted to a website hosted on a doctor's server and the website is authenticated. The doctor enters his login information to access the website. He can check on his patient's condition after being authenticated [13].

The current state of IoMT for the medical industry, which includes research and improvement plans and software, is discussed in this chapter. Worldwide adoption of the IoMT has grown exponentially, but there are still many technical and architectural issues to be resolved. To address the aforementioned challenges, this chapter illustrates a generic IoMT framework made up of three main parts: data gathering, interaction gateways, and network service. Finally, it highlightes the relevant open research issues and the practical possibilities and prospects of IoMT. The following is a discussion of some of the major problems and design issues in healthcare.

Power Consumption: The major concern with IoMT is its high power consumption. The majority of sensors and actuators used in IoMT application domains run on batteries, and the drawback of such systems is that they use a lot of energy. In a bid to reduce the total energy consumption, scientists have created some routing protocols and algorithms. But there is still a need for advancements and new technologies given the volume of data being generated.

Machine Intelligence, Decision, and Social Support: The advancement of future healthcare depends on the creation of an interdisciplinary innovation with monitoring systems and computation.

Communication and Network-Based System: Physical security of deployed networks and communication security are ongoing research topics. Newer friendly communication with the present technologies, communication, norms, and methodologies is also needed.

Security: Security is crucial for intelligent critical systems. Some of the challenges include communication security access mechanisms and authentication. Some issues are resolved by distributed solutions built on the blockchain, such as the requirement for trust in a central communication [14].

To strengthen IoMT's resistance to cyberattacks, the appropriate security precautions and learning competencies must be put into place. In addition, we examine the primary IoMT concerns about privacy as well as the available security system. There are two kinds of solutions: cryptographic and non-cryptographic. The different alternatives would then be examined and contrasted in terms of the computational difficulty and required resources. The security measures for IoMT show a barter between the level of security and the system's stability.

The right security measures such as efficient cryptosystem protocols and techniques that make use of free resources and computation are then covered. Despite its benefits, IoMT is vulnerable to a range of assaults, problems, and difficulties that primarily target patient privacy and integrity and connectivity of healthcare. The primary issues, difficulties, and disadvantages of IoMT were presented and examined in this chapter alongside the various safety precautions that can be put in place to protect and safeguard the IoMT sites, and they are involving a number of factors such as medical equipment mechanisms and public cloud services.

To ensure a more improved and robust application of these methods and improve the health and experience of the patients, various framework categorizations and approaches were additionally exhibited. Furthermore, it's critical to protect the various wireless transmission procedures of the IoT. Training healthcare and its staff are advised to protect them from physical and cyberattacks. In conclusion, the goal of this chapter is to strengthen the connection between various technical and non-technical elements to ensure a system that is much more advanced, safeguarded, and effective across all IoMT contexts [15].

The IoMT is a component of modern health coverage with extremely strict constraints and resources. Offering online privacy and verifying a patient's health information over a network infrastructure in a resource-effective way is a crucial aspect of trying to implement security for simulcasting patient data. Therefore, by removing the pulse rate from the ECG signal we created a fingerprint authentication security model for the source of energy portable health monitoring devices. The analysis demonstrates that the security of IoMT-based medical uses can be significantly improved by period-based biometric traitors. Additionally, a utility function-based resources optimization model is suggested for the IoMT's transmission of clinical information.

Sensor readings from 40 healthy volunteers were utilized in this study to create a research facility environment. We used a bio-keys component for healthcare encrypting data to provide stability in IoMT, which is advantageous for lowering scheme material requirements. The experimental findings show that biometric keys generated from various subjects are adequately arbitrary and distinct to be used to secure IoMT. Additionally compared to the roughly equivalent approaches, the proposed personality tests healthcare model utilizes less computation time and energy. In real-world hospital instances, the presented framework also provides a trade-off between privacy and resource use. This study guarantees the safe transmission of medical information between patients and their physicians while also reducing the cost of healthcare [16].

9.3 PROPOSED WORK

The AI and blockchain technology-based proposed model is collaborative chain-linked intrusion detection systems (CLIDS). The intrusion detection system detects suspicious and doubtful activities through the network chain and linked data. AI creates a model for the surveillance system for the IoMT device of ADHD children; if any intrusion is discovered, it checks the model with intrusion and finds the originality of the intrusion . Intrusion detection system (IDS)mainly focused on two things

1. Information is stored temporarily and monitored by the target objects.
2. Alert the authorized system about unauthorized access or suspicious things.

Blockchain technology is the end-to-end encrypted model for sharing transparent data over the open network. The data is recorded in blocks and each block grows continuously. These blocks are connected by chain using a cryptographic code. The proposed model works collaboratively with this blockchain to find out the unauthorized access and malware detection on the IoMT devices.

Figure 9.7 describes the working and importance of the CLIDS model. The proposed architecture is built collaboratively by an AI model and blockchain technique called a collaborative CLIDS. The monitoring device for ADHD children connects to an open network 24/7, so this device needs more protection to avoid threats to the children. As this network connects by an open communication system it can be hacked, and the hacker can mislead the children. Figure 9.8 shows the details of the CLIDS model working progress.

A CLIDS collaborative system was created that enables the device to be more secure and more protective. This proposed system works by the transparent data sharing by blockchain technique with the help of end-to-end encryption and it simultaneously stores the data with blocks; each block is connected by a chain link, and

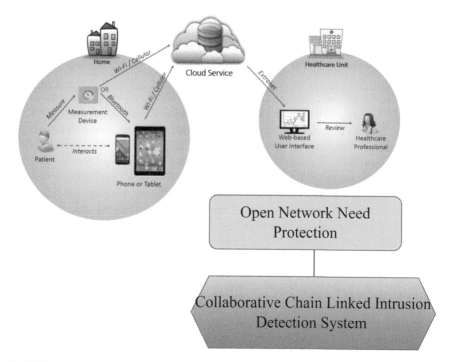

FIGURE 9.7   Importance of CLIDS model.

the next block alerts the system when an unauthorized person accesses the network or there are any suspicious activities in that link. It finds suspicious activities by checking the AI model with the whole system, so now it easily finds an intrusion by this model.

9.4   RESULT AND DISCUSSIONS

The proposed model CLIDS is a combination of an AI-powered intrusion detection system and blockchain temporary data storage method. This system helps to find intrusion and suspicious activities more accurately and efficiently. The existing system does not support the data temporary storage, so the hacker can change the data and remove the original data. Now the proposed model overcomes this issue and makes open communication safer and more protective.

Figure 9.9 depicts the accuracy range of intrusion detection. It achieves a 92.18% accuracy and the detection of mismatched data with an accuracy range of 89.08%. Intrusion detection over the network, communication systems, and IoMT devices by the work of CLIDS systems enables data safety more effective and also misleads children from unknown persons. The original data cannot be modified by unauthorized persons due to the security systems. With the help of this security system, the end user receives the original data without any modification.

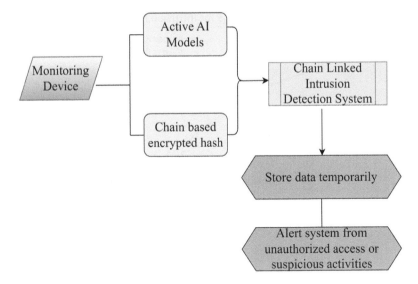

FIGURE 9.8 Work of CLIDS model.

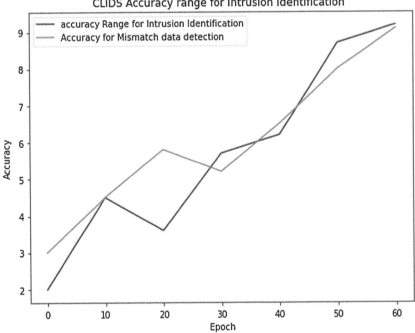

FIGURE 9.9 Accuracy range of CLIDS model.

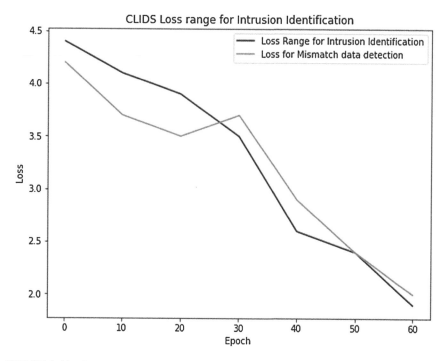

FIGURE 9.10   Loss range of CLIDS model.

Figure 9.10 displays the loss value of the proposed model compared to the existing method. The proposed model shows better performance and better results in intrusion detection. An IoMT monitoring device protects from data theft, intrusion, data modification, and unauthorized access and protects children from unknown persons by using this collaborative CLIDS model that achieves better performance and efficient work based on intrusion detection systems.

9.5   CONCLUSION

This chapter has analyzed intrusion detection over the open network, open communication systems, and IoMT monitoring devices. The communication between the patient, doctor, healthcare, and IoMT device data protected by the CLIDS model shows better results in intrusion detection and detection of mismatched data more accurately and more efficiently. In the future, this model will be used for more accurate results and technical communication through an open network safer and more protective from intruders and hackers who cannot intrude on the healthcare-based IoMT monitoring device. This model can protect open communication with open networks without any fear of Internet usage in the healthcare sector.

REFERENCES

1. Loh, H. W., Ooi, C. P., Barua, P. D., Palmer, E. Automated detection of ADHD: Current trends and future perspective. *Computers in Biology and Medicine*, 146, 105525, 2022.
2. Gagnon, A., Descoteaux, M., Bocti, C., Takser, L, Better characterization of attention and hyperactivity/impulsivity in children with ADHD: The key to understanding the underlying white matter microstructure. *Psychiatry Research: Neuroimaging*, 327, 111568, 2022.
3. Khare, S. K., Acharya, U. R., An explainable and interpretable model for attention deficit hyperactivity disorder in children using EEG signals. *Computers in Biology and Medicine*, 155, 106676, 2023.
4. Jayachitra, S., Prasanth, A., Hariprasath, S., AI enabled internet of medical things in smart healthcare. Springer. *AI Models for Blockchain-Based Intelligent Networks in IoT Systems: Concepts, Methodologies, Tools, and Applications*, 141–161, 2023.
5. Zhao, K., Duka, B., Xie, H., Oathes, D. J., A dynamic graph convolutional neural network framework reveals new insights into connectome dysfunctions in ADHD. *NeuroImage*, 246, 118774, 2022.
6. Kavitha, M., Roobini, S., Prasanth, A., Sujaritha, M., Systematic view and impact of artificial intelligence in smart healthcare systems, principles, challenges and applications. *Machine Learning and Artificial Intelligence in Healthcare Systems*, 21, 25–56, 2023.
7. Chang, V., Bhavani, V. R., Xu, A. Q., Hossain, M. A., An artificial intelligence model for heart disease detection using machine learning algorithms. *Healthcare Analytics*, 2, 100016, 2022.
8. Thang, P., Trang, T., Tai, B., Multimedia privacy, security, and protection within the blockchain: A review. *2022 5th International Conference on Contemporary Computing and Informatics (IC3I)*, 31171–31176, 2022.
9. Bhaskar, K. B., Prasanth, A., Saranya, P., An energy-efficient blockchain approach for secure communication in IoT-enabled electric vehicles. *International Journal of Communication Systems*, 35, 1–30, 2022.
10. Aljabr, A. A., Kumar, K., Design and implementation of internet of medical things (IoMT) using artificial intelligent for mobile-healthcare. *Measurement: Sensors*, 24, 100499, 2022.
11. Zikria, Y. B., Afzal, M. K., Kim, S. W., Marin, A., Deep learning for intelligent IoT: Opportunities, challenges, and solutions. *Computer Communications*, 164, 50–53, 2020.
12. Azad, M. A., Bag, S., Ahmad, F., Hao, F. Sharing is caring: A collaborative framework for sharing security alerts. *Computer Communications*, 165, 75–84, 2021.
13. Farahat, I. S., Tolba, A. S., Elhoseny, M., Eladrosy, W., A secure real-time internet of medical smart things (IOMST). *Computers & Electrical Engineering*, 72, 455–467, 2018.
14. Ray, P. P., Dash, D., Kumar, N., Sensors for the internet of medical things: State-of-the-art, security and privacy issues, challenges and future directions. *Computer Communications*, 160, 111–131, 2020.
15. Banerjee, M., Lee, J., Choo, K. K. R., a blockchain future for internet of things security: A position paper. *Digital Communications, and Networks*, 4(3), 149–160, 2018.
16. Rawat, R., A systematic review of blockchain technology use in e-supply chain in the internet of medical things (IoMT). *International Journal of Computations, Information, and Manufacturing (IJCIM)*, 2(2), 2022.

17. Moorthy, R. S. S., Nathiya, N., Botnet detection using artificial intelligence. *Procedia Computer Science*, 218, 1405–1413, 2023.

18. Saw, S. N., g, K. H., Current challenges of implementing artificial intelligence in medical imaging. *Physica Medica*, 100, 12–17, 2022.

19. Hussien, H. M., Yasin, S. M., Udzir, N. I., Ninggal, M. Blockchain technology in the healthcare industry: Trends and opportunities. *Journal of Industrial Information Integration*, 22, 100217, 2021.

20. Kumar, P., Gupta, G. P., Tripathi, R., An ensemble learning and fog-cloud architecture-driven cyber-attack detection framework for IoMT networks. *Computer Communications*, 166, 110–124, 2021.

21. Rasool, R. U., Ahmad, H. F., Rafique, W., Qayyum, A., Security, and privacy of the internet of medical things: A contemporary review in the age of surveillance, botnets, and adversarial ML. *Journal of Network and Computer Applications*, 201, 103332, 2022.

22. Pirbhulal, S., Samuel, O. W., Wu, W., Sangaiah, A. K., Li, G., A joint resource-aware and medical data security framework for wearable healthcare systems. *Future Generation Computer Systems*, 95, 382–391, 2019.

23. Al-rani, M., IoT and artificial intelligence implementations for remote healthcare monitoring systems: A survey. *Journal of King Saud University-Computer and Information Sciences*, 34(8), 4687–4701, 2022.

24. Wazid, M., Das, A. K., Chamola, V., Park, Y., uniting cyber security, and machine learning: Advantages, challenges, and future research. *ICT Express*, 2022.

25. Yamin, M. M., Ullah, M., Ullah, H., Katt, B., Weaponized AI for cyber-attacks. *Journal of Information Security and Applications*, 57, 102722, 2021.

26. Fontes, C., Hohma, E., Corrigan, C. C., Lütge, C., AI-powered public surveillance systems: Why we (might) need them and how we want them. *Technology in Society*, 71, 102137, 2022.

27. Deepa, N., Sathya Priya, J., Devi, T., Towards applying internet of things and machine learning for the risk prediction of COVID-19 in a pandemic situation using Naive Bayes classifier for improving accuracy. *Materials Today: Proceedings*, 2022.

28. Deepa, N., Devi, T., Gayathri, N., Kumar, S. R., Decentralized healthcare management system using blockchain to secure sensitive medical data for users. Springer. *EAI/Springer Innovations in Communication and Computing*, 265–282, 2022.

29. Devi, T., Alice, K., Deepa, N., Traffic management in smart cities using support vector machine for predicting the accuracy during peak traffic conditions. *Materials Today: Proceedings*, 62, 4980–4984, 2022.

30. Devi, T., Deepa, N., Jai Sharma, K., Client-controlled HECC-as-a-service. *Lecture Notes on Data Engineering and Communications Technologies*, 31, 312–318, 2022.

10 Smart Hand-Hygiene Compliance and Temperature Monitoring System to Tackle COVID-19-like Pathogens in Healthcare Institutions

Hari Krishnan Ramachandran,[1]*
Aravind Krishnaswamy Rangarajan,[1,2]
and Rajesh Kumar Dhanaraj[3]
[1]School of Mechanical Engineering, SASTRA Deemed to be University, Tamil Nadu, India
[2]Department of Environment, Faculty of Bioscience Engineering, Ghent University, Ghent, Belgium
[3]Symbiosis Institute of Computer Studies and Research (SICSR), Symbiosis International (Deemed University), Pune, India
*Corresponding Author: Hari Krishnan Ramachandran (Email: harikrishnan.r@mech.sastra.edu)

10.1 INTRODUCTION

The acute respiratory disease, coronavirus disease 2019 (COVID-19), which appeared in late 2019 has spread across the globe and has affected the normal life of every individual [1]. Toward the beginning of August 2023, almost 768,983,095 confirmed cases and 6,953,743 fatalities have been reported worldwide due to COVID-19 [2]. The World Health Organization (WHO) claims that frequent and proper handwashing is one of the foremost measures that may be utilized to reduce the spread of this virus [3]. This being the scenario, functional handwashing provisions with soap and water should be made available in homes and in public places, such as schools, healthcare institutions, markets, religious institutions, and bus/train stations. Among these locations, healthcare personnel including doctors and nurses working in healthcare institutions are more susceptible to this deadly disease. Moreover, the lack of proper hand-hygiene in healthcare institutions can also result in the transmission of COVID-19 virus and other pathogens that lead to hospital-associated infections (HAI), to people or patients who visit hospitals to cure their illness [4].

As per the interim guidance of WHO dated 25 January 2020, all healthcare personnel dealing with COVID-19 patients should keep their hands clean: (a) before wearing and after removing personal protective equipment (PPE), (b) while changing the gloves, (c) after any contact with the patient or their excreta, (d) after contact with any respiratory secretions, and (e) before eating and after using the toilet [5]. In addition, the WHO has also prescribed that hand-hygiene should be performed by following its 11-step handwashing guidelines [6]. Considering the current situation, a simple and reliable hand-hygiene compliance monitoring system is the need of the hour and this chapter explores an Internet of Things (IoT)-based system to track hand-hygiene habits of healthcare personnel. Several systems to ensure hand-hygiene compliance have been proposed in the past few years and a few of them are being discussed here.

The remainder of the chapter has been organized as follows: section 10.2 covers the related works, followed by a discussion on a pilot study to substantiate the correlation between hand hygiene and HAI in section 10.3. Further, the chapter elaborates on the conceptual design of the proposed system and detailed design of the same in section 10.4 and section 10.5, respectively. Finally, the concluding remarks are covered in section 10.6.

10.2 RELATED WORKS

A literature review emphasizing various designs reported in patent documents, research articles, and details about a couple of off-the-shelf technologies that are currently available to assure hand hygiene has been presented.

10.2.1 HAND-WASH SYSTEMS IN PATENT DOCUMENTS

The designs proposed by various inventors in patent documents have been categorized into two: (1) proximity sensing-based hand-wash systems and (2) vision-based hand-wash monitoring.

10.2.1.1 Proximity Sensing-Based Hand-Wash Systems

US Patent No. 5199118 discusses the design of a simple automated hand sanitizing workstation comprising of a washbasin, a soap dispensing system above the washbasin, a solenoid valve-operated water tap, and a hot air dryer for blowing hot air [7]. The device is equipped with two infrared (IR) sensors to detect the user's proximity. When the user places his/her hands within the proximity of the first sensor, the solenoid valves of the soap dispenser and the tap are energized to dispense liquidized soap solution and water. Once the hands are removed from the proximity of the first sensor, the soap dispensing will cease but the tap will continue to dispense water.

Subsequently, when the hands are placed within the proximity of the second sensor, the water dispensing will be ceased and the hot drier will be turned ON to dry the user's hands. Removing the hands from the proximity of the second sensor will turn OFF the drier. Even though the device is automated there are no provisions for monitoring the handwashing activities of the user.

A hand-wash monitoring system that can be interfaced with a computer has been proposed, in which the user is provided with an identification badge and a wristband [8]. The system consists of a plurality of sensors attached to the door of a lavatory to detect user's entry and a hand-cleaning station within the lavatory, both interfaced to a computer located distantly. When the user enters the lavatory, the identification badge worn by the user will be sensed by the sensors installed on the door of the lavatory and send the information about the user's entry into the lavatory to the computer. Following this, the user approaches the hand-cleaning station that is provided with sensors to sense the wristband worn by the user. When the user's hand along with the wristband comes to close proximity to the sensor, the system will dispense soap solution and the user can wash his/her hands. When the wristband is detected by the sensor, the system will also log into the database within the computer that the user has completed the hand-wash. If the wristband is not detected by the sensor, then it implies that the user has not washed his/her hands and this information will be logged into the computer and also issues a warning signal in visual or audible form. This system monitors the handwashing activities of the users but has limitations as it does not have provisions to issue timely reminders if the warning signal issued by the system goes unnoticed by the users.

A proactive hand-hygiene monitoring system has been proposed by Huang et al. [9], which basically consists of an active radio frequency identification (RFID)-based wristband worn by the user and pre-programmed soap dispensers located next to washbasins. It also has disinfectant dispensers mounted at hallways leading to controlled access areas like intensive care units (ICU), several sensors attached to the doors of the controlled-access areas, data transfer stations, and a central computer. The preprogrammed soap dispensers can be operated by both manual and automatic means. Each soap dispenser has a unique code representing its type and location that allows it to be identified by the program residing in the central computer. When a person wearing the wristband places his/her hand under the soap dispenser, an infrared proximity sensor will be triggered to activate the motor to dispense soap. Subsequently, the RFID reader within the soap dispenser reads a string containing the unique ID code of the band as well as the time of the most recent hand-wash activity. At the same time, the wristband will receive and record the unique ID code of the soap dispenser unit along with the hand-wash date and time generated by the internal timer circuitry.

Disinfectant dispensers also operate and record hand sanitization activities in a similar manner, with the only difference of dispensing alcohol-based sanitizing solution instead of soap. The entry–exit sensors attached to the doors of the ICUs record the unique ID code of the wristband as well as the date and time of entry and exit through the door. It will also check for the last hand-wash activity of the user and prompts for hand cleaning if required. The information recorded in the wristband can be downloaded using data transfer stations and then it will be transferred to the central computer for statistical analysis. Even though the system satisfies the requirements of automation of the hand-wash process, monitoring and recording of hand-wash activities, etc., it has a few disadvantages. In this system, after dispensing the soap, the user has to touch and turn ON and OFF the tap to dispense water. Pathogens accumulated on the tap handle may transfer to the user's hands while turning ON and OFF the tap after the hand-wash. An automated touchless water dispenser can be a solution to address this issue. Moreover, the system architecture is complicated and costly to be implemented in low- and middle-income nations.

A system and method to encourage hand-hygiene compliance was proposed by Hufton et al. [10]. It consists of a smart wearable disinfectant dispenser with a zone sensor and a controller with timer and alert functionalities. The disinfectant dispenser can be clipped onto the chest pocket on the user's clothing or can be worn over the sleeve by suitable means. It can also be mounted on a harness and worn off the user's shoulder. The dispenser has two parts: a replaceable dispenser cartridge part and a smart zone sensor part enclosed inside an external housing. The dispenser cartridge is responsible for dispensing the disinfectant solution when the resilient part of the cartridge is pressed against the external housing. The cartridge can be replaced, refilled, and reused. The zone sensor consists of an IR signal detector, a dispensing pressure sensor, an audible or visible alerting device, and a microprocessor-based control circuitry with data memory. The IR signal detectors are designed to be visible externally from the enclosure so that it can detect signals transmitted from various zone transmitters installed at various locations in a hospital.

The dispensing pressure sensor is used to detect the dispensing action of the cartridge when the user presses the same. The zone sensor is also designed to work in conjunction with specially designed wall-mounted disinfectant dispensers. When the user presses the wearable dispenser, the disinfectant will be dispensed from the cartridge and, subsequently, the pressure sensor detects the depression. At this time, the zone code to identify the location within the institution where the hand sanitization activity has been performed will be fetched by the controller from the zone transmitters. The zone code and the time at which the dispenser has been pressed to sanitize the hand will be logged on to the data memory and later this information can be transferred to a central computer for further analysis. An alert is issued whenever hand sanitization is required and when the system does not detect hand sanitization activity within a predetermined time after the user has moved from one zone to the other. The system has a complicated operational architecture and, moreover, the dispenser has to be operated bare hand, which is not recommended.

10.2.1.2 Vision-Based Hand-Wash Monitoring

US Patent Number 7818083B2 describes an automated washing and compliance verification system which comprises a washbasin with a tap, sanitizer or soap dispenser, an RFID reader, a video camera focused to pick hand-wash motions, a display screen, and an administration computer [11]. When the user wearing the RFID card approaches the washbasin, the RFID reader within the washbasin will fetch the user ID information. The user proceeds to dispense water and soap by manual or electronic means and starts the hand-wash procedure. The complete hand-wash motion will be monitored and recorded with the help of the camera. Various information such as user name, hand-wash time, duration, and status will be displayed on the screen provided and also will be logged on to the database in the administration computer for further analysis. The system is only meant for hand-wash monitoring and verification and it is unclear whether it incorporates automated water and soap dispensers. Also, the user is informed about his/her previous hand-wash status through the display screen within the washbasin, only when he/she approaches for the next hand-wash procedure. A timely reminder on hand-wash status is very much necessary to ensure proper hand hygiene.

US Patent Number 9721452B2 provides insights on an apparatus for managing hand-wash compliance [12]. The apparatus positioned near a washbasin consists of an IR, video or thermal imaging system, a processing unit, a front user interface including a display, and associated wireless communication facilities. When the camera detects the hands of the user within the range of the washbasin, an application is activated and tracks the hand motion during scrubbing or hand-wash. Based on hand-wash motions, several parameters such as the total number of hand-wash scrubs, scrubbing rate, and so on are estimated and will be displayed on the front user interface. The apparatus is designed to keep a log of hand-wash activities of each user and the same will be stored in its local database or a remote database. The apparatus is only meant for tracking hand-wash motion and displaying and storing statistics of the parameters identified based on the hand-wash motion. There are no water, soap, or disinfectant dispensers associated with the apparatus and moreover there exist no sufficient means to alert the user if proper hand-wash compliance is not met.

An infection control monitoring system has been proposed by Nelson et al. [13], which is a monitoring unit fixed next to a controlled access area or a washbasin. It includes one or more tracking and recognition sensors, optional non-biometric identification devices, a display screen, a speaker, a dispenser, and a control unit. Tracking and recognition sensors can be motion detector sensors, cameras, fingerprint sensors, or microphones, whereas RFID readers, touchpads, keyboards, etc., are the non-biometric identification devices that can be used. The dispenser is designed to automatically dispense disinfectant or soap if the user's hands are detected below the sensor. Provisions to provide UV treatment to the hands for improved sanitation have also been incorporated in the device. Considering that a camera and an RFID reader are used as tracking and recognition sensor and non-biometric identification device, respectively, the user stands in front of the camera and looks at it to achieve face recognition. Later he/she will be prompted to show his/her RFID badge against the RFID reader within the device.

Upon verification of the user, the dispenser automatically dispenses a pre-measured amount of soap or disinfectant when his/her hands are shown below the sensor. After the soap is dispensed and washed with water, the hands can be subjected to an optional UV light source to complete the hand disinfection process. The hand-wash time and technique can be monitored in real time by the authorities and corrective measures can be suggested if the hand-wash time and technique are found unsatisfactory. There are provisions to record hand-wash activities to determine individual and overall compliance. The monitoring system has a complicated design with multiple sensors and, moreover, it is unclear whether the information pertaining to the hand-wash activities is logged onto a database for further analysis and processing.

10.2.2   HAND-WASH SYSTEMS IN RESEARCH ARTICLES

Moving from various inventions as claimed in the patent documents to research articles, a variety of hand-wash monitoring systems have been developed and a few of them are discussed here. These systems are again categorized into two for better understanding.

10.2.2.1   Multi-Sensor and/or IoT-Based Systems

Harmony is a hand-hygiene reminder and monitoring system developed around a smartwatch embedded with sensors that can detect various hand gestures [14]. The design of the device is done in such a manner that it will be able to distinguish between hand-wash gestures and other hand gestures with an accuracy of 88%. Harmony comprises a smartwatch, Bluetooth beacons, liquid dispensers with Bluetooth communication facility, Bluetooth relays, and servers. Relays enable the smartwatch to communicate with servers and Bluetooth beacons are used to determine various zones within a healthcare institution. When a user wearing the watch washes his/her hands, the hand motion will be sensed by the sensors within the watch and an application records the hand-wash time, duration, and quality temporarily. Whenever the watch discovers a Bluetooth relay, it transfers this information to the server. Also, whenever the user moves from one zone to another, the watch detects the change in the zone with the help of Bluetooth technology and checks for his/her recent hand-wash activity. If his/her hands are not washed, it alerts the user through vibration, beeps, or a combination of both along with displaying a message on the screen.

Several IoT and/or RFID-based hand-hygiene monitoring and compliance systems have evolved over years and three recently reported systems are discussed here. One such system has been developed which comprises four functional units, namely, handwashing stations, prompting stations, door badge entry stations, and a central computer [15]. The handwashing station is basically a soap dispenser designed to operate closely with an RFID reader and a wireless data communication means. The door badge entry station detects the entry and exit of healthcare personnel to a controlled access area and it employs an RFID reader and a wireless data communication means to achieve its functionality. The personnel entering the controlled access area will be prompted visually to wash his/her hands by the prompting station installed in the area which communicates with the central computer using a wireless transceiver.

When the healthcare personnel washes his/her hands, the RFID reader picks up the user ID and the timestamp which will then be logged into the central computer's database. After washing the hands, if he/she enters the controlled access area, the RFID reader associated with the door badge entry station detects the entry, issues a *clean* status and no visual prompting is generated. If the healthcare personnel has not washed his/her hands before entering the controlled access area, the user entry will be detected, *unclean* status will be issued, and a visual prompting will be generated in the prompting station. He/she shall then clean his/her hands at a washbasin provided inside the controlled access area before attending the patient. The complete user activities will be logged into the database for further statistical analysis.

Bal et al. [16] had reported an IoT-based smart hygiene monitoring system that comprises a soap dispenser node and a faucet node. The dispenser node includes an automated soap dispenser employing an IR sensor for user's hand detection, an

RFID reader, and a transceiver based on ZigBee protocol. The faucet node, on the other hand, comprises an automated touchless faucet, a ZigBee transceiver, a Wi-Fi module, and a display screen. When the user shows his/her hands against the IR sensor within the soap dispenser, it dispenses a predetermined amount of soap solution and at the same time records the soap dispensing activity duration. Subsequently, the RFID reader reads the user information embedded in the RFID tag worn by the user and the control module of the dispenser node generates a data packet containing the user ID and date and time of dispensing activity. This data packet will then be transmitted to the faucet node using the ZigBee transceiver.

The faucet node receives the data packet from the dispenser node and replies with an acknowledgment message. The user now shows his/her hands under the faucet which will be detected by an IR sensor within the faucet unit and it will in turn trigger a solenoid valve to dispense water. The control unit of the faucet node records the duration of water dispensing. The user information along with the total hand-wash duration will be displayed on the screen provided and also will be updated in the cloud database for further analysis. Sagar et al. [17] have offered another practically viable RFID-based system for hand-hygiene compliance and monitoring. The system tracks and logs the hand-hygiene practices of the healthcare personnel and thus collected data can be downloaded as an Excel file for analysis.

An IoT-based hand-hygiene compliance system has been developed which employs Electronic Stability Program (ESP) modules and Bluetooth Low Energy (BLE) beacons to track the spatial position of healthcare personnel in a patient room [18]. In this system Bluetooth-enabled mobile phones act as BLE beacons. It is assumed that there will be at least one hand-wash station inside every patient room or ward. ESP nodes are placed inside the room or ward at three distinct locations. When a healthcare personnel carrying a mobile phone is identified by any one of the ESP nodes, it sends the identified device's address, the Received Signal Strength Indicator (RSSI) value, and ESP node's ID to the server. With the RSSI value, it can be determined to which ESP node the mobile phone is closer to. Using this location information, the number of times the healthcare personnel approaches the hand-wash station and patient beds can be determined and in this way hand-hygiene monitoring and surveillance can be achieved.

10.2.2.2 Vision-Based Hand-Wash Monitoring Systems Using Machine Learning

Llorca et al. [19] had developed a computer vision-based hand-wash quality measurement system that can be implemented in health care institutions and food processing industries. The system has a camera placed over the washtub collecting visual information on the handwashing activity. Whenever a user washes his/her hands, the system will acquire hand motion and for further processing, frames are grabbed at a rate of 20 per second. These frames are then pre-processed using segmentation techniques, k-means clustering, and particle filtering methods for the extraction of appearance and motion descriptor which will be provided to the Support Vector Machine (SVM) classifier to ensure the handwashing quality.

Another hand-hygiene compliance monitoring system employing deep learning techniques has been proposed by Camilus et al. [20]. The system which employs RFID technology and depth sensor such as Intel RealSense camera along with a deep learning algorithm which is a combination of RGB pre-training and depth re-training has resulted in an accuracy of 96.8%. RFID reader fetches user information from the RFID cards and the depth sensor captures the hand-wash motions. The user details, hand-wash duration, and status are updated to a cloud-based server. Both successful and failed hand-wash events will be alerted to the user by audio or visual means at the end of hand-wash.

10.2.3   OFF-THE-SHELF HAND-HYGIENE MONITORING SYSTEMS

An iPhone mobile application named iScrub has been developed based on Apple's Cocoa framework for monitoring and recording hand-wash activities of healthcare personnel [21]. The application allows easy management of data by reducing the processes and expenses associated with data logging and entry operations. It also has a web application with provisions to store, track, and view data once it is synchronized with the mobile application [22].

MedSense is an electronic hand sanitization compliance and monitoring system which consists of beacons placed next to patient beds, proximity sensor-embedded soap or sanitizer dispensers with data transfer capabilities and base stations wirelessly connected to a server [23, 24]. Every healthcare personnel is provided with an electronic badge and when he/she dispenses soap or sanitizer from the dispenser, the badge will record that he/she has sanitized his/her hands. When this healthcare personnel enters into the proximity of the beacon, the system understands that he/she is near the patient bed as the badge communicates with the beacon. The beacon will also sense whether he/she has sanitized his/her hands before approaching the patient. If the system detects a positive record from the badge, the hand-wash status is considered to be successful and if an unsuccessful record is detected, then an alert is issued to the badge of the concerned healthcare personnel. The successful and unsuccessful events are recorded in the database.

A comparison of all the systems mentioned in the previous sub-sections along with their limitations is presented in Table 10.1. It can be observed from Table 10.1 that most of the systems covered in the literature are merely hand-hygiene monitoring systems and only a very few systems ensure touchless dispensing of water or soap solution along with hand-hygiene monitoring. None of the systems discussed have an efficient and reliable real-time prompting strategy if hand-hygiene compliance is not met. Several researchers have reported that in low- and middle-income nations, the risk of HAI is 2 to 20 times higher than in high-income nations [25, 26, 27]. Moreover, controlling the transmission of HAI in low- and middle-income nations is very important as the general population in these nations may not have economic resources or awareness to receive appropriate timely medication [28, 29, 30]. There exist no affordable and smart strategies to monitor hand-hygiene compliance in healthcare institutions in these nations. Hence, developing a simple, cost-effective hand-hygiene monitoring and compliance system with an added feature of temperature monitoring which will overcome the limitations of existing systems is the need of the hour.

TABLE 10.1

Comparison of Hand-Wash Monitoring Systems

Sl. No.	System	Functionality	Sensors Used	Limitations
1	Cole and Mitre [7]	• Automated water and soap dispensing along with hot air blowing for drying	• Two IR sensors – one for detecting user's hands to dispense soap and the other again for detecting hands and dispensing water	• No monitoring of hand-wash activities
2	Verdiramo [8]	• Monitoring user's entry into the lavatory • Detecting user's hands to dispense soap • Logs the status of hand wash to the database and issues warning signal within the system for failed hand wash status	• RFID-type sensors to detect user's badge to determine the user's entry into the lavatory • Another RFID-type sensor to detect wristband worn by the user to dispense soap	• No touchless dispensing of water • No real-time prompting/ reminders if the user misses the warning signal issued by the system • Sensing just the user's entry and dispensing of soap is not a reliable method to monitor hand-wash compliance.
3	Huang et al. [9]	• Detects user's hands to dispense soap/ disinfectant • Monitors entry and exit to and from controlled access areas • Records hand wash activities of the user and prompt for hand sanitation, if required	• IR sensor and RFID reader in dispensers for detecting hands and for collecting user information, respectively • RFID readers indoors of controlled access areas to detect user's entry and to collect user information	• No touchless dispensing of water • No real-time prompting/ reminders if the user misses the warning signal issued by the system • Complicated system architecture • Unaffordable to be implemented in poor or developing countries

(continued)

TABLE 10.1 (Continued)
Comparison of Hand-Wash Monitoring Systems

Sl. No.	System	Functionality	Sensors Used	Limitations
4	Hufton et al. [10]	• Detects the dispensing of disinfectant and the zone/location at which the event occurred • The zone code and the time at which the event occurred will be first stored in the data memory and later will be transferred to a central computer • Issues an alert whenever hand sanitizing is required	• Pressure sensor to detect the pressing of the dispenser cartridge for dispensing disinfectant. • IR signal detectors to detect signals from zone transmitters	• No touchless dispensing of disinfectant. • Complicated design and operational architecture
5	Glenn and Swartz [11]	• Monitors the hand wash motion using a video camera. • User information, time of hand wash, hand wash duration, and hand wash status will be displayed on the screen • All this information will be logged on to the database	• RFID reader to fetch user information • Video camera for monitoring and recording the hand wash motion	• Unclear whether it incorporates touchless water and soap dispensers • No timely reminder on hand-wash status
6	Felch et al. [12]	• Tracking of hand motions during hand wash • Information such as the total number of scrubs, scrubs per minute, and so on will be displayed in the screen. • The same information will be stored in a database	• An IR, video, or thermal imaging system for hand detection and tracking motions	• Only meant for tracking hand-wash motion and displaying and storing information • No sufficient real-time prompting if hand-wash compliance is not met

TABLE 10.1 (Continued)
Comparison of Hand-Wash Monitoring Systems

Sl. No.	System	Functionality	Sensors Used	Limitations
7	Nelson et al. [13]	• Soap or disinfectant will be dispensed after face recognition and user verification • Hand wash duration and motions are monitored in real time and recorded. • Corrective measures are suggested if necessary	• Tracking and recognition sensor such as a camera • Non-biometric identification devices such as RFID • A proximity sensor to detect hands to dispense soap	• No touchless dispensing of water • Complicated design • Unclear whether the information pertaining to the hand-wash activities are logged on to a database for further analysis
8	Harmony [14]	• Senses hand wash motion using sensors embedded within a smartwatch • Records the time, duration and quality of hand wash activity and stores in the watch • Transfers this information to a server • Detects change in zone when the user moves from one zone to another • Checks for hand wash status and alerts if necessary	• Various sensors within a smartphone for hand wash motion tracking • Bluetooth beacons to determine zones	• Only meant for tracking hand-wash motion, displaying and storing information and alerting if hand-hygiene compliance is not met • No touchless dispensing of water/soap/disinfectant
9	Jain et al. [15]	• Fetches user information while performing hand wash • Logs the user information along with the time of hand wash to the database • Detects the user's entry into the patient ward.	• RFID reader in soap dispenser to fetch user information during hand wash	• Only meant for detecting hand hygiene status, logging the information to the database, and alerting if hand-hygiene compliance is not met

(continued)

TABLE 10.1 (Continued)
Comparison of Hand-Wash Monitoring Systems

Sl. No.	System	Functionality	Sensors Used	Limitations
		• Issues an alert to wash hands if the hand wash status is *unclean.* • All user activities are logged to a database	• RFID reader to detect entry of user into the ward	• No touchless dispensing of water/soap/disinfectant • No real-time prompting/reminders if the user misses the alert issued by the system
10	Bal and Abrishambaf [16]	• User's hands are detected to dispense soap and water automatically • Fetches user information, notes down the soap dispensing time and hand wash duration time • Displays this information on the screen provided and uploads it to the database	• IR sensors to detect the hands of the user to dispense soap and water • RFID reader to fetch user information	• No sufficient real-time prompting if hand-wash compliance is not met
11	Karimpour et al. [18]	• Monitors the location of the user using RSSI of the Bluetooth device he/she is carrying to determine the number of times he/she has approached the wash area and patient beds	• BLE beacons carried by the user • ESP nodes affixed at various locations in a patient ward	• Determining the number of times the user approaching a hand-wash area is not a reliable method to ensure hand sanitation. • No sufficient real-time prompting if hand-wash compliance is not met
12	Llorca et al. [19]	• Tracking hand wash motion to ensure hand wash quality	• Video camera to track hand wash motion	• Only meant for tracking hand-wash motion • No touchless dispensing of water/soap/disinfectant

TABLE 10.1 (Continued)
Comparison of Hand-Wash Monitoring Systems

Sl. No.	System	Functionality	Sensors Used	Limitations
13	Camilus et al. [20]	• Fetches user information and tracks hand wash motion to ensure hand wash quality • Updates user information, hand wash duration, and status to a cloud database • Alerts issued after the hand wash	• RFID reader to fetch user information • Depth camera for tracking hand-wash motion	• Only meant for tracking hand-wash motion, logging information to the database and alerting the user after hand wash • No touchless dispensing of water/ soap/disinfectant • No real-time prompting/ reminders if the user misses the alert issued by the system after hand wash
14	iScrub [21, 22]	• Monitoring and recording hand-wash activities • Easy data logging and management	• Various sensors in iPhone/iPad	• Only meant for tracking hand-wash motion and displaying and storing information • No touchless dispensing of water/ soap/disinfectant
15	MedSense [23, 24]	• A badge records hand sanitization activity when the user dispenses soap or disinfectant from the dispenser • Badge communicates with a beacon when the user comes near a patient • Checks whether hands are sanitized or not • Information is updated to a database • Issues a visual alert in the badge if not sanitized	• Proximity sensors in the dispenser to detect the proximity of the reader to it and thereby recording hand sanitization activity • Beacons near patient beds to check the proximity of the user with the patient	• Only meant for detecting hand hygiene status, logging the information to the database, and alerting if hand-hygiene compliance is not met • No touchless dispensing of water/ soap/disinfectant • Detecting hand sanitizing activity by merely sensing the proximity of the user to the dispenser is not a reliable method

As the world is going through a severe health crisis, any technological intervention, simple or complicated, can come in handy to support healthcare professionals in their fight against COVID-19. This chapter emphasized on the development of a simple smart hand-hygiene compliance monitoring system that will help healthcare professionals to ensure that their hands are sanitized properly and, on the other hand, helps the administration to monitor the handwashing activity of the healthcare personnel. The system also helps in monitoring the body temperature of the healthcare personnel and this will allow the hospital administration to take swift steps to keep the identified staff with higher body temperature in quarantine and subsequent observation. The complete system is also intended to be a cost-effective solution, aimed to be implemented in low- and middle-income nations.

10.3 RELATION BETWEEN HAND HYGIENE AND HAI – A PILOT STUDY

Before the development of the system, a pilot study on the role of hand-hygiene and infections acquired from the healthcare institution was performed. For this study, *Staphylococcus aureus* bacterial infection in hospitals was considered for analysis. The bacteria spreads through touching the infected person and inhaling droplets from the infected person which is similar to COVID-19. It is a major pathogen that causes a fatality rate of approximately 50%, which increases further without proper medication [31].

For this study, data related to the healthcare-associated *S. aureus* bacterial infection of the bloodstream from the Australian Institute of Health and Welfare were utilized for analyzing the relationship between hand-hygiene and infection (www.aihw.gov.au/reports-data/myhospitals/content/data-downloads). The data includes the hand-hygiene compliance rate, the number of people infected, patient days under surveillance, rate per 10,000 patient days, and peer group average for each year from 2011 to 2014. Data from 42 hospitals whose patient days were greater than 20,000 under surveillance were considered for the analysis. A linear regression model was used to analyze the relationship between hand-hygiene and HAI. Figure 10.1 shows the fitted curve along with the data and confidence bounds for the regression model.

The model resulted in the R^2 value of 0.934, which shows a strong correlation between hand-hygiene and *S. aureus* bacterial infection. It reported a root mean square error of 3.26. The p-value of the slope-intercept was 0.053, which states that it is statistically significant at the level of 0.1. It indicated a significant relationship between hand-hygiene compliance rate and the infection. Hence, this pilot study revealed the importance of hand-hygiene to prevent HAI.

10.4 CONCEPTUAL DESIGN OF THE SYSTEM

The conceptual block diagram of the smart hygiene compliance system is shown in Figure 10.2. It consists of four major units connected to the server, namely, (a) hand-wash unit, (b) temperature sensing unit, (c) patient side monitoring unit, and (d) administrative management and messaging unit.

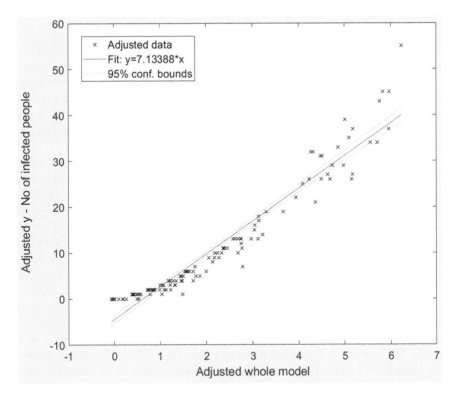

FIGURE 10.1 Scattered plot of the data with the fitted curve and confidence bound.

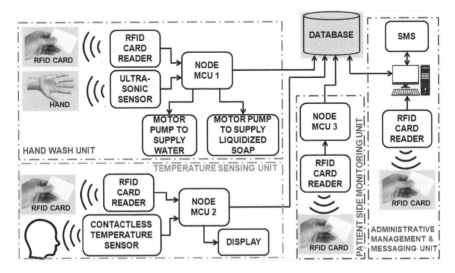

FIGURE 10.2 Conceptual block diagram of the hand-hygiene compliance monitoring system.

10.4.1 HAND-WASH UNIT

The hand-wash unit shall be installed at washbasins in staff washrooms, doctor's office/consultation rooms, operation theaters (OT), and handwashing areas in nursing staff rooms associated with each ward in a healthcare institution. The hand-wash unit includes an RFID reader, an ultrasonic sensor for hand proximity detection, a NodeMCU unit for overall control of the unit and for possible communication with the server and finally two motor pumps, one for supplying water and the other for supplying liquidized soap.

Each healthcare personnel will be provided with an RFID card having unique identification (ID) codes. As the personnel approaches the system after performing the previously mentioned activities or before and after attending a patient, the RFID reader detects his/her presence when he/she enters its range. An active or a passive RFID card/tag can be used for this. In this project, a passive RFID card is used and hence the user needs to subject the card to the close proximity of the reader. Later, he/she should place his/her hands under the tap, which will be detected by the ultrasonic sensor and turn ON the motor pump to supply water through the tap for 10 seconds. The user can rinse his/her hands with the water provided through the tap and after 10 seconds, the motor pump supplying the water will be turned OFF and the pump supplying soap will be turned ON to dispense a sufficient amount of liquidized soap through the tap. The user shall now rub his/her hands with the dispensed soap as per the WHO protocol. Subsequently, after a time delay of 20–25 seconds, the user can place his/her hands below the tap for the ultrasonic sensor to detect the same. This in turn will switch ON the motor to dispense water and wash off the lather to ensure proper and complete hand-wash. The details of the hand-wash activity of each staff member such as unique ID code, hand-wash time, and hand-wash duration are updated to the database. The complete functional flow diagram of the hand-wash unit is depicted in Figure 10.3.

10.4.2 TEMPERATURE SENSING UNIT

The temperature sensing unit shall be preferably installed at the main entrance of the healthcare institutions, doctor's office/consultation rooms, and nursing staff rooms associated with each ward. It comprises an RFID reader and a contactless temperature sensor interfaced to a NodeMCU module which in turn communicates with the server. The contactless temperature sensor can be fixed in such a way that temperature reading of the forehead of the staff can be obtained. The reading shall be obtained preferably twice a day: at morning while reporting to duty or during sign-off after the duty. First, the staff shall present his/her RFID card to the proximity of the RFID reader and, as a result, the employee ID of the staff will be displayed in the display provided. Subsequently, he/she shall stand facing the temperature sensor for it to sense the forehead/body temperature and the same will also be displayed on the screen. The details like unique ID code, temperature sensing time, and the body temperature of the staff will be updated to the database. If the temperature of a particular healthcare personnel is above the average normal temperature of 98.6°F, then the same will be alerted to the administration so that the staff can be quarantined

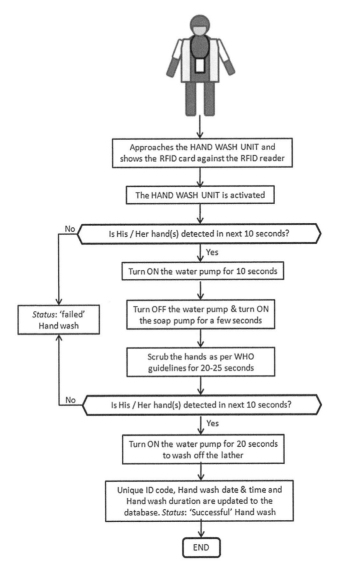

FIGURE 10.3   Functional flow diagram of hand-wash unit.

and observed. The concerned staff will also receive a message on this regard in his/ her mobile phone number, registered with the institution. Figure 10.4 illustrates the functional flow diagram of the temperature sensing unit.

10.4.3   PATIENT SIDE MONITORING UNIT

Patient side monitoring unit shall be installed near every patient bed within the healthcare institution. Before and after attending a patient, the healthcare

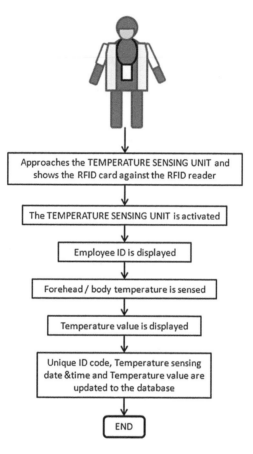

FIGURE 10.4 Functional flow diagram of temperature sensing unit.

personnel should present his/her RFID card to the proximity of the RFID reader in the patent-side monitoring unit. The NodeMCU in the unit will send the staff details with specific date and time of starting and ending of attending the patient to the database. After a preset duration post-attending the patient, if the system did not detect that particular staff washing his/her hands using the hand-wash unit, the same will be alerted through a message to his/her mobile phone. As the patient side monitoring unit operates in close conjunction with the hand-wash unit, the functional flow diagram will have elements of both the units as depicted in Figure 10.5.

10.4.4 ADMINISTRATIVE MANAGEMENT AND MESSAGING UNIT

The main purpose of the administrative management and messaging unit is to track and manage the healthcare and handwashing activities of the healthcare personnel registered in the system. This unit resides in an administrative office and is also used

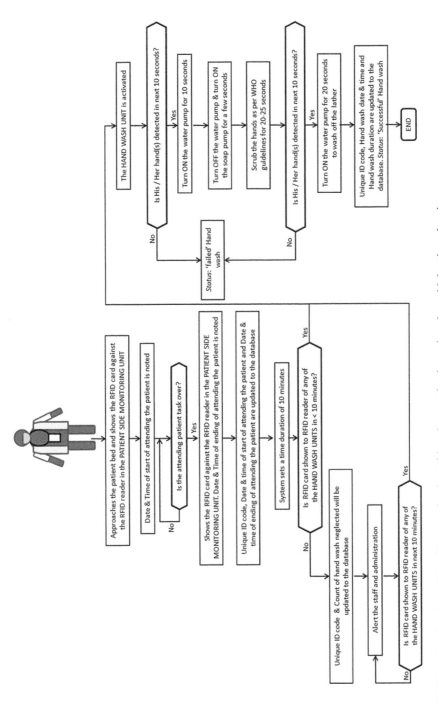

FIGURE 10.5   Functional flow diagram of patient-side unit operating in conjunction with hand-wash unit.

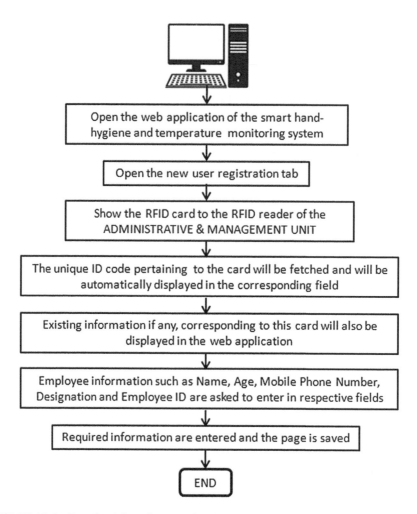

FIGURE 10.6 Functional flow diagram of registering a new user into the system.

for registering healthcare personnel with new RFID tags. Reminders and alerts for each staff are sent to their respective mobile phones as messages from this unit. Figure 10.6 shows the functional flow diagram of registering a new user into the system using administrative management and messaging units.

Adding to this, depending on the category of the healthcare personnel (e.g., a doctor or a nurse attending a patient in ICU or OT), an automatic alcohol-based sanitizer/hand rub dispensing unit can also be included in the system that can be installed in selected locations. This will help in optimized use of sanitizers and other handwash solutions, as a shortage in supply of these has been experienced in several countries during the COVID period.

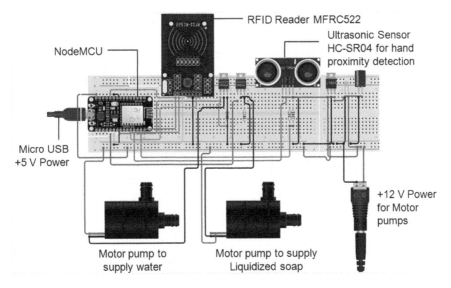

NodeMCU

RFID Reader MFRC522

Ultrasonic Sensor
HC-SR04 for hand
proximity detection

Micro USB
+5 V Power

+12 V Power
for Motor
pumps

Motor pump to
supply water

Motor pump to supply
Liquidized soap

FIGURE 10.7   Circuit diagram of hand wash unit.

10.5   DETAILED DESIGN OF SYSTEM

As mentioned in the previous section, the device is designed to have four dependent functional units. The first unit is the hand-wash unit which captures the unique ID code provided to the user from his/her RFID, detects the proximity of the user's hands using an ultrasonic sensor and operates motor pumps for water and liquidized soap dispensing in a sequence. The circuit diagram of the hand-wash unit is illustrated in Figure 10.7. The unit consists of an ESP8266 NodeMCU for controlling the unit and for communicating with the server using the HTTP protocol, an MFRC522-based RFID reader, an HC-SR04 ultrasonic sensor, and two 12 V motor pumps for water and liquidized soap dispensing. The +5 V required to power the NodeMCU is provided through the Micro USB port and a separate +12 V power source is provided to the circuit to operate the motor pumps.

When an RFID card or tag is subjected to the proximity of the reader, the NodeMCU receives the 16 bit unique ID code from the reader. Each unit is assigned a single character unit-type ID number. For example, for the hand-wash unit, the unit-type ID number assigned is 1. Thus, the obtained unique ID code and unit-type ID number will be written to the server using HTTP write operation. At the server, the unique ID code along with date and time of starting hand-wash, date and time of ending hand-wash, and hand-wash duration are written to the Structured Query Language(SQL) table pertaining to hand-wash tracking. The unit-type ID points to the SQL table to which the information should be entered. In this case, unit-type ID number 1 points to the hand-wash tracking table. The structure of the hand-wash tracking table is shown in Figure 10.8(a).

Figure 10.9 shows the circuit diagram of the temperature sensing unit which consists of an ESP8266 NodeMCU, an MFRC522 RFID reader, an MLX90614 IR

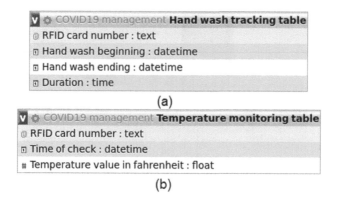

(a)

(b)

FIGURE 10.8   Structure of (a) hand wash tracking table and (b) temperature monitoring table.

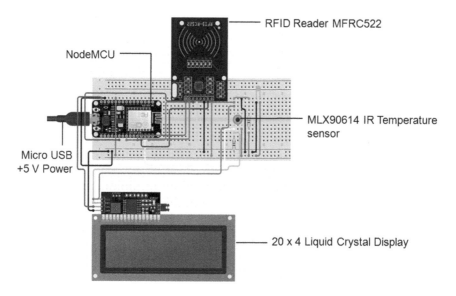

FIGURE 10.9   Circuit diagram of temperature sensing unit.

temperature sensor, and a 20x4 Liquid Crystal Display (LCD). During operation, the 16-bit unique ID code of the health personnel and unit-type ID number (e.g., 2 in this case) are processed the similar way in the server as mentioned previously. Based on the unit-ID type, that is, 2, information such as unique ID code, temperature check time, and temperature value in Fahrenheit will be written to the temperature monitoring SQL table depicted in Figure 10.8(b).

The construction of the patient-side monitoring unit and the administration and messaging unit is relatively simple. The circuit diagram of the patient-side monitoring unit is shown in Figure 10.10 and it consists of an ESP8266 NodeMCU and MFRC522 RFID reader. The power for the operation of the unit is provided through the micro USB port.

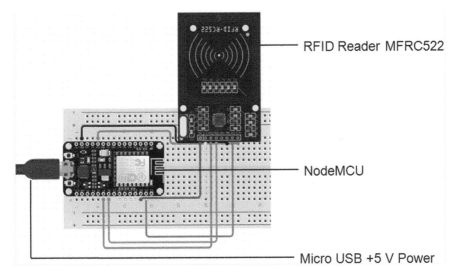

FIGURE 10.10   Circuit diagram of patient-side monitoring unit.

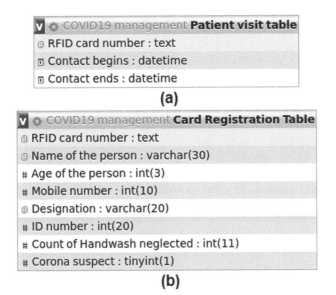

FIGURE 10.11   Structure of (a) patient visit table and (b) card registration table.

Figure 10.11(a) depicts the structure of the patient visit SQL table to which the information pertaining to the patient-side monitoring unit is entered as per the unit-type ID number returned. In this case, for the unit-type ID number 3, information such as unique ID code, date and time of the start of patient care, and date and time of the end of patient care are written to the patient visit SQL table.

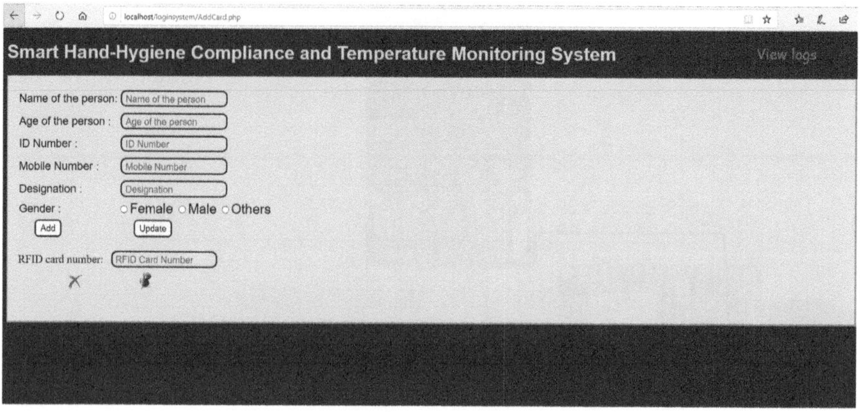

FIGURE 10.12   New user registration page in the website created.

The circuit diagram of the administration and messaging unit is similar to the patient-side monitoring unit, with the only difference that the former is connected to a computer via a micro USB port. This unit is meant for registering a new user and also for monitoring and controlling the activities of the entire system. If any failure in compliance with hand hygiene or high temperature is detected, it is from this unit that an alert message is sent to the concerned health personnel's mobile phone via a short message service (SMS) A web application-based SMS service can be used for this purpose.

Figure 10.11(b) shows the card registration SQL table pertaining to the administration and messaging unit with unit-type ID number 4 . For registering a new user, first the RFID reader reads the 16-bit unique ID code and various information of the health personnel such as name, age, designation, employee ID, and mobile phone number. This information will be written to the card registration table. This table also fetches and enters the count of hand-wash neglected by a particular employee, during a predetermined duration. In addition to this, if the temperature of an employee is above 98.6°F, this information is also fetched from the database and entered into this table.

A website has been constructed and hosted using Apache and MySQL services in XAMPP server software. The complete handwashing activity and body temperature status of each staff member in a healthcare institution can be monitored by the concerned authorities through this website. Date- wise staff log can be downloaded from the website in .csv format. The page for registering a new user in the website is shown in Figure 10.12.

10.6   CONCLUSION

Healthcare personnel are forefront warriors in this war against COVID-19. Any technological interventions, simple or complex, can be of great help for these warriors. Considering this fact, development of a smart hand-hygiene compliance and temperature monitoring system is described in this chapter. Prior to the development, a brief literature review has been conducted covering a few hand-wash systems available in patent documents, research articles, and a couple of off-the-shelf technologies. It was found that the existing systems have several limitations. A pilot study was also performed using a linear regression model to substantiate the correlation between hand hygiene and HAI and a significant relationship between hand-hygiene compliance rate and the infection was indicated. The system proposed is a humble yet powerful contribution as an arm in the current war against pathogens similar to COVID-19. The device is cost-effective and hence can be implemented in healthcare institutions in low- and middle-income nations.

REFERENCES

1. Shereen, M. A., Khan, S., Kazmi, A., Bashir, N., Siddique, R., COVID-19 infection: Emergence, transmission, and characteristics of human coronaviruses. *Journal of Advanced Research*, 24, 91–98, 2020.
2. WHO Coronavirus (COVID-19) Dashboard, who.sprinklr.com, 2021. [Online]. Available: https://who.sprinklr.com/. [Accessed: 04 August 2023]
3. Water, sanitation, hygiene, and waste management for SARS-CoV-2, the virus that causes COVID-19, who.int, 2021. [Online]. Available: www.who.int/publications/i/item/water-sanitation-hygiene-and-waste-management-for-the-covid-19-virus-interim-guidance. [Accessed: 28 Oct 2021]
4. Onyedibe, K. I., Shehu, N. Y., Pires, D., Isa, S. E., Assessment of hand hygiene facilities and staff compliance in a large tertiary health care facility in northern Nigeria: A cross sectional study. *Antimicrobial Resistance & Infection Control*, 9(30), 2020.
5. Infection prevention and control during health care when novel coronavirus (nCoV) infection is suspected, who.int, 2021. [Online]. Available: www.who.int/publications/i/item/10665-331495. [Accessed: 28 Oct 2021]
6. WHO guidelines on hand hygiene in health care, who.int, 2021. [Online]. Available: www.who.int/publications/i/item/9789241597906. [Accessed: 28 Oct 2021]
7. Cole, C., Mitre, C., Hand wash station, US Patent No. 5199118, 1993.
8. Verdiramo, C., Hand wash monitoring system and Method, US Patent No. 7443305B, 2008.
9. Huang, C., Peng, J., Hwang, F., Proactive hand-hygiene monitoring system, US Patent No. 20090195385A1, 2009.
10. Hufton, G., Levchenko, O., Fernie, G., Hand hygiene compliance system, US Patent No. 7898407B, 2011.
11. Glenn, J., Swartz, D., Automated washing system with compliance verification and automated compliance monitoring reporting, US Patent No. 7818083B, 2010.
12. Felch, A., Boyd, M., Bessire, J., Movitz, A., Dahlberg, C., Hand-wash management and compliance system, US Patent No. 9721452B, 2017.
13. Nelson, W., Nelson, R., Nickele, G., Infection control monitoring system, US Patent No. 10482753B, 2019.
14. Mondol, M., Stankovic, J., Harmony: A hand wash monitoring and reminder system using smart watches. *Proceedings of the 12th EAI International Conference on Mobile and Ubiquitous Systems: Computing, Networking and Services*, 2015.

15. Jain, S., Mane, S., Lopez, J., Lie, D. Y. C., A low-cost custom HF RFID system for hand washing compliance monitoring. *Proceedings of the 2009 IEEE 8th International Conference on ASIC*, 2009.

16. Bal, M., Abrishambaf, R., A system for monitoring hand hygiene compliance based-on Internet-of-Things. *Proceedings of the 2017 IEEE International Conference on Industrial Technology (ICIT)*, 2017.

17. Sagar, P. S., Krishnan, R. H., RFID based smart hand hygiene monitoring system for health care institutions. *Proceedings of the 2020 International Conference on System, Computation, Automation and Networking (ICSCAN)*, 2020.

18. Karimpour, N., Karaduman, B., Ural, A., Challenger, M., IoT based hand hygiene compliance monitoring. *Proceedings of the 2019 International Symposium on Networks, Computers and Communications (ISNCC)*, 2019.

19. Llorca, D. F., Parra, I., Sotelo, M. A., Lacey, G., A vision-based system for automatic hand washing quality assessment. *Machine Vision and Applications*, 22(2), 219–234, 2009.

20. Camilus, S., Lee, Y., Automated hand hygiene compliance monitoring. *Proceedings of the 2020 2nd International Conference on Image, Video and Signal Processing*, 2020.

21. Hlady, C. S., Severson, M. A., Segre, A. M., Polgreen P. M., A mobile handheld computing application for recording hand hygiene observations. *Infection Control & Hospital Epidemiology*, 31(9), 975–977, 2010.

22. Hlady, C. S., Fries, J. A., Curtis, D. E., Segre, A. M., iScrub online: A system for standardized hand-hygiene observation and feedback. In *Proceedings of the Fifth Decennial International Conference on Health-Care Related Infections*, 2010.

23. Cheng, V. C., Tai, J. W., Ho, S. K., Chan, J. F., Introduction of an electronic monitoring system for monitoring compliance with Moments 1 and 4 of the WHO "My 5 Moments for Hand Hygiene" methodology. *BMC Infectious Diseases*, 11(1), 2011.

24. Al Salman, J., Hani, S., Marcellis-Warin, N., Isa, F., Effectiveness of an electronic hand hygiene monitoring system on healthcare workers' compliance to guidelines. *Journal of Infection and Public Health*, 8(2), 117–126, 2015.

25. Phan, H. T., Tran H. T. T., Tran, H. T. M., Dinh, A. P. P., An educational intervention to improve hand hygiene compliance in Vietnam. *BMC Infectious Diseases*, 18(1), 2018.

26. Matar, M. J., Moghnieh, R. A., Awad, L, S., Kanj, S. S., Effective strategies for improving hand hygiene in developing countries, *Current Treatment Options in Infectious Diseases*, 10(2), 310–329, 2018.

27. Loftus, M. J., Guitart, C., Tartari, E., Stewardson, A. J., Hand hygiene in low–and middle-income countries. *International Journal of Infectious Diseases*, 86, 25–30, 2019.

28. Maiti, R., Bhatia, V., Padhy, B. M., Hota, D., Essential medicines: An Indian perspective. *Indian Journal of Community Medicine*, 40(4), 223–232, 2015.

29. Grover, A., Citro, B., India: Access to affordable drugs and the right to health. *The Lancet*, 377(9770), 976–977, 2011.

30. Krishnan, R., A brief review on lavatory cleaning devices and their feasibility in public toilets in developing countries. *International Journal of Intelligent Robotics and Applications*, 4(3), 354–369, 2020.

31. Tong, S. Y. C., Davis, J. S., Eichenberger, E., Holland, T. L., *Staphylococcus aureus* infections: Epidemiology, pathophysiology, clinical manifestations, and management. *Clinical Microbiology Reviews*, 28(3), 603–661, 2015.

11 LDS–LVAT
Lie Detection System– Layered Voice Technology

Veena K.,[1] Meena K.,[2] D. Rajalakshmi,[3] Fathima M.,[4] and Thamarai Selvi K.[5]*
[1]Department of Computer Science and Engineering, Sathyabama Institute of Science and Technology, Chennai, India
[2]Department of Computer Science and Engineering, GITAM University, Bengaluru, India
[3]Department of Computer Science and Engineering, Sri Sairam Institute of Technology, Chennai, India
[4] Department of Computer Science and Business Systems, Sri Krishna College of Engineering and Technology, Coimbatore, Tamil Nadu, India
[5]SRM Medical College Hospital and Research Centre (SRMMCH&RC), Kattankulathur, India
*Corresponding Author: Veena K (Email: veenakanagaraj07@gmail.com)

11.1 INTRODUCTION

Cybercrime is the use of a computer to facilitate illicit activities such as identity theft, child pornography trafficking, and privacy invasion. Cybercrime is divided into three categories:

- Violent Crimes against People: These violations incorporate digital following and provocation, the transmission of child erotic entertainment, financial frauds, illegal exploitation, mocking, and online defamation or criticism.
- Theft of Personal Property.
- Governmental Offenses.

Occasions of cybercrime incorporate getting to a personal computer (PC) without the proprietor's consent, surpassing the degree of one's approval to get to a data framework, adjusting or erasing PC information, and using PC time and assets without suitable assent. In order to achieve one's political or ideological goals, cyberterrorism means engaging in similar activities. Terrorist oppressor exercises on the Internet could be executed by people or terrorist groups, and also by states against one another. As a result, cyberterrorism blends in with other types

DOI: 10.1201/9781003405450-11

of terrorism. Denying service, sabotage, fraud, eavesdropping, intellectual property theft, and private information are all examples of potential threats. This chapter intends to give a wide outline of the world's concerns with cybercrime, as well as the issues addressed by law enforcement agencies and information and communication technology innovation security experts in cyber investigations, and also the advantages that the global local area, and specifically, public–private partnerships, can bring to cybercrime counteraction, detection, and arraignment, as well as how underdeveloped nations should remain aware of the implications of cybercrime [1].

11.1.1 CYBERCRIME TOOLS

Digital forensic tools are available in a variety of configurations.

11.1.1.1 Kali Linux

A Linux-based operating system Kali is used for penetration testing. Kali.org has just released an upgrade to its software that includes numerous new capabilities. There are a lot of tools included with Kali Linux that may be used to carry out a wide range of activities.

11.1.1.2 Oph Crack

This program is mostly used to crack hashes that are generated by the same Windows files that are used to generate them. With a secure user interface and the ability to work across several platforms, it is an excellent choice.

11.1.1.3 EnCase

For the most part, this program is used to decode hashes created using the same Windows files that were used to generate them. It includes a secure graphical user interface and may be used on a variety of different computers and devices.

11.1.1.4 SafeBack

SafeBack is used to image Intel-based computer hard drives and restore them to other hard drives.

11.1.1.5 Data Dumper

It's a forensic command-line tool. It's a free UNIX application that allows you to produce exact disc copies for digital forensics.

11.1.1.6 Md5sum

This is a check tool that helps you determine if data has been correctly duplicated.

11.1.2 NECESSITY OF DETECTION OF CYBERCRIME

The threat of cybercrime has become pervasive globally, presenting a significant risk of criminal or terrorist activity that can jeopardize both domestic and international security, including military operations. Addressing these threats requires a collaborative, multi-agency approach, rather than relying on a single authority for policing. Networks are responsible for facilitating access from various points, allowing malicious users to engage in a variety of illegal activities, resulting in a rise in territorialism in nations/regions or specific authorities within nations, further aggravating the exploitation of communications technology. The velocity of electronic crime has developed to the point where private information and commodities spread too quickly for traditional law enforcement measures to keep up with. If a cybercrime goes unnoticed, personal and financial information is lost. This can include gaining access to and exploiting a person's financial accounts and credit cards.

11.1.2.1 Techniques for Detecting Cybercrime

1. Cybercrime detection methods – machine learning-based method
   Artificial intelligence (AI), or machine learning, is the study of algorithms that develop over time as a consequence of experience and data.
2. Cybercrime detection methods – neural networks-based system
   Neural Network Techniques: The human brain's operation is simulated using a neural network (NN) technique [2]. The amount of research that has been done on using NN to recognize computer instructions is extremely limited [3]. The neural network has the ability to solve some of the problems that other instruction detection systems have.
3. Strategies for detecting cybercrime – based on deep learning
   With deep learning, it is possible to identify Arabic cyberbullying using a feed forward NN trained on tweets as the data set.
4. Cybercrime detection – neural networks algorithm-based fuzzy logic
   Fuzzy Neural Network: It is a hybrid framework that performs multiple functions in the classification of patterns, including the identification of abnormal or anomalous behavior. The employment of fuzzy systems is required when a traditional logic method to solve the problem is no longer viable due to the problem's complexity [4].
5. Data mining approaches – for detecting cybercrime
   Data mining methods in fraud recognition can assist with fostering the scam identification model and afterward start the information model with any classifier that is proper. Data mining is primarily concerned with the extraction of data from data sets and the identification of examples from which affiliation rules might be built. Data mining is characterized as the method involved in separating or mining data from a lot of information to produce helpful data.

11.1.3 LAYERED VOICE TECHNOLOGY

LVA is a contentious technology marketed as a tool for detecting stress and other emotions through voice analysis. The human voice is made up of sounds generated by a person's vocal tract. The frequency of the human voice is a component of human sound production in which the vocal folds are the primary source of sound. When paired with the articulators, the vocal folds may form incredibly complex sound patterns. Changing the tone of one's voice can communicate anger, surprise, fear, happiness, and sadness. The human voice may convey emotion as well as disclose the speaker's age and gender. Singers utilize the human voice as a musical instrument.

11.1.3.1 Working of Layered Voice Analysis Work

By recognizing emotional indicators in the suspect's speech, LVA technology allows you to have a deeper understanding of his or her mental state and emotional makeup at any given time.

11.1.3.2 Accuracy of Voice Lie Detector Test

According to the study, these algorithms had an average accuracy rate of roughly 50%. According to the study, users may be discouraged from lying if they believe their comments can be "proven" false.

11.1.3.3 Voice Stress Analysis

Voice stress analysis (VSA) and computer voice stress analysis are unreliable methods that claim to detect deception by analyzing voice stress data. These techniques involve using a microphone to capture the speaker's voice and extracting information on the presenter's physiological and psychological state from the voice's nonverbal, low-frequency content. Generally used in investigative contexts, the technology makes a distinction between stressful and non-stressful responses to stimuli (such as questions asked), with high stress considered indicative of deceit.

It is controversial if VSA can be used to detect deception. The reliability of VSA in identifying stress and its connection with deception has been the subject of debate. Some critics contend that even if VSA accurately detects stress from speech, the criticisms against polygraph testing also apply to VSA since both methods share similar limitations. In other words, they argue that VSA is analogous to polygraph testing.

LVA Test: Officials claim that the LVA uses voice frequency to determine whether or not someone is lying. Officials stated the program takes a sample of the suspect's speech to determine his "emotional state," and that it can "assist detectives during questioning." The voice sample is available both online and offline.

11.1.3.4 LVA 6.50 – Modes of Operation

There are two modes of operation for the LVA 6.50 system. This can be done in person, over the phone, or via a microphone during a face-to-face interview.

11.1.3.4.1 Real-Time Analysis

During investigations, real-time analysis is performed. When real-time analysis is required, the online mode allows you to conduct investigations. This can be done in person, over the phone, or via a microphone during a face-to-face interview. This mode allows you to concentrate on troublesome speech chunks in real time and ask follow-up questions if necessary. It also saves time throughout the investigation by allowing you to swiftly narrow down a suspect list by screening a large number of people. Because it is nearly totally automated, this is the simplest option to use. The findings of the top layer analysis are shown as simple terms such as "Truth," "Inaccuracy," or "High Stress," and they provide a clear indication of the subject's level of honesty and general emotional condition. In real time, each phrase is analyzed. This is the ideal choice to utilize while working with LVA for first-time or novice users after finishing the LVA training class. You can also record your discussion in online mode. Please bear in mind that recording conversations under certain or all circumstances may be unlawful in some countries. If you choose to take this option, you should get legal assistance and clarity.

11.1.3.4.2 *Post-Analysis of Pre-Recorded Material*
Pre-recorded information is examined in detail. Offline mode can be used to review previously collected data and develop a thorough psychological protocol for a given sample. There are many different types of sources that may be used to analyze vocal sections. Tape recordings, digital audio tape recordings, film, radio, television, live people, and phone calls are all examples of sources that can be utilized. Using the Offline Wizard, you may examine each section on its own and in connection with prior segments, allowing you to conduct an "emotion over content" examination of the video. You can access interactive graphs, reports, and statistics data while you are not connected to the Internet in offline mode. However, training courses will be required in order to fully comprehend the findings of the offline mode.

11.1.3.5   **LVA 6.50 Features**
11.1.3.5.1   *Online Mode Features*
- The question and the answer can be replayed and a detailed analysis can be done. Thus, a replay discussion segment can be done with a complete analysis.
- It allows you to type in pertinent questions and compare and contrast with any set of parts. A part of the question can be compared with the existing samples got and thus a detailed analysis of a particular section can be done.
- When some discussions cannot be made face to face, a bar display can be used which represents a colored graphic depiction of the fundamental parameters in the form of a histogram.
- A Segment Map depicts a segmented examination of the dialogue, complete with appropriate reaction and authenticity assessment. A CRITICAL SEGMENT occurs when the propositional substance of the segment is directly related to the interview's most important subjects.
- The questionnaire process can be recorded online and further analysis can be done.

11.1.3.5.2   *Offline Mode Features*
Before creating a cut, a new segmentation technique allows you to control and prolong the segment. This prevents the loss of important audio files. Sexual arousal factor analysis has been added, which is appropriate for sexually oriented crime investigations. Find out why the crime was committed. Additional segmentation tools, as well as remedies for a number of previous issues are examined. New advancements and tools

enable you to analyze offline findings in a variety of ways for maximum reliability. Work with multiple databases to better organize your files and recordings.

LVA utilizes a unique mathematical technique to detect patterns and anomalies in speech flow and classify them as different emotional states, such as stress, excitement, and bewilderment. These emotional states have been identified as strongly linked to the patterns observed in the study. The proprietary approach employed by LVA enables the identification and classification of various significant emotional states based on the analyzed speech data.

LVA technology offers users the ability to delve into different levels of emotional intensity, unveiling additional layers of concealed information. By leveraging this technology, users can gain deeper insights and understand subtle nuances that might otherwise remain unnoticed. This capability enables a more comprehensive exploration of emotional states and enhances the understanding of emotional dynamics. This information can help you save time as you work through the investigation.

11.1.3.6 LVA and "Lie Detection"

Experts in the field of lie detection acknowledge the absence of a definitive "true" lie detector due to the non-uniform nature of lying, which can vary across individuals and circumstances. Lying is not a consistent reaction that unfolds uniformly in every instance. The polygraph, widely recognized as a "Lie Detector," is constrained to function effectively only within its predefined settings and specific context. Its reliability as a lie detector is limited to those predefined conditions and circumstances. Connecting a polygraph to a person watching a film or engaging in any type of physical activity will provide nonsensical findings. Lying is the product of a complex logical process carried out with a specific goal in mind. One might lie to protect themselves, while others may lie for financial gain or to make a joke. There are no specific physiological or psychological traits that can differentiate between lies and truths. Nevertheless, using LVA can help identify the emotions associated with deception, enabling one to identify and report significant falsehoods.

11.1.4 GENERAL QUESTIONING AND TESTING TECHNIQUES

1. Survey questionnaire method: A sample of 1,000 persons are hired to be monitored. In the survey questionnaire method of obtaining the solutions, a face-to-face questionnaire is done and analyzed through intuition. This method requires a human expert who has to pay for the services.
2. Deception: When it comes to detecting deception by psychophysiological measures, the polygraph is the most well-known tool. All of these procedures are aimed at identifying dishonesty by examining evidence of changes in the body that aren't normally evident to the human eye, such as those caused by stress.
3. The guilty knowledge exam and the control question test: The guilty knowledge test is a psychophysiological questioning method that may be used in conjunction with a polygraph examination to determine if suspects are concealing "guilty knowledge" by assessing physiological reactions while answering to a set of multiple-choice questions.

4. Polygraph: For a price, trained polygraph examiners give lie detector examinations. As of March 2020, the average cost is between $200 and $2,000 according to Google.

5. Cognitive polygraph: A polygraph test can be considered to be a type of working memory training. This shows the presence of mental aid activities corresponding to the discrete knowledge strategy (DKS) model. As such, the DKS model might contain a discrete information base (DKB) of critical task components, however, the DKB is inadequate in the non-discrete knowledge strategy (nDKS)model, coming about in a "worldwide" or bi-hemispheric search. A "lie detector" system was fabricated in view of the last option premise, as depicted in US Patent No. 6,390,979. Because of inquiries with right and mistaken replies, an example of blood-stream velocity changes is found. Bi-hemispheric actuation will be inspired by the inaccurate response, while one-sided initiation will be evoked by the right response. The cognitive polygraphy of this framework is without any abstract command over mental cycles, and thus, this framework's cognitive polygraph is liberated from emotional control of mental cycles, bringing about superb dependability and particularity; regardless, it still can't seem to be tried in legal practice. Biometrics of comprehension is one more term for cognitive biometrics.

6. Event-related possibilities (ERP) are utilized to assess acknowledgment, and therefore, they could conceivably be viable in identifying deception. P3 amplitude waves are estimated in ERP examinations, and these waves are huge when a thing is perceived [5]. In any case, P100 amplitudes have been found to have a significant relationship with reliability assessments, which will be analyzed in more detail in the electroencephalogram (EEG) area. This, alongside other examinations, has driven some to guarantee that ERP examinations are "fundamental to the identification of double-dealing" since they depend on a quick perceptual process [6].

7. EEG: Machine learnings applied to EEG information were likewise used to decide if a member accepted or questioned a recommendation with a precision of 90%. This study is based on past work by Sam Harris and others, showing that conviction preceded belief as far as time, suggesting that the brain might acknowledge claims as true portrayals of the world (belief) prior to dismissing them (disbelief). Seeing how the brain assesses the honesty of a truthful assertion may be an essential advance in step in lie detection procedures in view of neuroimaging [7].

8. Eye tracking: A near-infrared light source and high-definition cameras are used to throw light onto the cornea of the eye and record the direction in which the light is reflected off the cornea. The location of the eye is then calculated using advanced algorithms to establish exactly where it is focused.

9. Voice stress analysis: Using these percentages, we evaluated the two VSA systems' total accuracy rates and found that they could detect recent drug use dishonesty to within 50%. This study used MATLAB®.

10. Functional magnetic resonance imaging (fMRI) identifies fluctuations in blood flow. This strategy uses the relationship between cerebral blood flow and neuronal activity. When a portion of the brain is utilized, its blood flow increases.

11.2 RELATED WORKS

Criminology is an interesting area but full of obstacles. Investigating a criminal case needs a tool which can aid in the process and lie detection can help [8]. Lying is a sort of human character, especially when it comes to criminals and is one of the primary topics that the science of criminology focuses on. Because there are insufficient external responses from educated criminals, analyzing human lying or deception features is a key difficulty for crime researchers [9].

"Deception" is a well-known term that refers to deceiving another person into believing something that is not true. In everyday life, deception is all too widespread. While some researchers rely solely on verbal strategies to detect dishonesty [10], others investigate people's physical and emotional actions using nonverbal elements [11]. Another set of researchers, on the other hand, uses both verbal and nonverbal elements [12].

In fact, liars experience more anxiety, dread, embarrassment, and rage than truth tellers [13]. In addition, using syntactic stylometry, some researchers were able to detect dishonesty in writing with 91.2% accuracy [14]. Based on their favorable performance in earlier research, the qualities chosen for this study have proven to be successful in this application [15]. According to Dalibor et al. [16], a neural network can be trained by utilizing a regulated set of progression functions in a designated layer of a chosen pattern. Following that, the classifier's accuracy is improved by selecting the optimal combinatorial feature vector. Finally, multi-layer perceptron (MLP) and k-nearest neighbour (KNN) are used to classify the study's innocent and guilty participants. According to the findings of this process, an accuracy of 89.73% can be obtained in detecting deception. This score is significantly higher than earlier methods [17].

In [18], a feature abstraction technique suitable for Graphics Processing Unit (GPU) has been proposed, which considers the computational time to enhance the performance of feature extraction at different stages. It also mentions how the algorithm has been enhanced. The NN is set up for "direct" or "relaxation" request inputs and an expected set of outputs. There are numerous approaches for configuring network assets. Using prior knowledge, the process is utilized to set the weights. Next, the neural network is expedited by presenting it with instruction patterns and enabling it to adjust its weight based on specific information, as suggested by Roshni et al. [19]. The Artificial Neural Networks model has revealed the existence of a more advanced classification validation model that can function optimally with an appropriate number of neurons and a distinct parameter set. Additionally, the guilty knowledge test, which utilizes forensic EEG, has been employed as a reliable and potent alternative to the conventional comparison question test in lie detection. Multiple people who have completed the guilty knowledge test paradigm will be required to participate in the method's evaluation. Following that, their brain signals were recorded.

Plaintiffs have endeavored to incorporate human input-based deception detection through voice analysis. A comprehensive examination of current cases and scientific research on this subject has been conducted, which examines the obstacles posed by the need for scientific evidence to demonstrate its validity and reliability. Additionally, this investigation acknowledges the crucial limitations of science as expert testimony.

11.3 PROPOSED WORK

11.3.1 OVERVIEW

The method's fundamental idea is to obtain the tested person's input voice signals recorded using a concealed information test. In the process of signal acquisition, a few basic filtering procedures are applied to the acquired data in order to enhance the signal's signal-to-noise ratio (SNR) and reduce its noise content. The powerful Independent Component Analysis technique can assist to distinguish the refined and independent signals from the mixed other undesirable signals in a human voice signal, which is made up of several overlaid signals. The use of a lie detection system aids in the creation of a clear image of the signal and the extraction of features. Time, frequency, amplitude, and eigenvalues are some of the properties that may be retrieved from EEG signals. The features are applied to the NN classifier after the feature extraction phase.

Amir Liberman invented Nemesysco's main technology, layered voice analysis. By identifying emotional clues in the suspect's speech, LVA technology allows for a better understanding of the user's mental state and emotional makeup at any one time. The LVA technology has two modes of operation. The LVA technology analyzes recorded voice files in the offline mode. Liberman explains that LVA technology identifies and assesses diverse psycho-physiological responses that indicate alterations in the tested individual's perception. This alerts the trained operator to search for new indications and leads. The Forensic Science Laboratory began employing the LVA tool which is supposed to aid in the detection of falsehoods and the screening of suspects. LVA relies on speech fluctuations and does not require cables or sensors to be affixed to a suspect's body. The voice sample is available both online and offline. Earlier lie detection technologies took days or months to provide findings, but the new programme is projected to produce data "within minutes," which may be analyzed by forensic psychology specialists.

11.3.1.1 Voice Analysis

Lie detection software often employs voice analysis techniques, such as layered voice analysis, which may detect various sorts of stress, emotional reactions, and cognitive processes in the subject's voice. Researchers discovered that the human voice has frequencies that are sensitive to honesty. For example, when someone is being honest, the average sound in that range will be less than 10 Hz, and only when dishonesty is present would it be over 10 Hz.

All of our muscles, including our voice chords, vibrate between 8 and 12 Hz. This is commonly referred to as a feedback loop, and it works in the same way as a thermostat or heater that maintains an average temperature by oscillating between higher and lower temperatures. Our muscles tighten and loosen in the same way to maintain constant tension.The frequency of vibration will grow from 8–9 Hz to 11–12 Hz, which is a stressful range..

As a result of our bodies preparing for fight or flight, for example, if we are telling a lie and don't want to be detected, we increase the readiness of our muscles for action and protection anytime we feel stressed. The frequency of vibration will increase from 8–9 Hz to 11–12 Hz, which is a difficult range of frequencies to operate within.

11.3.1.2   Research Methodology

Step 1: Lie Detection using layered voice technology

Step 2: Lie detection confirmation using neural network

11.3.1.3   Algorithm of Overall System of Lie Detection System

Step 1: Input the sample

Step 2: Use the guilty knowledge test

Step 3: Preprocess

Step 4: Feature extraction

Step 5: Forwards Features to NN classifier

Step 6: Training and testing

Step 7: Classification

11.3.2   Signal Preprocessing

The first step involved in signal processing is input voice preprocessing, which is used as a filtering technique. Low frequency is removed through the use of high-pass filters. EMG activity is a high-frequency noise which can be removed using low-pass filters. The removal of noise from the power supply is usually performed. The average mean reference method is used to reduce noise from power line interference, electronic amplifiers, and external amplifiers.

Channels are evaluated to calculate mean values. This mean value is later deducted from the original raw signal value. To diminish the impact of individual disparities that take place because of fundamental frequency rhythms and also to minimize the complexity of computations, the process of normalization is performed. During the process, all the values related to the different elements are normalized as they lie within a range between zero and one.

11.3.3   Feature Extraction

Features are the fundamental qualities of signals that help to characterize the raw signals. Feature extraction is critical in sound recognition systems and is regarded as the system's heart. Feature extraction plays a significant role since it is a way for extracting a small quantity of data from human speech sounds that can then be used to describe each sound. Feature extraction is a method for obtaining feature values from a prepossessed human EEG signal. The method of detecting unknown human speech by comparing extracted characteristics from voice input with known sound is known as feature matching. This is something that MFCC can perform in this project.

11.3.4   Mel-Frequency Cepstrum Coefficient

The most well-known approach for extracting features from sound signals is MFCC. The MFCC technique is where the audio signal is mostly discovered. The audio stream is analyzed using a codebook and a species sound. This is a sound recognition function which is derived from the MFCC feature extraction. The utilization of MFCC

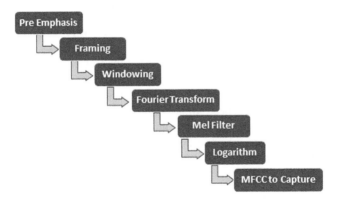

FIGURE 11.1 MFCC technique for speech recognition.

matrices has enhanced the training procedures for each human voice input amidst background noise. A sound recognition framework is the most fundamental degree of element extraction and coordination. The primary goal was to use the MFCC to detect lying speech in human input sounds. Figure 11.1 depicts the Sequential diagram of the MFCC mechanism.

11.3.4.1 Pre-Emphasis

Analysis of modulation frequency indicates a higher degree of noise compared to other cases. To enhance the SNR, higher frequencies are pre-emphasized. If the sound signal is $x(n)$, then the output of the filter is $X2(n)$, and the normalization factor is a.

11.3.4.2 Framing

The sound recognition of the input voice signal is nonstationary. When the frame is too big, temporal resolution suffers, and when it's too tiny, frequency resolution suffers. The frequency resolution and temporal resolution have a good connection. When the signal is coupled to smaller signals, framing is highly important for effective outcomes. It may be modified from amplitude.

11.3.4.3 Hamming Window

To eliminate a break, this causes disruptions in the Hamming window's start and end frames. These will have a negative impact on the frequency response. When compared to other windowing strategies, all frames are expanded with a Hamming window to preserve the connection. The human voice input signal is denoted by $X(n)$, where $n=0,1,2,...N-1$. Prior to being segmented, the signal is subjected to Hamming windowing to amplify it.

11.3.4.4 Fast Fourier Transform

A time domain signal is converted to a regularity domain signal using the fast Fourier transform. The signal is interrupted in frame as a result of this change. If the sound signal is not stopped during frame calculation, a transform with a gap appears at the beginning and end of the frame. There are two options for comprehending this circumstance: (1) aggregating the frames with a Hamming window for continuous collective signal at start and final locations and (2) creating a set of equal sizes. Disturbances are reduced in windowing at the beginning and end of the frame. The continuous human speech signal is converted into windowed frames when this stage is completed. These windowed frames are put through a fast Fourier transform, which turns them into a magnitude spectrum. A Mel spectrum is synthesized by specifying a resolution and a subjective frequency scale for spectral analysis. This spectrum is converted to a frame, which, in contrast to the fast Fourier transform, yields Mel cepstrum as the final output. The Mel cepstrum has properties that can be used to detect lies in speech.

11.3.5 NEURAL NETWORKS AND LIE DETECTION

Using NNs, the network creation is done to solve classification challenges. The NN approach is used in the training and testing of red palm weevil noises. There are three layers in an NN. The first layer receives the gathered features and computes the input vector and training input vector spaces. This will make it easier to build vector components that show the training data. As its ultimate output, the second layer merges all of the inputs into a single vector possibility. Each human speech signal is capable of being processed by the system. The last layer is carried out in order to enhance the detection of lies in human speech signals. The system was trained in a noise-free setting to ensure that the findings were accurate.

Sound recognition is performed using the voice signal from human talks, which is trained on by a computer system. Recognizability is achieved by the employment of two types of sounds. The following sounds are recognized: for training purposes, the input sound is utilized. Noises that have not been recognized include the sounds that are not utilized during training.

11.4 DISCUSSIONS

In the testing phase of epileptic seizure detection, the test input is the speech signal. The correctness of the findings after experimenting with the proposed technique is shown in Figure 11.2.

Figure 11.2 presents a comparison between the efficacy of human input voice in feature extraction and alternative approaches including Hidden Markov Model (HMM), Gaussian mixture modeling (GMM), and MFCC. Figure 11.2 evaluates the relative effectiveness of these methods in the given context. The suggested technology which employs MFCC produces superior results than any other technique now available.

Figure 11.3 exposes the time spent variously on feature extraction techniques. The quiet sound must be eliminated in order to analyze the speech, which is done using the preprocess approach shown in Figure 11.4. Figure 11.5 depicts the feature extraction process, while Figure 11.6 depicts how the voice signal is trained and tested using a neural network. The results of the proposed model are demonstrated in Figures 11.7–11.9. Thus, the outcome of lie detection is done and this classification method depicts the outcome depending on the input voice signal (normal or lie).

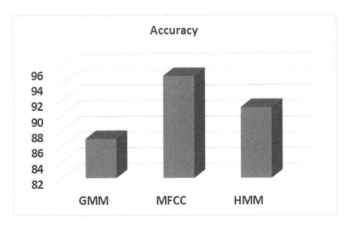

FIGURE 11.2 Accuracy of the methods utilized to extract features from data.

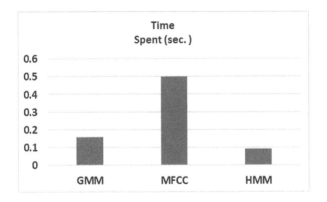

FIGURE 11.3 The time spent on various feature extraction techniques.

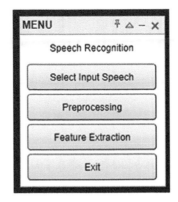

FIGURE 11.4 Menu bar option for speech recognition The vocal input of an emotional speech in humans encompasses a wide range of expressive features, including variations in pitch, tone, intensity, rhythm, and articulation. These vocal cues convey the speaker's emotions, such as happiness, sadness, anger, fear, or excitement, and play a crucial role in conveying the intended emotional message to the listener.

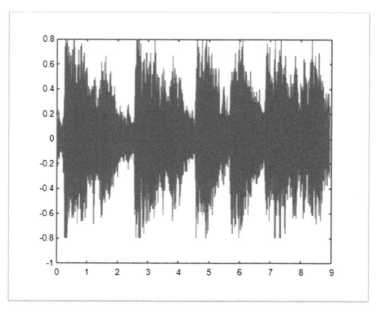

FIGURE 11.5   Vocal input of an emotional speech in human.

Information of the speech file "inpt1.wav":

Duration = 8.92493 seconds

Sampling rate = 8192 samples/second

FIGURE 11.6   Information of the emotional speech.

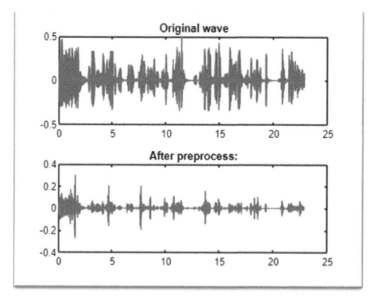

FIGURE 11.7   The preprocessing of the emotional speech.

Information of the speech file "inpt1.wav":

Duration = 8.92493 seconds

Sampling rate = 8192 samples/second

Output = Lie Speech

FIGURE 11.8   Information of the emotional speech after preprocessing.

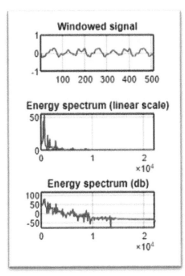

FIGURE 11.9   The extraction of features from emotional speech with energy spectrum.

11.5   CONCLUSION

An effective approach, also known as electroencephalography, may be used to understand brain activity in relation to the stimuli. Internal stimuli such as lie detection cause a reaction in which the appropriate part of the brain is activated. The thinking stimulus may be used to assess deception status, which is linked to the lying section of the brain. Prior to the detection procedure, the EEG data set was utilized to do preprocessing. Following this preprocessing, the NN was trained and a test was conducted. After that, MFCC is used to extract the response characteristics. In this study, statistical metrics such as variance, power, and root mean square are computed for both the contemplative and standard segments of the vocal input signal. The results indicate that the temporal lobe signals exhibit a more pronounced impact due to cognitive activity. These metrics provide insights into the influence of cognitive processes on the vocal input signal. As a result, the NN classifier aids in identifying discrepancies between replies that might be false or true.

ACKNOWLEDGMENT

When it comes to criminal proceedings, detecting lies and deception is a huge difficulty in today's environment. When it comes to detecting cybercrime, lie detection comes in handy. As a result, we would like to assisting in the discovery of criminals by using vocal signals as input. I appreciate all of the folks that assisted me in drafting this chapter.

REFERENCES

1. Sekgwathe, V., Talib, M., Cyber crime detection and protection: Third world still to cope-up. *Technologies and Networks for Development ICeND 2011 Communications in Computer and Information Science*, 171–181, 2011.
2. Wadha, A., Somaya, M., Abdulghani, A, Muhammad, K., Comprehensive review of cyber crime detection techniques. *Proceedings of IEEE Access, Special Section on Emerging Approaches to Cyber Security*, 1–19, 2020.
3. Li, J., He, P., Detection and prevention of cyber crime based on diamond factor neural network. *Journal of Physics: Conference Series*, 1437, 1–6, 2020.
4. Batista, L., Gabriel, S., Vanessa, A., Rezende, T., Fuzzy neural networks to create an expert system for detecting attacks by SQL Injection. *The International Journal of Forensic Computer Science*, 13(8), 8–21, 2018.
5. Heussen, Y., Ferdinand, B., Jacob J., The semantics of the lying face–An EEG study. *International Journal of Psychophysiology*, 77, 206–208, 2010.
6. Douglas, Pamela K., Edward, L., Ariana, A. Single trial decoding of belief decision making from EEG and fMRI data using independent components features. *Frontiers in Human Neuroscience*, 7, 1–8, 2013.
7. Daniel, D., Langleben, D., Jane, C., Using brain imaging for lie detection: Where science, law, and policy collide. *Psychology, Public Policy, and Law*, 19(2), 222–234, 2013.
8. Lakshmi, T., Prasad, T., Exploration of recent advances in the field of brain computer interface. *IOSR Journal of Computer Engineering*, 8(2), 1–8, 2012.
9. Enos, F., Detecting deception in speech. *Dissertation Abstracts International, B: Sciences and Engineering,* 70, 1–250, 2009.
10. Farah, M. J., Hutchinson, J. B., Phelps, E. A., Wagner, A. D., Functional MRI-based lie detection: Scientific and societal challenges. Nature Publishing Group. *Nature Reviews Neuroscience,* 15, 123–131, 2014.
11. An, G., Literature review for deception detection. Doctoral dissertation, The City University of New York, 1–110, 2015.
12. Oppenheim, A., Discrete-time signal processing. *Electronics and Power*, 23, 157–159, 1977.
13. Huang, G., Introduction to extreme learning machines, *Hands on Workshop on Machine Learning for Bio Medical Informatics 2006*, 1–8, 2006.
14. Padhy, P., Avinash, K., Vivek, C., Kalyan, R., Feature extraction and classification of brain signal. *World Academy of Science, Engineering, and Technology*, 55, 1–6, 2011.
15. Reynolds, D., Speaker verification using adapted Gaussian mixture model. *Digital Signal Processing*, 10, 19–41, 2016.
16. Dalibor, M., Matthias, Z., Christian, B., Features for content–based audio retrieval. *Advances in Computers*, 78, 71–150, 2010.

17. Sheeba, S., Bhavana, H., A review on statistical signal processing of EEG signals for lie detection. *International Journal of Advanced Research in Electrical, Electronics and Instrumentation Engineering,* 4(4), 1–8, 2015.

18. Joshi, S., Cheeran, A., MATLAB® based feature extraction using mel frequency cepstrum coefficients for automatic speech recognition. *International Journal of Science, Engineering and Technology Research,* 3(6), 1820–1823, 2014

19. Roshni, D., Tale., Harne, B., Deception detection method using independent component analysis of EEG signals. *International Journal of Advanced Research in Electronics and Communication Engineering,* 4, 1–5, 2015.

Index